Mount Washington

Mount Washington

Narratives and Perspectives

Edited by Mike Dickerman

BONDCLIFF BOOKS · LITTLETON, NEW HAMPSHIRE

To

Chris Schneider

Friend, skier, and mountain victim.

Contents

Introduction

ALTHOUGH I grew up in northeastern Vermont, a little more than an hour's drive from the Presidential Range, Mount Washington has always been a part of my life.

As a kid growing up, the mountain was brought into my living room every night courtesy of Channel 8 out of Poland Spring, Maine. Sometime shortly after six, there would appear on the television screen the fuzzy, black & white image of Marty Engstrom, who would give a live report from the top of the mountain, detailing prevailing weather conditions at the summit. Being just kids, though, with little interest in meteorology, it wasn't the weather update we were interested in; it was Marty's signature grin that would keep our eyes peeled to the screen. Just before he would sign off for the night, Marty would flash that goofy smile of his directly into the camera, and all of us, mom and dad included, would immediately crack up with laughter, even though we'd seen it a hundred times before.

It was hard to take Marty seriously—and still is—and that made it difficult to accord the mountain as much respect as it obviously warranted. It wasn't until 1982, when I suddenly became interested in hiking, that I really gave much thought about what it was truly like on the mountain. I had to assume there was more to it than just a television camera pointed in Marty's face, but I needed to find out for certain, so my older brother organized a fall expedition up the mountain and I got to see in person what Mount Washington was really about.

Ever since that crisp, clear October day on the top of New England there has existed in me a curious fascination with this 6,288-foot mountain. The fact that it is the tallest mountain in New England (and one of the highest in the entire Appalachian Mountain chain), that it is home to some of the worst weather on earth, and that it has a history that is perhaps unrivaled among all North America peaks, makes Mount Washington one of the most visited and most written about mountains in the world. It goes without saying I am not alone in having a fascination with this mountain.

It has been my fortune these past 17 years to get to know Mount Washington in a variety of ways. I have seen it from a hiker's perspective, dragging one foot after another up its steep, rocky cone, wondering if my legs or heart would give out before I reached the summit. I have seen it from a journalist's perspective, chronicling enough tragic events on the mountain over the years to fill a book of its own. And more recently, I have seen it from an aspiring historian's perspective, who has gobbled up every morsel of information he can find in hopes of learning everything about the mountain's storied past.

It is no wonder then that I am still drawn to its summit every year, even though I remain intimidated by this mammoth mound of rocks. Despite years of hiking and climbing in the White Mountains, I find every trip up to heights as exhausting and exhilarating as that first one. And even when I am not on the mountain itself, but instead find myself plodding along some footpath elsewhere in these White Mountains of northern New Hampshire, Mount Washington beckons. It is always there on the horizon, standing head and shoulders above all else, its summit structures pointing skyward, and in summer, the tell-tale puffs of black smoke drifting upwards from the Cog Railway engines.

The mountain is hardly pristine, for humankind's presence is obvious most everywhere, and it is certainly not hospitable. Still, for all its faults and foibles, Mount Washington remains a lifelong acquaintance, and I am glad I have gotten to know it better over the years.

When I began working on this book a year ago, it was not my intention to focus solely on Mount Washington. This project started out as an anthology of White Mountain literature, but soon developed into a book solely devoted to pieces related to the Rock Pile, as the mountain is commonly known.

I like to think of this as a prewritten history of the mountain, for it tells the story of Mount Washington through the words of those who knew and wrote about the mountain long before I'd ever seen or heard of the Presidential Range. Most of the mountain's major events—from Darby Field's historic climb of 1642 to the tragic Cog Railway crash of September 1967—are chronicled on these pages. Sure, there are a few events I have skipped over, and certainly some readers may feel too much of the mountain's morbid past is covered. By and large, though, I think you will come away with a good sense of why this particular White Mountain peak has captured my imagination, and the imagination of many others, for so many years.

For the most part, the republished works appearing here are in their original form, with the spelling and punctuation virtually unchanged. It is my intent, in keeping things as they were, to give readers a flavor of the times in which these words were first written.

Acknowledgments

Until I began piecing together this book I had no idea how much time and energy would be required. Like any project of this sort, I suppose, the work was both fun and frustrating. Certainly tracking down the various pieces which comprise this anthology was the most time-consuming but enjoyable part of the journey. Likewise, finding photographs to match the written words was a thoroughly enjoyable challenge. At the same time, eliminating deserving articles or photographs—primarily because I'd run out of space— was a wrenching experience, especially knowing how much time and effort went into choosing these items in the first place.

That I've made it this far with the book is a true testament to the encouragement and assistance offered by numerous individuals throughout northern New Hampshire, most of whom share my interest in Mount Washington and the entire White Mountains region. Without these folks, who I'll get to in just a moment, the stories you are about to read and photographs you are about to view would never have come together.

First and foremost I'd like to thanks the staffs of the New Hampshire State Library, the Littleton Public Library, Pease Public Library of Plymouth, and the Bethlehem Public Library. At each library, staff members went out of their way to help me find whatever I was searching for.

Contributing authors such as Floyd W. Ramsey, Peter Crane, Warren and Ginny Martin, and Laura and Guy Waterman were equally helpful, not for just allowing me to reprint their invaluable contributions to this book, but also for loaning me photographs and suggesting other worthwhile pieces.

Descendants of two of the White Mountains' most famous 20th century photographers, Winston Pote and Guy L. Shorey, need to be thanked for providing a dozen or so vintage photographs. In the case of the Winston Pote photos appearing in this volume, it was Norma Andrews of Gorham who searched her archives for just the right images. Susan Hawkins of Lancaster was also exceptionally cooperative, even inviting me to her Lost Nation home to rifle through boxes and boxes of treasured photos and White Mountain ephemera from the extensive Guy Shorey collection.

Other vintage photographs were supplied by people such as the ever encouraging David Govatski of Jefferson, and Littleton bookstore owner Bob Cook (Titles & Tales). The Mount Washington Observatory, accomplished Lincoln, N.H. photographer Robert Kozlow, the Littleton Area Historical

Society, Littleton Public Library, and local photographer George Mitchell also helped in my quest for Mount Washington images.

Thanks must also go out to the Trustees of Dartmouth College, Gordon Hardy of the Appalachian Mountain Club, and dear friend Eleanor Stephenson of Bethlehem, who all graciously agreed to let me publish previously written pieces.

The Amherst College Alumni Association needs to be recognized as well for providing invaluable biographical information on several of the authors whose work appears in this book, while Art Tighe and the crew at Foto Factory of Littleton did a superb reprinting dozens of old photographs appearing elsewhere in this volume.

Finally, I owe big thank yous to Trish Ilacqua for her hours on the keyboard typesetting much of the copy for this book, Scott Cahoon and Passumpic Publishing for the excellent layout design, and the entire staff at Sherwin Dodge Printers.

Littleton, N.H.   Mike Dickerman

Mount Washington

July 30, 1877

The Objective Point

From *Among the Clouds*

Among the Clouds, the mountaintop tourist newspaper published daily during the summer months from atop Mount Washington, was founded by Henry M. Burt in 1877. The idea of publishing such a newspaper came to Burt in 1874, while he was storm-bound atop the mountain's Summit House. Mr. Burt, whose previous newspaper publishing experiences found him in Boston, Massachusetts and Bellevue, Nebraska, among other places, served as editor of Among the Clouds *until his death in March 1899. His son, Frank H. Burt, took over as editor/publisher that summer and stayed with the newspaper until the devastating 1908 summit fire, which destroyed the paper's summit offices. The paper was revived in 1910 by Reginald Buckler, a former* Among the Clouds *employee. Operating from the Cog Railway Base Station, he ran the paper until its final year of publication in 1917.*

THE SUMMIT of Mount Washington is the objective point of every White Mountain traveler, as no one can afford to leave the mountains without making a trip to it; but of those who come, how few really understand how to get the most out of their visit. The average American seems bent on doing his sight-seeing in a hurry, as he does his business. That certainly is an absurd way to get the real enjoyment that the opportunity affords. Here, from this grand eminence, there is more to be seen and learned than any other place in New England, and it seems almost profanity to rush here and back, as though the mere act of coming and going was the principal pleasure. The ride up and down is exhilarating and not to be forgotten; but beyond there lies a hidden and wonderful beauty that must be studied to be understood and appreciated. The grand view itself never wearies the beholder; there is so much to be seen it requires time to comprehend all that lies within the range of human vision. The mountain ranges and their peaks are almost countless, and time is required to learn their names and forms so as to carry away a recollection of them. Here lies before the visitor all the grandeur of New England, and who can take into his soul its poetry and beauty in a single day at the Summit? This view awakens the tenderest and noblest feelings of humanity; and who can be so unappreciative as to pass it by with a rude feeling of business? These mountains tell of the countless ages that have come and gone before man had development and existence—they are God's great alphabet, and how can one read this great book of nature in a single day? It should not be forgotten, also, that the elements at this great altitude are fickle and uncertain, and that a passing cloud at any hour is liable to limit the view and shut out the grandeur of the scene. With its passing away their [*sic*] comes the compensation. The magnificence and beauty come in a single moment—all the more beautiful from having been obscured. The cloud and the storm are the drop curtains to the great play that is waiting to be enacted. Let no one who comes here get impatient; the clear sky that is sure to follow the storm will make everything more beautiful, and reveal the mountains and valleys so minutely that a view of them under such conditions are worth more than a day of misty vagueness. To get the most out of a visit to Mount Washington one should spent at least a week on the Summit, coming up in a cloud just at the close of a storm. The sudden lifting of the curtain, the flashing rays of light that follow brings a scene that no one can describe, and there is more enjoyment in it than can possibly come from any other condition.

1890

The Glory of Mount Washington

Julius Ward

From *The White Mountains: A Guide to Their Interpretation*

The White Mountains: A Guide to Their Interpretation *was published in
1890. Its author, Rev. Julius H. Ward (1837–1897) was an editorial writer for the*
Boston Sunday Herald. *Most of the passages appearing in* The White Mountains *had first appeared in the Boston newspaper. The Appalachian Mountain
Club, of which Ward was a member, said of the author in its 1891 review of the
book, "Mr. Ward seems to be as much at home all through the mountainous parts
of New England as common folk are in their own gardens, and his love for the hills
is genuine and inspiring. He has learned their secrets in lonely climbing."*

APPROACHED from whatever point of view, Mount Washington stands
alone for grandeur and isolation among its kindred peaks. Seen from North
Conway, it lies in majestic repose against the northern sky—now enveloped
in clouds, now brightened in the sunshine, but always in an attitude of dig-
nity and strength, the monarch of the hills; seen from the Glen, its massive
shoulders, its enormous ravines, and its length and breadth and height dwarf
everything within its range; seen from Fabyan's, its magnitude is lost in
comparison with the companions that lend themselves to its greatness; seen
from Bethlehem or Jefferson Highlands, the distance lends enchantment to
the view, and the imagination kindles with its greatness and with the
grandeur of the whole Presidential range; seen in the distance from Moosilauke, it lies hard against the eastern sky, and holds the mountains in its embrace as a shepherd keeps his flock. There is no part of northern New Eng-

land where a sight of it does not thrill the soul with its serenity and power. It is so high it stands sentinel of the country round-about; if the highest mountain in New England, it is far from being the highest in North America, and in the west it would sink into insignificance; but here it represents to the distant observer that outreach of the earth to the heavens for which we have no better symbol than the mountain whose peak pierces the blue.

The danger is, that in visiting Mount Washington this fascination of distance may be lost and nothing put in its place. It is with mountains as it is with great men—at a distance and at their best they are towers of strength. Nothing of their weakness is discovered. It is a different thing to live with them, to bear with their foibles, to ignore their defects, to admit their superiority. Only the greatest and noblest of men can endure the ordeal of being known for what they truly are. It is so with the mountains. It is easy to invest them with the colors of the spirit, but the difficulty is to trace these colorings when you are climbing them or enjoying the outlook from their summits. The nearness and the reality oppress the imagination. Mount Washington is approached with the feeling that the majesty and grandeur are to be revealed without personal effort, and people carry away nothing like the impressions which they had hoped to obtain. One sees in the mountains only what he is prepared to see. A quick sensibility to the beauty and glory of the outer world is a great help to seeing them, but even this gift needs to be trained and developed before the mountains reveal their secrets and have their full effect upon our sensitive life. One must not be disappointed if Mount Washington fails at first to meet his expectations. It is so unlike any other summit, except Jefferson and Adams and Madison in its own range, that one is at a loss to compare it with anything that he has known; and if it is his first acquaintance with the White Hills, he is like a man who has suddenly inherited a fortune—he is ready to enjoy it if he only knew how.

The interpretation of Mount Washington is as much an undertaking as the following of the frescoes of Michael Angelo in the Vatican, or the entering into fellowship with the genius that created The Divine Comedy. Both are understood only as you enter into the mind of the artists or the poet and give to him the sympathy of a kindred spirit. The greatest things in literature and art are the commonest, and yet the power of mind and soul that goes into them takes them out of the common order and calls us up to their level. This represents the situation to one who visits Mount Washington. There is nothing here which is not common to our life. The rocks, the sky, the clouds, the light, the darkness—all these one is familiar with; and when you begin to exchange the feelings with which you have regarded this grandest of our mountains for the hard and bleak and desolate realities of its daily

WINSTON POTE

Snow-covered Mount Washington and Pinkham Notch.

existence, the imagination is set its hardest task to rise above the awful nakedness of the summit and invest it with the ideal majesty which belongs to it when seen from afar. Ruskin says that "all the power of Nature depends on subjection to the human soul." It is not difficult to comprehend the great poem or the masterpieces of the painter and the musician. They are human, and if we follow the laws of creative effort we can interpret them; but in subjecting the mountains to the soul, in interpreting them as we enter into the works of man, how do we find the thread of intelligence that leads us to the comprehension of their motive, their feeling, their part in the plan of Nature, their kinship with the mind of man? The key is ready for the hand that knows how to use it, and many a one has turned it through the wards of the lock that opens to us the divine order which prevails no less in the inorganic than in the organic world.

Nothing in the outer realm is without its laws, its combinations, its sympathies, and when you begin to see and feel them, whether in the dew-drop or in the uplifted mountain, you have caught the thread of intelligence that leads you into the inner kingdom of Nature and gives the suggestion that turns the earth and the water and the sky into vital instruments in the hands of God. In knowing and feeling this one begins to have a reverent spirit toward the mountains with a sufficient cause. The imagination is as true a part of the intellect as the reasoning faculty, and it is with the imagination that we best enter into the life of the mountains and learn how to bring them into proper relations with the human soul.

At first Mount Washington said nothing to me. It was a great pile of broken rock, desolate, passionless, without appeal, without response, and the outlook was so vast and unusual that I could do nothing with it. The key to its grand life was not given; there was nothing to compare it with, and even the naming of the peaks within the reach of the eye brought no relief. Ordinarily the ascent of a mountain gives pleasure, but Mount Washington is haughty in its mood and will encourage no familiarity. Its immense desolation is the only impression that the naked peak makes upon the newcomer, and for most persons this is all that they take home with them. So you meet with people reputed to be great in the world, and measure them from the outside; so the casual man met Goethe and took his impression of the chief modern man from the surface; but he knew not Goethe as did those who by kindred studies and like culture were prepared to share his life. It was my duty to wait in the outer courts of the temple till I could be initiated and prepared to enter into the veil. I had not long to wait. Cold and passionless as the mount is to those who do not approach it with intelligent devotion, it finds its way quickly enough to those who are responsive to its grand moods. The attitude of one who is drinking in the sky and feels the exhilaration of the morning and opens his heart toward Nature—the attitude of sympathetic and intelligent approach—is the way to win the secrets of Mount Washington.

An awakening, slow and sure, as when a great thought gradually makes its way to the conquest of one's life, passed over my whole existence. I felt myself lifted into a new consciousness. I could not read; I could not stay indoors; I could not talk with friends. It seemed as if the tides of life were rising to a new altitude. The commonness of the peak disappeared; the great rough fragments of rock lost their individuality; the huge shoulders and ravines lost their terribly bleak wildness; and there came the consciousness of the grand and sublime in Nature which I had never known before. It was the unconscious exhilaration that comes to a lover of the mountains when they enter into his soul and raise his life to their level. Then Mount Washington began to speak to me in a language that I could understand; the sky and the peak kissed and embraced; then the mountains and the morning stars sang and danced together; then the mountain was instinct with life, and an awful reverence stilled the soul of its solitude. More and more this feeling, as if there were a divine Presence, came upon me and lifted everything out of common. My mind and heart were in tune with the music of the spheres, and I could hear what the mountain had to say.

It was in this mood that the glory of Mount Washington passed before me. It passed many times, and first it presented itself in this wise. The sky had been thick with haze for several days, so that the surrounding peaks lost their significance and the sunrise had given no hint that a clearing was to come in the early morning. It did not seem as if there were clouds in the air. It was rather mist than cloud. The sun stood on the horizon half an hour high, when suddenly the atmosphere was alive with movement. The shifting of the scenery of the heavens and the earth had begun. Not often do the clouds assume greater majesty or break into wilder beauty than did the cloud mists which formed in column and rose for their morning homage. They lay like immense coils of impalpable reality over the neighboring peaks which they half concealed and half revealed—so near that it seemed as if you could almost take them in your arms, and yet they moved with the majesty and order of the winged chariots of the Most High. It was as if the earth and the sky were in motion—not in the conflict of battle, but in the tremor of silent adoration. One thinks and feels intensely at such moments. The rare displays in the life of Nature have their responses in the minds of men. It was so on this morning. I was not alone. Others were by my side enjoying the beauty of the heavens and the mountains as keenly as myself; but still I was alone. The soul was apart by itself, and would only have its own company. The pageant was as unreal as the baseless fabric of a dream, and yet it was intensely real. The clouds marched as if to the music of the morning, and the imagination was aroused to its highest sympathy with that something in the outer world that stimulates our feelings of unlimited life. In that picture, which no artist could paint, I felt as St. Paul is said to have felt when he had the ecstatic vision. I was caught up out of my usual self, and found things not ordinarily within my grasp so near that it seemed as if I had never known anything else. These are the moods that the mountains induce in the minds of those who are prepared to enter into their life. No one who has ever read Wordsworth's Excursion will doubt their reality or feel that too much is made of them by those who have the vision of spiritual things.

At morning and at evening the mountains put on their glorious apparel, and Mount Washington, slumbering like a giant at midday, is never so alive to the imagination as when the sunbeams shoot out of the east and cross the great ravines to kiss the summit, or as when, tired out with his day's work, the Sun lingers to caress the two or three peaks of the Presidential range that are most in touch with one another, while the western valley and the great table-land are almost invisible in the gathering darkness. The morning brings light and joy to the world, and on Mount Washington these may come upon the wings of the wind or break in golden color through folds of mist, or make the peak resplendent, while the ravines are sending up their incense to mark the opening of the day. No one can tell what the revelation may be. If you are watchful for the vision, it will come, but you can no more coax it then you can hurry the footsteps of the hours. One must be like Samuel, watching through the night for the divine call, if the glory of the mountain is to be his portion. If you wait on the mountain until the moment of vision comes, it is as if the glory of earth and sky had passed before your eyes.

The evening on Mount Washington touches a note different, indeed, from that of the morning, less radiant, not paling away into the noonday glare of the eternal hills, but even more accordant with one's sober experience, and with the national pulse of life. The evening, too, has the point of advantage. The Green Mountains, behind which the sun goes down, are lower than Mount Washington, and the dip is just enough to give the peak a final flash of light before the chill of the night comes on. What a change then begins! A few moments before there was—

> A sense sublime
> Of something far more deeply interfused,
> Whose dwelling is the light of setting suns,
> And the round ocean, and the living air,
> And the blue sky, and the mind of man.

Then comes the slow, lingering twilight, darkness below and the fading light above, when the peaks seem to rise out of the dark ravines like great created forms and advance and recede in dumb pantomime than which nothing can be more impressive. Again and again have I watched Jefferson and Adams and Madison, under the spell of the deepening night, just across the Great Gulf, which is so foreshortened that you feel as if you could almost step across it, until they had settled themselves for the night, and seemed like giant children going to sleep. The lonely lea in the neighborhood of the hamlet in the country has its grateful hush at nightfall, when you wait for the darkness and are glad at its coming. The mountains in their vaster silence and loneliness repeat the feeling at the country side with an intensity that is proportioned to their vastness, and the human spirit clings to their summits in the summer darkness with an indescribable sense of protection.

What a world it is which greets the eye in the starry night on Mount Washington! The distant peaks are shut out of sight, and the welkin comes down to your feet and you live among the lights of worlds not ours. Sit down on one of these rough rocks and tell the number of stars, trace the courses of the constellations, separate the planets and the great stars from the inferior host of the sky, and identify yourself with the systems — greater than our own — by which God ministers to his outer worlds. It is wholesome to thus lose yourself in the universe and make a journey with the travelers in the sky. It is thus that you live into the life of the mountains by night as by day, and they take possession of you in such a way that in your turn you obtain their secrets and translate their messages into a personal experience. There is never a moment by night or by day that the mountains are not waiting upon one with their messages, but one must empty himself of himself again and again before the voice is heard in the deeper recesses of the spirit.

The lighting up of the clouds on the approach of sunset is one of the moments when Mount Washington is the centre of glory. The great height and immense horizon respond to this display of strength and beauty and power of color with magnificent results. The combinations are like visitations of the ethereal light, and at times they surpass all the resources of expression. The splendor and the glory are as intense as they are evanescent, and the only display that surpasses the sunsets is that of the gathering of a storm from the lowlands and its march upon the mountain. Then the sublime and the grand and the awful and the terrible are all wrought up to a fearful intensity at the same moment, and when the powers of Nature are unleashed it is as if the whole world were to be devoured at once. The spirit quails at such moments before the fury of the elements. Ruskin and Wordsworth have done most to teach us how to interpret the connection of the clouds with the mountains, but neither of them has helped us to interpret them in the hours of storm. Mostly the clouds reveal their beauty in the sunshine or at the critical moments when storms begin or end, but there is a truth of life in the storm which is as important as the revelation of glory in the clouds at the altars of the morning and the evening sacrifice. Artistically, the storm refuses full expressions, but the clouds lend a strength to the storms on Mount Washington which matches the storm crisis of the human spirit at every point; and one can better understand himself after he has lived through them than he could before.

The clouds in their great throes of power and agony and fury are not beautiful. Their beauty is in their relation to the sky and the earth in the light. In the storm they are not our best symbols of the divine Will, and join with the wind and the rain to chastise the mountains. Mount Washington is always expecting this chastisement. All the world may be at peace with the higher Powers, but not so the monarch of the hills. The clouds drop their fatness in rain or sleet at the slightest invitation, and the gentle *susurrus* of the valleys becomes on the mountain summit the trumpet blast that drives all the forces of the heavens before it. There are no adequate terms to describe a storm on Mount Washington. The shrouding of the summit in mist so that day is turned into night expresses its power to create gloom. The wind blowing a gale that treats a man as if he were a feather expresses a fury that is only matched by a tempest at sea. The chained buildings, the crowding in of the mist, the feeling of the infinity of nothing that comes with it, the roar and rage of the elements, the continuous gloom, the utter helplessness of man, the sense of unmeasureable terror, make a picture of desolation in which man is nothing and the Will that rules the storm is supreme. Nothing but the mountain itself, weighted down with its millions of broken rocks, can survive the contest in which the strongest forces of Nature are engaged. Secure as one may be within the hotel, the spirit aches and moans and rages like the tempest outside. The battles in the air are like the battles between living men.

One feels in the great storms as if he were in command of the host; his spirit is raised to the concert pitch; it is a battle in which no one can be a disinterested spectator. Imagine the most terrible storm that you have ever witnessed in the lowlands, and then imagine it seven times as terrible as that, and you have a most imperfect conception of a storm at its height on Mount Washington. It is as if all the evil in the world were seeking to devour you; it is not the wind or the darkness or the pelting of the storm or the trembling of the hotel or the feeling that the world is up in arms, but the sense of terror, the wildness of the beasts of power, the let-looseness of everything that swells the fury of the elements; and yet all the while it is raging there is a satisfaction in this display of might and strength that is comforting; it tells you that Nature in these savage moods is only the reflex of your own unruled will tearing its way through the world in constant conflict; and when the storm subsides and the mists clear off and the old mountain is again what it was before, the gladness is not unlike the joy of one who has been through a terrible tumult in his soul and has finally risen above it and again reached tranquillity of spirit. A mountain in its expression of the moods of Nature is not unlike a man in his life with himself.

There are times when Mount Washington is simply great in its beauty and glory. This is not in its storm period, not in its revelations to the spirit at the opening and the close of the day, but in the hours of a sunny afternoon when the clouds are level with the peak and encircle the horizon and look as if they were waiting to be reviewed by the father of the hills. The forces of the sky are then in their best array. The artillery, the thunder and the lightning, are dismissed, and the great clouds are waiting for the nod of approval from the monarch of the kingdom in which they move. Then you take your seat reverently upon a great rock on the peak, or better still on top of the observatory, and watch. At the moment the universal stillness alone comes to you; but wait and watch. The clouds do not move, and yet they move. The picture is that of still pageantry, and yet it is not long before you discover that the whole welkin is quietly shifting before your eyes. Do not be in a hurry. Wait an hour or two. Turn from the clouds to the near mountains—Clay, Jefferson, Adams, Madison. They do not move. Oh no, they are the everlasting hills, and never move; and yet they have caught the enchantment of the sky and are moving too. In a bit of wood the branches bend and the leaves are in a gentle quiver when there is not a breath of air to stir them, and Emerson used to say that it was the good manners of the trees in the presence of man, and bowed his head in response. So in this glorious pantomime between the sky and the mountains, the peaks catch the manners of the silent clouds and go through their silent and graceful response, and the great ravines in their changing shadows fill the air with their spirit.

There is never a moment on this grand old summit in which God does not use it for impressions upon the sensitive mind and heart. The highest reaches of the imagination here find their adequate response, and the strongest emotions are stirred to a still stronger life. One who opens himself through all the range of his conscious life to Mount Washington, in its brightness and beauty at the ushering in of day or at the coming on of evening, or in the lingering and softening twilight, or in the hours of storm, or at the moments of the cloud majesty, or when cherubim and seraphim beam upon it through the clouds in the glory of a summer afternoon, will find himself, after his visits to this visible throne of God, so purged of the false, the evil, the untrue and the unreal that on his return to the world his face will be like the face of Moses on his return from Mount Horeb, radiant with the revelations which God gives through the mountains to the souls of men.

1784

A Description of the White Mountains

Jeremy Belknap

From *The History of New Hampshire*, Vol. III

An explorer, clergyman and historian, Rev. Jeremy Belknap (1744–1798) of Dover was the author of the three-volume History of New Hampshire, *published between 1784 and 1792. Included in this early state history is an extensive accounting of the first persons to see and visit the forbidding White Mountains. Belknap, a Massachusetts native, visited Mount Washington in 1784 as part of a scientific expedition. He was accompanied by Manassah Cutler of Ipswich, Massachusetts, Rev. Daniel Little of Wells, Maine, and several others.*

FROM THE earliest settlement of the country, the White Mountains have attracted the attention of all sorts of persons. They are undoubtedly the highest land in New-England, and in clear weather, are discovered before any other land, by vessels coming in to the eastern coast; but by reason of their white appearance, are frequently mistaken for clouds. They are visible on the land at the distance of eighty miles, on the south and southeast sides; they appear higher when viewed from the northeast, and it is said, they are seen from the neighborhood of Chamble and Quebec. The Indians gave them the name Agiocochook: They had a very ancient tradition that their country was once drowned, with all its inhabitants, except one Powaw and his wife, who, foreseeing the flood, fled to these mountains, where they were preserved, and that from them the country was re-peopled. They had a superstitious veneration for the summit, as the habitation of invisible beings; they never ventured to ascend it, and always endeavoured to dissuade every one from the attempt. From them, and the captives, whom they sometimes led to Canada, through the passes of these mountains, many fictions have been propagated, which have given rise to marvellous and incredible stories; particularly, it has been reported, that at immense and inaccessible heights, there have been seen carbuncles, which are supposed to appear luminous in the night. Some writers, who have attempted to give an account of these mountains, have ascribed the whiteness of them to shining rocks, or a kind of white moss; and the highest summit has been deemed inaccessible, on account of the extreme cold, which threatens to freeze the traveller, in the midst of summer.

Nature has, indeed, in that region, formed her works on a large scale, and presented to view, many objects which do not ordinarily occur. A person who is unacquainted with a mountainous country, cannot, upon his first coming into it, make an adequate judgment of heights and distances; he will imagine every thing to be nearer and less than it really is, until, by experience, he learns to correct his apprehensions, and accommodate his eye to the magnitude and situation of the objects around him. When amazement is excited by the grandeur and sublimity of the scenes presented to view, it is necessary to curb the imagination, and exercise judgment with mathematical precision; or the temptation to romance will be invincible.

The White mountains are the most elevated part of a ridge, which extends N.E. and S.W. to an immense distance. The area of their base, is an irregular figure, the whole circuit of which, is not less than sixty miles. The number of summits within this area, cannot at present be ascertained, the country around them being a thick wilderness. The greatest number which can be seen at once, is at Dartmouth, on the N.W. side, where seven summits appear at one view, of which four are bald. Of these, the three highest are the most distant, being on the eastern side of the cluster; one of these is the mountain which makes so majestic an appearance all along the shore of the eastern counties of Massachusetts: It has lately been distinguished by the name of *Mount WASHINGTON.*

To arrive at the foot of this mountain, there is a continual ascent of twelve miles, from the plain of Pigwacket, which brings the traveller to the height of land, between Saco and Amariscoggin rivers. At this height there is a level of about a mile square, part of which is a meadow, formerly a beaver pond, with a dam at each end. Here, though elevated more than three thousand feet above the level of the sea, the traveller finds himself in a deep valley. On the left is a steep mountain, out of which issue several springs, one of which is the fountain of Ellis river, a branch of Saco, which runs south; another of Peabody river, a branch of Amariscoggin, which runs north. From this

meadow, toward the west, there is an uninterrupted ascent, on a ridge, between two deep gullies, to the summit of Mount Washington.

The lower part of the mountain is shaded by a thick growth of spruce and
fir. The surface is composed of rocks, covered with very long green moss,
which extends from one rock to another, and is, in many places, so thick and
strong, as to bear a man's weight. This immense bed of moss, serves as a
sponge, to retain the moisture brought by the clouds and vapours, which are
frequently rising and gathering round the mountains; the thick growth of
wood, prevents the rays of the sun from penetrating to exhale it; so that
there is a constant supply of water deposited in the crevices of the rocks, and
issuing in the form of springs, from every part of the mountain.

The rocks which compose the surface of the mountain, are, in some parts,
slate, in others, flint; some specimens of rock crystal have been found, but
of no great value. No lime stone has yet been discovered, though the most
likely rocks have been tried with aquafortis. There is one precipice, on the
eastern side, not only completely perpendicular, but composed of square
stones, as regular as a piece of masonry; it is about five feet high, and from
fifteen to twenty feet in length. The uppermost rocks of the mountain, are
the common quartz, of a dark grey colour; when broken they shew very small
shining flecks, but there is no such appearance on the exterior part. The
eastern side of the mountain, rises in angle of 45 degrees, and requires six or
seven hours of hard labour to ascend it. Many of the precipices are so steep,
as to oblige the traveller to use his hands, as well as feet, and to hold by the
trees, which diminish in size, till they degenerate to shrubs and bushes;
above these, are low vines, some bearing red, and others blue berries, and
the uppermost vegetation is a species of grass, called winter-grass, mixed
with the moss of the rocks.[1]

1. "At the base of the summit of Mount Washington, the limits of vegetation may with
propriety be fixed. There are indeed, on some of the rocks, even to their apices scattered specks
of a mossy appearance; but I conceive them to be extraneous substances, accidentally adher-
ing to the rocks, for I could not discover, with my botanical microscope, any part of that plant
regularly formed. The limits of vegetation at the base of this summit, are as well defined as
that between the woods and the bald or mossy part. So striking is the appearance, that at a
considerable distance, the mind is impressed with the idea, that vegetation extends no farther
than a line, as well defined as the penumbra and shadow, in a lunar eclipse. The stones I have
by me, from the summit, have not the smallest appearance of moss upon them.

"There is evidently the appearance of three zones—1, the woods—2, the bald mossy
part—3, the part above vegetation. The same appearance has been observed on the Alps, and
all other high mountains.

"I recollect no grass on the plain. The spaces between the rocks in the second zone, and
on the plain, are filled with spruce and fir, which, perhaps, have been growing ever since the
creation, and yet many of them have not attained a greater height than three or four inches,

Having surmounted the upper and steepest precipices, there is a large area, called the plain. It is a dry heath, composed of rocks covered with moss, and bearing the appearance of a pasture, in the beginning of the winter season. In some openings, between the rocks, there are springs of water, in others dry gravel. Here the grous or heath bird resorts, and is generally out of danger; several of them were shot by some travellers in October, 1774. The extent of this plain is uncertain; from the eastern side, to the foot of the pinnacle, or sugarloaf, it is nearly level, and it may be walked over in less than an hour. The sugar loaf, is a pyramidal heap of grey rocks, which, in some places, are formed like winding steps. This pinnacle has been ascended in one hour and a half. The traveller having gained the summit, is recompensed for his toil, if the sky be serene, with a most noble and extensive prospect. On the S.E. side, there is a view of the Atlantic ocean, the nearest part of which is fifty-five miles, in a direct line. On the W. and N. the prospect is bounded by the high lands, which separate the waters of the Connecticut and Amariscoggin rivers, from those of Lake Champlain and St. Lawrence. On the south, it extends to the southern-most mountains of New-Hampshire, comprehending a view of Lake Winipiseogee. On every side of these mountains, are long winding gullies, beginning at the precipice below the plain; and deepening in the descent. In winter, the snow lodges in these gullies; and being driven, by the N.W. and N.E. wind, from the top, is deepest in those which are situated on the southerly side. It is observed to lie longer in the spring on the south, than on the N.W. side, which is the case with many other hills in New-Hampshire.

A ranging company, who ascended the highest mountain, on the N.W. part, April 29th, 1725, found the snow four feet deep on that side; the summit was almost bare of snow, though covered with white frost and ice, and a small pond of water, near the top, was hard frozen.

In 1774, some men, who were making a road through the eastern pass of the mountain, ascended the mountain to the summit, on the 6th of June, and on the south side, in one of the deep gullies, found a body of snow thir-

---

but their spreading tops are so thick and strong, as to support the weight of a man, without yielding in the smallest degree. The snows and winds keeping the surface even with the general surface of the rocks. In many places, on the sides, we could get glades of this growth, some rods in extent, when we could, by sitting down on our feet, slide the whole length. The tops of the growth of wood were so thick and firm, as to bear us currently, a considerable distance, before we arrived at the utmost boundaries, which were almost as well defined as the water on the shore of a pond. The tops of the wood, had the appearance of having been shorn off, exhibiting a smooth surface, from their upper limits, to a great distance down the mountain." MS. of Dr. Cutler.

teen feet deep, and so hard, as to bear them. On the 19th of the same month, some of the same party ascended again, and in the same spot, the snow was five feet deep. In the first week of September, 1783, two men, who attempted to ascend the mountain, found the bald top so covered with snow and ice, then newly formed, that they could not reach the summit; but this does not happen every year so soon; for the mountain has been ascended as late as the first week in October, when no snow was upon it; and though the mountains begin to be covered, at times, with snow, as early as September, yet it goes off again, and seldom gets fixed until the end of October, or the beginning of November; but from that time it remains till July.[2] In the year 1784, snow was seen on the south side of the largest mountain, till the 12th of July; in 1790, it lay till the month of August.

During this period, of nine or ten months, the mountains exhibit more or less of that bright appearance, from which they are denominated white. In the spring, when the snow is partly dissolved, they appear of a pale blue, streaked with white; and after it is wholly gone, at the distance of sixty miles, they are altogether a sky colour; while at the same time, viewed at the distance of eight miles or less, they appear of the proper colour of the rock. These changes are observed by the people who live within constant view of them; and from these facts and observations, it may with certainty be concluded, that the whiteness of them is wholly caused by the snow, and not by any other white substance, for in fact, there is none. There are indeed in the summer months, some streaks, which appear brighter than other parts; but

2. The following is a journal of the appearances of the mountain, in the autumnal months of 1784, observed by Rev. Mr. Haven, of Rochester, whose house is in plain view of the south side of the mountain, distant about sixty miles.

Sept. 17 and 18. a N.E. storm of rain.

20, Mountain appeared white.

22, Of a pale blue.

Oct. 3 and 4. Rain, succeeded by frost.

5, Mountain white.

8, Of a pale blue.

9, White at the west end.

10, White in the morning, most part blue P.M.

22 and 24, Blue.

28, White at the west end, the rest blue.

Nov. 2, A spot of white at the west end.

4, Uniformly white.

5, Very white.

From this time, to the 23rd, when the weather was clear enough to see so far, the lower part of the mountain appeared very white; the summit involved in squally clouds.

N.B. the west end is the highest part.

these, when viewed attentively with a telescope, are plainly discerned to be the edges of the sides of the long deep gullies, enlightened by the sun, and the dark parts are the shaded sides of the same; in the course of the day, these spots may be seen to vary, according to the position of the sun.

A company of gentlemen visited these mountains in July, 1784, with a view to make particular observations on the several phenomena which might occur. It happened, unfortunately, that thick clouds covered the mountains almost the whole time, so that some of the instruments, which, with much labour, they had carried up, were rendered useless. These were a sextant, a telescope, an instrument for ascertaining the bearings of distant objects, a barometer, a thermometer, and several others for different purposes. In the barometer, the mercury ranged at 22,6, and the thermometer stood at 44 degrees. It was their intention to have placed one of each at the foot of the mountain, at the same time that the others were carried to the top, for the purpose of making corresponding observations; but they were unhappily broken in the course of the journey, through the rugged roads and thick woods; and the barometer, which was carried to the summit, had suffered so much agitation, that an allowance was necessary to be made, in calculating the height of the mountain, which was computed in round numbers, at five thousand and five hundred feet above the meadow, in the valley below, and nearly ten thousand above the level of the sea.[3] They intended to have made a geometrical mensuration of the altitude; but in the meadow, they could not obtain a base of sufficient length, nor see the summit of the sugar loaf; and in another place, where these inconveniences were removed, they were prevented by the almost continual obscuration of the mountains, by clouds.

Their exercise, in ascending the mountain, was so violent, that when Dr. Cutler, who carried the thermometer, took it out of his bosom, the mercury stood at fever heat, but it soon fell to 44°, and by the time that he had adjusted his barometer and thermometer, the cold had nearly deprived him of the use of his fingers. On the uppermost rock, the Rev. Mr. Little began to engrave the letters N.H. but was so chilled with the cold, that he gave the instruments to Col. Whipple, who finished the letters. Under a stone, they left a plate of lead, on which their names were engraven. The sun shone clear while they were passing over the plain, but immediately after their arrival at

---

3. This computation was made by the Rev. Dr. Cutler. Subsequent observations and calculations have induced the author to believe the computation of his ingenious friend too moderate, and he is persuaded, that whenever the mountain can be measured with the requisite precision, it will be found to exceed ten thousand feet, of perpendicular altitude, above the level of the ocean.

the highest summit, they had the mortification to be inveloped in a dense cloud, which came up the opposite side of the mountain. This unfortunate circumstance, prevented their making any farther use of their instruments. Being thus involved, as they were descending from the plain, in one of the long, deep gullies, not being able to see to the bottom, on a sudden, their pilot slipped, and was gone out of sight, though happily, without any other damage, than tearing his clothes. This accident obliged them to stop. When they turned their eyes upward, they were astonished at the immense depth and steepness of the place, which they had descended by fixing their heels on the prominent parts of the rock, and found it impracticable to reascend the same way; but having discovered a winding gully, of a more gradual ascent, in this they got up to the plain, and then came down on the eastern side; this deep gully, was on the S.E. From these circumstances, it may be inferred, that it is more practicable and safe, to ascend or descend on the ridges, than in the gullies of the mountain.

These vast and irregular heights, being copiously replenished with water, exhibit a great variety of beautiful cascades; some of which fall in a perpendicular sheet or spout, others are winding and sloping, others spread, and form a bason in the rock, and then gush in a cataract over its edge. A poetic fancy may find full gratification amidst these wild and rugged scenes, if its ardor be not checked by the fatigue of the approach. Almost every thing in nature, which can be supposed capable of inspiring ideas of the sublime and beautiful, is here realized. Aged mountains, stupendous elevations, rolling clouds, impending rocks, verdant woods, crystal streams, the gentle rill, and the roaring torrent, all conspire to amaze, to soothe and to enrapture.

1916

Early Explorations

Frederick W. Kilbourne

From *Chronicles of the White Mountains*

In 1916, Frederick Kilbourne (1872–1965) penned what is generally regarded as the finest overall history of the White Mountains. The piece that follows, along with one other in this volume, are excerpted from that book. The native New Englander, born in Wallingford, Connecticut, attended Yale University, and, following in the footsteps of early Yale president Timothy Dwight, frequently found himself exploring the scenic White Mountain country of northern New England. For many years Kilbourne served as director of publications for the Brooklyn (N.Y.) Library. He was also a life member of the Appalachian Mountain Club and a charter member of AMC's Connecticut Chapter. His writings on mountain history frequently appeared in AMC's journal, Appalachia.*

In July, 1784, a journey to the Mountains was accomplished, which is noteworthy for the number and character of the members of the party who made it and because of the purpose for which it was undertaken. I refer to the expedition made by the Reverend Dr. Jeremy Belknap, the historian of New Hampshire, then a resident of Dover; the Reverend Daniel Little, of Wells, Maine; the Reverend Manasseh Cutler, of Ipswich, Massachusetts; Dr. Joshua Fisher, of Beverly, Massachusetts; Mr. Heard, of Ipswich, and two young collegians, Hubbard and Bartlett, who set out to make a tour of the White Mountains "with a view to make particular observations on the several phenomena that might occur." For this purpose they were equipped with various instruments, including barometers, thermometers, a sextant, and surveying compasses. They were thus the first of a considerable line of scientific inquirers to visit these hills.

The historian has left several records[1] of the trip. Let me briefly advert to these, noting their character and provenience. In the first place, much of the Reverend Doctor's correspondence with his friend Ebenezer Hazard, of Philadelphia, has been preserved and printed in the "Collections" of the Massachusetts Historical Society.

Among these letters we find a record of Belknap's intention to make such a journey, for under date of July 4, 1784, he writes, "I expect, next week, to set out on a land tour to the White Mts., in company with several men of a scientific turn. I may write you again once before I go; but, if I live to come back, you may depend on such a description as I may be able to give." Dr. Belknap's letters to Mr. Hazard, giving an account of his tour are, unfortunately, not preserved among the Hazard letters. The want of such a narrative, however, is fully supplied, as has been intimated. There is extant, first, a memoir, "Description of the White Mountains," which was sent by him to the American Philosophical Society of Philadelphia, and to which "great attention was paid," writes Hazard. This was published in 1786, in the second volume of the Society's "Transactions," and in substance is similar to the account afterwards published in the third volume of Dr. Belknap's "History of New Hampshire." Both of these records are very different in form from the third account, which consists of the original notes kept by the doctor in the form of a diary. These have been printed with the correspondence above mentioned, and on them I shall largely rely for my summary of this notable trip. In the chapter on the White Mountains, given in the "History," the author refers to the visit to the Mountains made by a party of gentlemen in 1784, but gives no intimation that he was one of the company A few additional particulars are, however, there given.

The historian's account of the trip recorded in his dairy is so naïve and detailed that one may be pardoned for thinking that it may be of sufficient interest to give rather fully.

At Conway the travelers found Colonel Joseph Whipple, of Dartmouth (later Jefferson), and Captain Evans, who was to be their pilot, ready to go with them. Thence they journeyed through what is now Jackson and "along the Shelburne Road" to apparently about three fourths of a mile beyond the Glen Ellis Falls, where they encamped for the night. The next day, Saturday, July 24, the party undertook the ascent of "the Mountain" from the east-

---

1. Dr. Cutler also left an account of the journey, which is graphic and well written and which may be found in his *Life, Journals, and Correspondence*, published in 1888. Belknap was indebted to Cutler for his information about the ascent and descent of the chief peak. Cutler's manuscript breaks off before the description of the return is finished, but the remainder is covered in an account of the tour written by Mr. Little.

ern side. Dr. Fischer soon gave out, owing to a pain in his side, and returned to camp, where Colonel Whipple's negro man had been left in charge of the horses and baggage. After about two hours more of climbing, "having risen many very steep and extremely difficult precipices, I found my breath fail," says Dr. Belknap,[2] and in a consultation of the party it was decided that inasmuch as many stops had had to be made on his account and as the pilot supposed they were not more than halfway up to "the Plain," he should return. Refusing to deprive those who offered to go back with him of their expected pleasure, the good doctor came down safely alone in about an hour and a half and arrived "much fatigued," at the camp, "about 10 o'clock." It came on to rain toward night, so those at the camp repaired their tent with bark, took all the baggage into it, and anxiously awaited the return of their friends. The rain increased and continued all night, but although the tent leaked and the fire "decayed," they managed to keep the fire going and themselves dry.

It ceased raining at daylight on Sunday and soon thereafter the report of a gun partly relieved the anxiety of Drs. Belknap and Fisher. Shortly after the party of climbers arrived safely at camp. They reported that they passed the night around a fire, which was their only defense against the rain, and that "they had ascended to the summit, but had not had so good a view as they wished, the Mountain being most of the time involved with clouds, which rolled up and down in every direction, above, below, and around them." Their scientific observations were by "this unfortunate circumstance" for the most part prevented. They arrived at the pinnacle of the Sugar-Loaf at 1.06, their actual time of climbing from the tent being five hours and thirteen minutes. On the highest rock they found an old hat, which had been left there in June, 1774, by Captain Evans's party. They dined at 2 o'clock, we are told, on partridges and neat's tongue, cut the letters "N.H." on the uppermost rock and under a stone left a plate of lead[3] on which were engraved their names. The descent was a particularly difficult one, as, owing to the clouds, even the guide could not find the way down. Soon after their return to the camp they left for Dartmouth.

Their course in ascending the mountain was evidently through Tuckerman's Ravine, probably over Boott Spur, and up the east side on the cone, their route in the lower part being indicated by the stream which bears Dr.

---

2. "The spirit was willing but the flesh (i.e., the lungs) weak," he says in a letter to Hazard, and in the same letter, "You will not wonder that such a quantity of matter ('180 or 190 lbs. of mortality') could not ascend the White Mountains farther than it did."

3. The finding of this plate eighteen years later was "the source of great mystification to the villagers of Jackson." (Sweetser.)

Cutler's name.[4] Dr. Cutler estimated the height of the "pinnacle" or sugar-loaf," as Belknap calls it, to be not less than three hundred feet. From some unsatisfactory observations with the barometer, the elevation of the principal summit above the sea was computed to be nearly ten thousand feet. The party were disappointed in their attempt to measure the altitude geometrically from the base, because "in the meadow they could not obtain a base of sufficient length, nor see the summit of the sugar-loaf; and in another place, where these inconveniences were removed, they were prevented by the almost continual obscuration of the mountains by clouds."

"It is likely," says Professor Tuckerman, "that the plants of the higher regions were observed, and Mr. Oakes possessed fragments of such a collection made, either now or later, by Dr. Cutler, but the latter did not notice them in his memoir on the plants of New England published the next year in the transaction of the Academy,[5] nor is there any mention of them in the six small volumes of his botanical manuscripts which have come to my knowledge."

As the name of Mount Washington is found in Dr. Cutler's manuscript of 1784, it is probable that the appellation was given to the mountain by the party whose journey has just been described. The name first appears in print in Belknap's "History of New Hampshire," in the third volume, which was published in 1792.[6]

Dr. Cutler again visited the Mountains in July, 1804, this time chiefly to collect botanical specimens, in company with several friends, among whom were Dr. Nathaniel Bowditch and Dr. W. D. Peck, afterward professor of natural history at Cambridge. The party encamped on the side of Mount Washington on the night of the 27th, and on the next day Cutler, Peck, and one or two others made the ascent, arriving at 12.30. There were no clouds about the mountain, but the climbers were much chilled, and the descent

---

4. Given to the river, it is said, by Dr. Cutler's express desire. According to Belknap, another tributary of the Ellis River, "falls from the same mountain," a short distance to the south, and is called New River. Belknap's map makes Cutler's River flow from the present Tuckerman's Ravine. The account of Dr. Bigelow, a later explorer, agrees with this. In later maps, however, the names of the streams were transposed, the error being noticed by Mr. Sweetser, who was confirmed in his decision in the matter by Professor Tuckerman. New River got its name from the fact of its recent origin, it having been formed in October, 1775, during a great flood.

Some general observations on the vegetation of the Mountains, set down by Dr. Cutler in a manuscript preserved by Belknap, are quoted in Belknap's *History* and Dwight's *Travels*.

5. The American Academy of Arts and Sciences, of which Dr. Cutler was a member.

6. "It has lately been distinguished by the name of *Mount Washington*," is Belknap's statement.

was extremely fatiguing. Barometrical observations made at this time were computed by Dr. Bowditch to give an elevation of 7055 feet for the highest summit.

Dr. Peck made during this trip a collection of alpine plants, the citations of which in Pursh's "Flora of North America," published in 1814, "enable us," says Professor Tuckerman, "to determine the earliest recognition of several of the most interesting species."

Of early travelers to the Mountains one of the most distinguished was the Reverend Dr. Timothy Dwight, president of Yale College from 1794 to 1817. Dr. Dwight made two journeys on horseback to this region, the first in 1797 and the second in 1803.[7] His companion on the first expedition ("Journey to the White Mountains") was a Mr. L., one of the tutors of Yale College, and their objects were to examine the Connecticut River and to visit the White Mountains. Their first objective point was Lancaster, whence they proposed to proceed through the Notch to their second, Portland. They reached Lancaster on the morning of September 30. They left there on October 2, stayed overnight at Rosebrook's, and on October 3 passed through the Notch, of which Dr. Dwight gives a vivid description. It is "a very narrow defile," he says, extending two miles in length between two huge cliffs, apparently rent asunder by some vast convulsion of nature. This convulsion," he continues, "was, in my own view, unquestionably that of the deluge." He gives interesting information about the size and character of the mountain towns, describes Mount Washington and other features of the landscape graphically, and, altogether, has provided a very readable narrative of his tour. In his visit to the Mountains in 1803, President Dwight had as companion two graduates and a senior of Yale College, and their object was to ride up the Connecticut River as far as the Canadian boundary ("Journey to the Canada Line"). In the course of the tour, however, the party left the Connecticut, went up the lower Ammonoosuc, turned aside from the latter to visit Bethlehem, whence they returned to the Ammonoosuc, and then went on to the Notch, which they visited on September 30. "I renewed," says the traveler, "a prospect of all the delightful scenes, which I have mentioned in a former account." It was at this time that he gave to one of the waterfalls near the Gate of the Notch the name "Silver Cascade," which it still bears. He visited Rosebrook's, and then went by way of Jefferson to Lancaster and thence onward to Canada.

7. Dr. Dwight also made two horseback journeys to Lake Winnepesaukee. The first of these was made in the autumn of 1812 and the second in the same season of the next year. In both excursions he touched the fringe of the White Mountain region, passing through Plymouth in both and ascending Red Hill on the second.

Another early scientific explorer of the White Hills, who has left us an account of his excursion and a record of his observations, and who deserves a brief mention, was Dr. George Shattuck, of Boston. He was one of a party of six, which set out from Hanover, July 8, 1807, taking along various scientific instruments. On Saturday the 11th the members of the party started from Rosebrook's to ascend Mount Washington, at the summit of which they arrived the following day. Dr. Shattuck notes that the temperature there at noon was 66° and that the day was not very clear, the distant horizon being smoky. He describes briefly the plants, the character of the surface of the summit, and rareness of the atmosphere, and other phenomena. Unfortunately, his attempts to make barometrical observations for the purpose of estimating the height of the mountain were, he says, "defeated by an accident, the prevention of which was beyond my controul."

The next noteworthy American explorer of the White Hills was Dr. Jacob Bigelow. Botany was the particular interest of this famous Boston physician, who was born in 1797 and who lived to the ripe old age of ninety-two. His tour to the Mountains was made in 1816, in company with Francis C. Gray, Esq., Dr. Francis Boott, in whose honor a spur of Mount Washington has been named, Nathaniel Tucker, and Lemuel Shaw, Esq., afterward Chief Justice of Massachusetts. On their way they climbed Monadnock and Ascutney. The ascent of the White Mountains "was at that time," says the doctor,[8] "an arduous undertaking, owing to the rough state of the country and the want of roads or paths." "We were obliged," he says further, "to walk about fifteen miles and to encamp two nights in the brushwood on the side of the mountain." Each man of the party having carried up a stick, they were enabled to build a fire on the summit and to prepare a meal from such supplies as their guides had brought up. The day (July 2) was a fine one, but the atmosphere was hazy, so that their view of distant objects was very indistinct. The temperature at noon was 57° F. From the registration of a mountain barometer at that hour, calculations were made which gave the height within a few feet of the correct altitude. As a memorial of their achievement of the ascent they left their names and the date inclosed in a bottle cemented to the highest rock. In the afternoon they descended in

8. Dr. Bigelow published an account of the journey and a list of the plants collected in the *New England Journal of Medicine and Surgery*, for October, 1816. The quotations in the text are taken from some autobiographical notes, quoted in a *Memoir of Jacob Bigelow, M.D., LL.D.*, by George E. Ellis (1880). Writing these notes about fifty years after the event, Dr. Bigelow's memory must have played him false, for he gives the year of the journey as 1815 and states that it was the 4th of July when the party was on the summit and that in celebration of the day, Mr. Gray was invited to deliver an impromptu address.

about five hours to their camping place, and the following day they reached Conway.

This expedition, besides achieving the most satisfactory determination of the height of Mount Washington that had been made, was noteworthy as a natural history survey. Dr. Bigelow's article "Some Account of the White Mountains of New Hampshire," provided a statement of all that was known of their mineralogy and zoology, but is especially important from a botanical standpoint, for his lists of plants, or florula, "determined," says Professor Tuckerman, "in great measure the phaenogamous botany of our Alps." Very appropriately Dr. Bigelow's name has been since given to a grassy plot (Bigelow's Lawn), rich in alpine plants, below the cone of Mount Washington on Boott Spur. Dr. Boott returned to the Mountains in August of the same year, and as a result of his trip added a "considerable" number of species to the botanical collection.

Another noted botanist to explore the Mountains was William Oakes,[9] who visited them, in company with his friend Dr. Charles Pickering, in 1825, again in 1826, and from 1843 on, every summer. To him we are indebted for additions to our botanical knowledge, but especially for one of the classics of White Mountain literature, his "Scenery of the White Mountains," a book consisting of descriptive letterpress accompanying large lithographic plates from drawings by Isaac Sprague.[10] His purpose of publishing a smaller volume to be called "The Book of the White Mountains" and to consist of descriptions of things of interest, a flora of the alpine plants, with the mosses and lichens, and a complete guide for visitors, was frustrated by his tragic death the year (1848) of the publication of his "Scenery."

9. There is a memoir in the *American Journal of Science and Arts* for January, 1849, by Asa Gray, who calls him "the most distinguished botanist of New England." Oakes was born in Danvers, July 1, 1799, and was drowned by falling overboard from a ferryboat between Boston and East Boston, July 31, 1848, it is supposed as a result of a sudden attack of faintness or vertigo. He graduated in 1820 from Harvard, where his previous fondness for natural history was developed under the instruction of professor W. D. Peck. Oakes named Mounts Clay and Jackson, sending his guide to the summit of the latter to kindle a bonfire there to celebrate the event. His own name is perpetuated in the Mountains by Oakes Gulf, the deep ravine to the east of Mounts Pleasant and Franklin.

10. There are in all sixteen full folio pages of plates. The sixteenth plate and a part of the fourteenth are from paintings by G. N. Frankenstein, a well-known artist of Cincinnati, after whom a cliff and a railroad trestle in the Crawford Notch are named.

1855

The White Mountain Giant

John H. Spaulding

From *Historical Relics of the White Mountains*

A North Country native, born and raised in Lancaster, N.H., John Hubbard Spaulding (1821–1893) went on to become manager of two of Mount Washington's early summit hotels—the Tip-Top House and Summit House. It was during his tenure as hotel manager that he published Historical Relics of the White Mountains, Also, a Concise White Mountain Guide. *This early history and guide to the region went through three different editions between 1855 and 1862. Mr. Spaulding made his last visit to the mountain in 1891, when he successfully climbed to the summit at the age of 70. He died on his 72nd birthday in nearby Whitefield.*

THE NAME of E. A. Crawford is deeply chiselled upon the rocks of this granite Mount built by nature (Mount Washington); and the lady who shared in life his joys and sorrows has, in her "White Mountain History," reared a testimonial to his memory. Will not my humble tribute of a stone, laid in silence upon his grave, be accepted by all who pleasantly cherish the remembrance of *"Ethan of the Hills,"* or the *"White Mountain Giant"*?

The subject of this sketch was born in Guildhall, Vermont, in the year 1792. When but a mere lad his parents moved to the White Mountains, and here he grew up a giant mountaineer, illustrating by his hardy habits, how daring enterprise and pure mountain climate nerve the man and stamp the *hero* upon mortality. Inheriting the house on the westerly end of the "Giant's Grave," with an encumbrance that made him worse than destitute of all worldly goods, he was one day shocked, when returning from hunting on the hills, to see his home burned down, and his wife and infant sheltered only by an open shed. Twelve miles one way, and six the other, to neighbors, here he was with his little family in the wilderness, destitute of every comfort, save that of hope. The sunshine of joy, unclouded by sorrow, and the warm smiles of good fortune, seem ever attendant upon the lives of some, constantly beckoning their favorites forward to the green fields of abundance, and bowers of pleasure and ease. Others, perchance born under a less favoring star, in their growth rise up like giants, breasting manfully, step by step, the wrecking storms of adversity, and by their own heroic exertions, hew out for themselves characters deeply lined, amid the black shadows of sorrow and disappointment. Of such a mould was the spirit of Ethan A. Crawford. The inconveniences of poverty, that come like a strong man armed upon poor mortality, and sickness and the many hardships linked with every-day life in a new settlement, fell to this man's share. Yet he cheerfully performed the duties of life with an iron resolution, that stood misfortune's shocks as firmly as his own mountains stand storms and the changes of time. He was a tall, finely-proportioned man; and, though called by many the "White Mountain Giant," beneath the rough exterior of the hardy mountaineer glowed constantly, in a heroic heart, the warm fire of love and manly virtue. The artless prattle of his little children was sweet music to his spirit, and his ambitious aspirations were constantly invigorated by social comfort with his little family.

Carrying the Kettle and Deer.

The first display of Ethan's *giant strength* recorded is of his carrying on his head, across the Amonoosuc river, a potash-kettle, weighing four hundred pounds.

In 1821 he caught a full-grown deer, in a wild gorge, four miles from his home; and as the trap had not broken his leg, and he appeared quite gentle, he thought to lead him home. Failing in his attempt to do this, he shouldered him and trudged homeward, over hill and through tangled brushwood, feeling by the way, perchance, like Crusoe, with his lamas, how fine it would be to have a park and many deer to show his visitors. But his day-visions vanished; for, on arriving home, he found the deer so much injured that he died.

Another time, he *caught a wild mountain-buck* in a snare; and, finding him too heavy to shoulder, he made him a halter of withes, and succeeded in halter-leading him so completely, that, after nearly a day spent in the attempt, he arrived at home with his prize, much to the wonder of all.

The Giant Lugging the Old Bear.

In 1829 Ethan caught a good-sized bear in a trap; and thought to bind him with withes, and lead him home as he had the buck. In attempting to do this, the bear would catch with his paws at the trees; and our hero, not willing to be outwitted by a bear, managed to get him on his shoulder, and, with one hand firmly hold of his nose, carried him two miles homeward. The bear, not well satisfied with his prospects, entered into a serious engagement with his captor, and by scratching and biting succeeded in tearing off his vest and one pantaloon-leg, so that Ethan laid him down so hard upon the rocks that he died. That fall he caught ten bears in that same wild glen.

The first bear kept in the White Mountains for a show was caught by Ethan, while returning from the Mountain with two young gentlemen he had been up with as guide. Seeing a small bear cross their path, they followed him to a tree, which he climbed. Ethan climbed after, and, succeeding in getting him, tied his mouth up with a handkerchief, and backed him home. This bear he provided with a trough of water, a strap and pole; and here he was for a long time kept, as the first tame bear of the mountains. This was about the year 1829.

Ethan caught a wild-cat with a birch withe! Once, when passing down the Notch, he was attracted to a tree by the barking of his dog, where, up among the thick branches, he discovered a full-grown wild-cat. Having only a small hatchet with him, he cut two long birch withes, and, twisting them well together, made a slip-noose, which he run up through the thick leaves; and while the cat was watching the dog, he managed to get this noose over his head, and, with a sudden jerk, brought him to the ground. His dog instantly seized him, but was willing to beat a retreat till reinforced by his master, who with a heavy club came to the rescue. The skin of this cat, when stretched, measured over six feet.

Ethan's *two close shots* are worthy of note. One fall, while setting a sable line, about two miles back of the Notch, he discovered a little lake, set, like a diamond, in a rough frame-work of beetling crags. The fresh signs of moose near, and trouts seen in its shining waters, was sufficient inducement to spend a night by its shady shore. About sunset, while engaged in catching a string of trouts, his attention was suddenly arrested by a loud splashing in the still water around a rocky point, where, on looking, he saw two large brown moose pulling up lily-roots, and fighting the flies. Prepared with an extra charge, he fired; and before the first report died in echoes among the peaks, the second followed, and both moose fell dead in the lake. Ethan labored hard to drag his game ashore; but late that evening bright visions of marrow-bones and broiled trouts flitted like realities around him. That night a doleful dirge rose in that wild gorge; but our hero slept soundly, between two warm moose-skins. He cared not for the wild wolves that scented the taint of the fresh blood in the wind. That little mountain sheet is now, from the above circumstance, known as "*Ethan's Pond.*"

Ethan was always proud to speak of how he *carried a lady two miles down the mountain on his shoulders.* It was no uncommon affair for him to shoulder a man and lug him down the mountain; but his more delicate attempts to pack a young lady down the steep rocks, he seemed to regard as an important incident in his adventurous career. Miss E. Woodward was the name of the lady who received from the Mountain Giant such marked attention. By a wrong step she became very lame, and placing, as well as he could, a cushion of coats upon his right shoulder, the lady became well seated, and he thus brought her down to where they left their horses.

By Adino N. Brackett's Journal, published in Moore's His. Col., vol. 1st, page 97, it appears that Adino N. Brackett, John W. Weeks, Gen. John Willson, Charles J. Stuart, Esq., Noyes S. Dennison, and Samuel A. Pearson, Esq., from Lancaster, N.H., with Philip Carrigan and E. A. Crawford, went up, July 31st, 1820, to name the different summits. Gen. John Willson, of Boston, is now, 1855, the only survivor of that party. "They made Ethan their pilot, and loaded him with provisions and blankets, like a pack-horse; and then, as they began to ascend, they piled on top of this load their coats." This party had a fine time; and, after giving names of our sages to the different peaks, according to their altitude, they drank health to these hoary cliffs, in honor to the illustrious men whose names they were, from this date, to bear; then, *curled down among the rocks,* without fire, on the highest crag, they doubtless spent the first night mortals ever spent on that elevated place. In the morning, after seeing the sun rise out of the ocean far, far below them, they descended westerly from the apex about a mile, and came to a beautiful sheet of water (Lake of the Clouds), near a ridge of rocks, which, when they left, they named "*Blue Pond.*" It doubtless looked blue to them; for something they carried in bottles so weakened the limbs of one of the party that Ethan was, from this place, burdened with a back-load of mortality, weighing two hundred pounds, down to the Amonoosuc valley. Thus we find Ethan most emphatically the "*Giant of the Mountains.*" He never hesitated to encounter any danger that appeared in his path, whether from wild beasts, flood, or mountain tempest.

The *First Bridle-path* on the White Mountains was made in 1819. As there had got to be ten or twelve visitors a year, to see these mountains, at this date, Ethan thought, to accommodate his company, he would cut a path

The gravesite of Ethan Allen Crawford can be found in Bretton Woods, N.H., not far from the site of his former home in the White Mountains.

as far as the region to scrub vegetation extended. It had been very difficult to go without a road, clambering over trees, up steep ledges, through streams, and over the hedgy scrub-growth; and accordingly, when the act of a path being made was published, the fame of this region spread like wildfire. This path was started at the head of the notch near Gibb's House, and, extending to the top of Mount Clinton, reached from thence to the top of Mount Washington, nearly where Gibb's Path now is. Soon after the completion of this path, the necessity of a cabin, where visitors could stop through the night, was perceivable by Ethan; and accordingly be built *a stone cabin,* near the top of Mount Washington, by a spring of water that lives there, and spread in it an abundance of soft moss for beds, that those who wished to stop here through the night, to see the sun set and rise, might be accommodated. This rude home for the traveller was soon improved, and furnished with a small stove, an iron chest, and a long roll of sheet-lead; —the chest was to secure from the bears and hedge-hogs the camping-blankets; and, according to tradition, around that old chest many who hungered have enjoyed a hearty repast. That roll of lead was for visitors to engrave their names on with a sharp iron. Alas! *that* tale-telling old chest was buried by an avalanche. How all things pass away!

In 1821 the *first ladies* visited Mount Washington. This party, of which these ladies numbered three, had Ethan for its guide, and, proceeding to the stone cabin, waited there through a storm for several days, that they might be the first females to accomplish the unrecorded feat of ascending Mount Washington. This heroic little party was the Misses Austin, of Portsmouth, N.H., being accompanied by their brother and an Esq. Stuart, of Lancaster. Everything was managed as much for their comfort as possible; the little stone cabin was provided with an outside addition, in which the gentlemen staid, that their companions might be more retired and comfortable. This party came near being what the sailor might call "weather-bound." They were obliged to send back for more provisions; and at last the severe mountain-storm passed away, and that for which they had ambitiously endured so much exposure was granted them. They went to the top, had a fine prospect, and, after an absence of five days, returned from the mountains, in fine spirits, highly gratified with their adventure. This heroic act should confer an honor upon the names of this pioneer party, as everything was managed with so much prudence and modesty that there was not left even a shadow for reproach, save by those who felt themselves outdone; so says record.

In the summer of 1840 the first horse that ever climbed the rocks of Mount Washington was rode up by old Abel Crawford. The old man was then seventy-five years old, and, though his head was whitened by the snows of many winters, his blood was stirred, on that occasion, by the ambitious animation of more youthful days. There he sat proudly upon his noble horse, with uncovered head, and the wind played lightly with his venerable white locks. Truly that was a picture worthy an artist's skill. Holding that horse by the rein, there stood his son Ethan, as guide to his old father. The son and the parent!—worthy representatives of the mighty monument, to the remembrance of which, their pioneer exertions have added fadeless fame. From that day a new era dawned on these mountains. Forget not the veteran Abel, and Ethan *"the White Mountain Giant."*

The White Mountain Guides should all be remembered. In our lengthy notice of Ethan, *the White Mountain Giant*, we do not mean to eclipse the worthy deeds of other noble mountain spirits, who have followed his old path, and even made new ones for their own feet. This mountain region is truly haunted, as it were, by peculiar influences, that call to its attractions as dauntless men for guides as our New England mountain-land can boast. Ethan A. Crawford came here when this was a wilderness-land, unknown to fame. The fashionable world knew nothing of its peculiarities. He spent much time, even the energies of his life, exploring the wild gorges and dangerous peaks of the mountains, and became a mighty hunter. He was, in fact, the bold pioneer who, with his old father, opened the way whereby the "Crystal Hills" became known to the world. "Honor to whom honor is due!" Then let us not be unmindful of Ethan, who grappled with nature in her wildness, and made gigantic difficulties surmountable; and let us remember the names of "Tom Crawford," "Hartford," Hall," "Cogswell;" "Dana, and Lucius M. Rosebrook," "Leavitt," "Hayes," and others, who have followed piloting for a series of years on these mountains. These are all men in whose hands the tourist was comparatively safe; and, though the most of the above names are with the past, others are on the stage, who have an ambitious desire to outdo, even, in skill and management, those whose footsteps they follow. We will not praise the living guides of the White Mountains; their actions speak monuments of honor to their own names. Have confidence in their integrity; and may they never betray their trust!

1960

Dolly Copp
and the Glen House

F. Allen Burt

From *The Story of Mount Washington*

Like his father and grandfather before him, Frank Allen Burt (1885–1971) had a passion for Mount Washington and the White Mountains, and that passion led to the 1960 publishing of the book, The Story of Mount Washington, *by Dartmouth College. Burt's epic biography of New England's most celebrated peak was a natural project for him to undertake, seeing how his grandfather, Henry M. Burt, and his dad, Frank H. Burt, were the editors of the summit newspaper,* Among the Clouds, *from its inception through the great mountaintop fire of 1908. Drawing on the wealth of documents his family had gathered over the years, along with his extensive personal experiences on the mountain, Burt was able to write the definitive history of the mountain. Frank Burt was also a well-known Boston writer, teacher and advertising expert, who was affiliated with both Boston University and Northeastern University. Prior to penning the Mount Washington history, Burt wrote several other books, mostly about advertising.*

ALTHOUGH the Crawfords in the early 1800s were making the valley to the west of Mount Washington popular with tourists, it was not until 1827 that anybody had the hardihood to settle in the wilderness on the eastern slope of the great mountain, then known as the "Eastern Pass," now "Pinkham Notch" or "The Glen."

Even the early owners of the Glen made no effort to settle there. During the French and Indian Wars Thomas Martin served the English Crown so faithfully as a purchaser of military stores for the British army that King

George III in 1775 deeded to him a tract of land in the Glen along the banks of Peabody River. Contained in Martin's Location is the now famous Dolly Copp Camp Grounds five miles south of Gorham on the Glen Road.

Jackson, the first town near the lower end of Pinkham Notch, was first settled by Benjamin Copp, in 1778. The original name given the town was New Madbury, for the early settlers came from Madbury, New Hampshire. In 1800 the town was incorporated as Adams. Some years later its name was changed to Jackson, all of its voters but one being for Jackson, when the question was whether he or Adams should be president.

Little is known of Copp and his family. They lived entirely alone in a vast wilderness for twelve years before any other inhabitants joined them. Then in 1790, a year before Abel Crawford moved into Nash and Sawyer's Location, Captain Joseph Pinkham, of Madbury, with four neighboring families, migrated to New Madbury and its rich lands on the lower part of Ellis River.

But the real pioneer of what was to become Pinkham Notch—the man who single-handed, hewed a home out of the virgin forest—was a young fellow twenty-four years of age, small of stature, with bent, sloping shoulders, a shapely head under a curling shock of yellow hair, pale blue eyes set deep under shaggy brows, a sound heart in a barrel chest, and long arms with rippling muscles. Born in 1804, in Stow, Maine, near the New Hampshire line, Dodifer Hayes Copp was the son of Lieutenant Samuel Copp of Lebanon, Maine, and the former Hannah Hayes. Christened "Dodovah Hayes Copp," he later changed the spelling to "Dodifer." Most generally he was known as Hayes, or "Haze," by his intimates. Whether or not Hayes Copp was related to Benjamin is uncertain.

Hayes Copp, before he was twenty, had made his way through Fryeburg to the blooming farm lands of Bartlett and Jackson. There he heard tales of the rich black soil seventeen miles up the notch from Jackson, where wealth was waiting only for the axe, the torch, and the plowshare.

Even then young Copp was a hard, unyielding man, whom neither hardship nor danger could turn from his determined course. Negotiating with the New Hampshire Legislature, he secured a deed to a future farm in the forest lands of Martin's Location. In place of money, of which he had none, the boy pledged wheat, oats, and barley, to be raised when the land was ready, and which through years of toil he paid to the last bushel.

It was in 1827 that Hayes Copp, a pack on his back, his long-barreled flintlock gun over his shoulder, his axe in his hand, set off up the blazed trail that followed the Ellis River up the Notch and then went down the Peabody River, crossing the stream where later was built the Dolly Copp Bridge, since

Hayes Copp (left) and his bride, Dolly (right), were pioneer settlers in the area known as Glen Peabody between Pinkham Notch and Gorham.

removed. Somehow he found the surveyors' blazes on the trees, telling him that here along the river was the land which was to be his farm and home. And here he built his shelter, a lean-to of poles, roofed, and walled on three sides with strips of hemlock bark. In front of the open side he built a great fireplace of flat stones — his cook stove and his only source of warmth through the long winter nights that lay ahead of him

Food was abundant: trout in the brooks, bears in the berry thickets, deer coming morning and night to drink in the river, and game birds aplenty. Salt pork, Indian meal, salt — the pioneer's priceless commodities — he traded for on infrequent trips to Jackson, carrying down in exchange the furs he had dressed.

In the Glen the summer is short. The snow lies late into the spring in this deep valley, and comes again early in winter. Those few weeks of warm weather between snow and snow were filled with grinding toil, felling, piling, and burning the great trees. The second spring Hayes "scratched in" round the blackened stumps in his little clearing turnip and pumpkin seeds and perhaps a few patch of wheat. The black soil, the humus of ages of fallen trees, awoke in the sunshine and gave the toiler a harvest.

Where a butternut once shaded the road, the young man "rolled up" a one-room log cabin, and a little nearer the river a log barn for the sheep and

GUY SHOREY

The boarded-up homestead of Hayes and Dolly Copp
as it appeared earlier this century.

cows he hoped to soon buy. No one driving up the smooth road from Jackson to Gorham can picture the savagery with which nature fought back at this invader of the Glen. It took from three to five years for him to wrest from the wilderness a farm and a home. Then he was ready for a helpmate.

On one of his rare visits down the notch Hayes had met Dolly Emery, a girl just his own age, small in stature, with flaxen hair, light blue eyes that had a flash of keenness, and glib tongue. They were married in Bartlett 3 November 1831.

In 1824 Durand, six miles beyond the mountain wall to the west, was incorporated as the town of Randolph, known for its prosperous farmers and lumbermen. To link Randolph with Jackson, early in the thirties the legislature of New Hampshire made a contract with Daniel Pinkham to build a wagon road along the old blazed trail. It was rough going, the work of several years, with few laborers and fewer tools. It taxed the resourcefulness of a man, who as a boy, had taught his pig to haul a sled, but he carried it through. Daniel received a grant of land on both sides of the road, extending from just above Glen Ellis Falls to Emerald Pool in the Peabody River, and embracing the present-day site of the Appalachian Mountain Club's Pinkham Notch Camp, the Notch having been given its name from this grant. So the road came to the Copps' farm, and made just a bit lighter the life of this man and woman whose perfect health, great strength, and un-conquerable will fitted them for the everlasting battle to enlarge their clear-ing and make for themselves and their flocks more lands to till and wider pastures for grazing. As George Cross tells us:

> But they needed all their strength and pluck to fight the bears from the young lambs in spring, the wolves from the young cattle in the fall, the foxes, coons and skunks from the poultry yards, the deer from the ripening grain. They must expect the late and early frosts of the too-short summers. They must face the intense cold, terrific winds and deep snows of the always long win-ters. And they well knew that every year the fight with some of these enemies would be a losing battle.

But year after year their farm and their flocks increased. The one-room log cabin gave place to a long low frame house, neatly painted and connected by an ell with a roomy frame barn.

As for Dolly Copp's part in this household—in the spring she saw to the setting of the hens and raised fine broods of chickens. She helped Hayes shear the sheep, cleansed and carded the wool, spun the snowy rolls into yarn, wove the yarn on her clumsy loom into cloth or knit it into socks for the whole family. In the corner of the ell room stood the brass kettle in which in the fall she made hundreds of "tallow dips." Ranged along the barnyard wall were the barrels and tubs, and the kettle swung over the out-door fireplace where in the early spring she made the year's supply of soap. In the winter evenings, by the light of her tallow dips burning on the light stand before the fireplace, she knit or darned and made or mended the gar-ments of the whole family.

A tradition says that Joseph Jackson brought on his back from Canter-bury, New Hampshire, a sackful of little apple trees to grow into the first apple orchard in Shelburne Addition (now Gorham). Dolly's orchard, now rows of gnarled and decaying tree trunks, was started not long after Jackson planted his first trees. But she found her trees in the woods along the river banks, the "Johnny Appleseed" trees that grow everywhere. From the "wild-ings" she selected the best, and by care and cultivation they grew to great size and bore apples of many fine varieties.

During the forty years that the Pinkham Notch road was the only high-way from Jackson to Randolph, the Copps' home served as an inn for the wayfarers who stopped for a meal or for the night. Dolly's comfortable beds and good food became widely known. The price was "a shilling all round"—that is, twenty-five cents for a meal, the same for a bed for each person, and a quarter for the feed and care of a horse.

In 1836 Shelburne Addition became the town of Gorham. A good wagon road took the place of the old blazed trail from the Copp farm to this prosperous town. In 1852 the Atlantic & St. Lawrence Railway (operated first by the Grand Trunk Railway and now a part of the Canadian National System) connected Gorham with Portland. At the same time the Boston, Concord & Montreal Railway pushed up as far as Conway. Daily mail stages started running through Pinkham Notch between these two mountain towns.

A little earlier, a family of English descent by the name of Barnes built their home and farm a quarter of a mile up the Randolph road from the Copps'. Soon after, Patrick Culhane took up a claim about midway between the Copp and Barnes farms. Across the river in Green's Grant had settled Frederick and Sally Spaulding with their four lively youngsters, who were a little older than the Copp children. After so many years of neighborless isolation, the pioneers of the Glen were to know neighbors and human friendship.

Mail coaches and trains meant travelers. In 1852, quick to see the future possibilities of the Glen, came John Bellows to build the first hotel at the eastern base of Mount Washington.

Colonel Joseph M. Thompson, who in 1853 succeeded John Bellows as owner of the Glen House, had learned the hotel business as proprietor of the Casco Bay House in Portland, Maine. At the time of his purchase at the Glen he was living in New Gloucester, Maine. Under his genial and able management—aided materially by the excellence of Mrs. Thompson's cooking—the Glen House became increasingly popular, and required enlargement.

Dolly was ready to reap her own harvest from this new summer-visitor business. Her own little inn was full of city folk summer after summer. And besides she found a ready market at the Glen House for her bolts of woolen homespun, her yards of linen, her dyes of delicate blue, her golden butter, rich cheese, and maple syrup.

Among summer folk there was a belief that the one perfect view of the profile on Imp Mountain, then becoming known as "Dolly Copp's Imp," was to be had in the dooryard of the Copp farm. So the great six-horses stages, as they rolled along the Glen road laden inside and out with eager sightseeing visitors, usually turned aside, crossed the river, and drew up before the Copp house. There the smartly-dressed vacationers divided their attention between Dolly's Imp, standing out clear against a screen of white cloud, and Dolly herself and her modest family gathered shyly about, the father with his pinched, hard face wearing the grim smile of years of endurance,

COURTESY BOB & FLORENCE COOK

The first Glen House, built in 1850 and enlarged several times afterwards, was operated by Joseph M. Thompson from 1853 to 1869, when he drowned in a fall flood. The hotel was destroyed by fire in 1884.

Dolly standing in the doorway, clad in her pale blue dress of homespun, nervously fingering her gold beads, pretty Sylvia shyly peering out over her mother's shoulder, small Daniel clinging to his mother's skirt, Jerry and Nat modestly answering a babel of questions. Thus the name and fame of Dolly Copp and her family went forth throughout New England and far beyond.

One of Colonel Thompson's early improvements was the building of the Glen Bridle Path up Mount Washington, climbing to the summit in seven miles by the ridge on which the carriage road was afterwards built. The zigzag route of the path through the woods for the first few miles has long since been wiped out and forgotten, but between the Halfway House and the summit much of the course may still be traced, some portions in a deep trench among the rocks, others in thickets of scrub. Within a mile of the top it crossed a broad, grassy area called the Cow Pasture, where are still seen the stone walls of a corral in which cows were kept during one summer before 1860 to supply the Tiptop House with milk.

The elegant dining room of the first Glen House
could accommodate as many as 600 guests.

For the stage lines to Gorham and North Conway and for riders on the Glen Bridle Path, Thompson needed a large number of horses. In his great stable at New Gloucester he kept a splendid array of animals, and their departure for the mountains each summer was one of the great events of the village. A long rope was laid along the principal street, a pair of fine horses harnessed as leaders at one end, with a rider on one of them. Then at regular intervals the remaining horses were tied to the ropes in pairs, one on each side, a carriage with driver bringing up the rear. As there were as many as a hundred horses in all, they were divided into several bunches, each group tied to a long rope. It is said that the cavalcade would be two or three days in reaching the Glen House.

Landlord Thompson had much of the showman in his make-up. His big Concord coaches of the tallyho variety, which met the Grand Trunk trains at Gorham, were drawn by eight perfectly matched white horses. His expert driver had his arrival so timed that just at the moment the passengers commenced to alight from the train at the Gorham station, they were surprised and fascinated by the sight of the great coach, often loaded with departing guests, sweeping in a great circle up to the platform, the eight beautiful horses on a full gallop, brought to a standstill directly in front of the train.

Colonel Thompson continued to run the Glen House with increasing patronage until his death by drowning in 1869 during a terrific rainstorm and flood in the Peabody River.

In December of 1874, their children having married, Dolly and Hayes Copp once more were left alone in the home they had fought so hard to build in Martin's Location. The wilderness was tamed. Their work as pioneers was finished. They were approaching the Golden Jubilee of their marriage. It would have seemed a fitting time for relaxing and contentment and joy. But this couple were like sunlight and storm. Dolly was a dynamo of happy energy, her twinkling blue eyes seeking needs for service her ready hands might perform, her wide mouth turning up at the corners in mirthful appreciation of the fun of living.

But Hayes was a dour character who, in all his life, had never had time for fun. His gimlet eyes were always boring into some problem that was to mean hard, laborious work. His forehead was puckered up above his hawk nose, while his straight bitter lips slanted downward at each end towards the unrelieved hardness of his jaw. There is no story told of Hayes being unkind to his family, but it was not in such a nature to be sympathetic or kindly or to have the least fun in life. And it is not mere coincidence than an old timer in Gorham recalled that "Haze Copp was the meanest man I ever knew in all my life."

Dolly was not one to speak ill of any one, least of all her husband of fifty years. All she told her friends was: "Hayes is well enough. But fifty years is long enough for a woman to live with any man."

So, without rancor, and with scrupulous care, they divided between them the savings of a lifetime. Leaving the fields, the orchard, and the garden they had made together, they separated and went their chosen ways. Hayes returned to his native town of Stow, while Dolly found a home with her daughter Sylvia in Auburn, Maine. There, far from each other, and far from the scenes of their life work, they lived out their remaining years.

It was in 1915 that the Federal Government added to the White Mountain National Forest the old farms in the Glen, and laid out the Dolly Copp Recreational Area, which has become a favorite vacation spot for hundreds of campers. In the spring of 1951 it was placed under the management of the Appalachian Mountain Club, to become the largest of its camping facilities.

In 1933 citizens of Gorham joined to erect a monument to the memory of Hayes and Dolly Copp, the Pioneers of the Glen.

1916

Summit Hospitality

Frederick W. Kilbourne

From *Chronicles of the White Mountains*

THE STEPS in two connected enterprises—one the supplying of shelter for visitors to Mount Washington and the other the providing of means of making the ascent for others than persons coming on foot or on horse-back—form perhaps the most interesting series of events in White Mountain history. The joint story covers a long period of time and is a record worthy of the strong men who by their courage and energy have made New Hampshire famous. I have already told of the building of the earlier foot-paths and the bridle path and of the first shelter erected on the Mountain. This latter, it will be recalled, consisted of Ethan Allen Crawford's three stone cabins, which, soon after their erection in 1823, were abandoned. Mr. Crawford followed these with a large tent, which he spread near a spring of water not far from the Summit and which was provided with a sheet-iron stove. Because, however, of the violent storms and wind, this new shelter could not be kept in place and soon wore out.

Soon after the bridle path was opened, a rude wooden shelter of about a dozen feet square was built, but its existence was short,[1] and it is not known what became of it. This is the "Tip-Top House," that Dr. Edward Everett Hale tells of entering, in September, 1841.

The first hotel on Mount Washington was built in 1852, and owed its construction to the enterprise of Nathan R. Perkins, of Jefferson, and Lucius M. Rosebrook, and Joseph S. Hall, both citizens of Lancaster. This difficult

1. Colonel Charles Parsons, of St. Louis, who visited Mount Washington in 1900 for the second time, remembered that this shelter was in existence in 1844, when he walked up the Mountain. (From his "Reminiscences" in *Among the Clouds*.)

work was begun in May, and on July 28 the hotel, the "Summit House," was open to the public.

All the lumber for the sheathing and roof had to be carried upon horses from a sawmill near Jefferson Highlands. A chain was hung over the horse's back and one end of each board was run through a loop at the end of the chain, two boards being carried on each side of the horse. The drivers, D. S. Davis and A. Judson Bedell, walked behind carrying the farther ends of the boards. Mr. Rosebrook, it is said, carried the front door up the Mountain on his back from the Glen House. Such were the obstacles that were overcome by these energetic men.

This structure, which stood on the north side of the peak, was built largely of rough stones blasted from the Mountain and was firmly secured to its rocky foundation by cement and large iron bolts. Over the low, sloping gable roof passed four stout cables. It was enlarged the following year, when Mr. Perkins was in charge and a half-interest had been sold to Nathaniel Noyes and an associate, and an upper story with a pitched roof was added. It withstood the storms of winter for more than thirty years, being used, after the building of the second Summit House, as a dormitory for its employees until 1884, when it was demolished.

The success of this undertaking led to the erection of a rival house, the famous Tip-Top House, which was opened in August, 1853. Samuel Fitch Spaulding, of Lancaster, was the builder, and his associates in the project and in the management of the hotel were his sons and a nephew, John Hubbard Spaulding, the author of "Historical Relics of the White Mountains." It was built of rough stones, similarly to the Summit House, measured eight-four by twenty-eight feet, and had originally a deck roof, upon which the visitor might stand and thus have an unobstructed view. A telescope was kept there in pleasant weather. Competition between the two hotels was keen the first common season, but in 1854 Mr. Perkins disposed of his interest in the Summit House to the Spauldings, who managed the two houses for nine seasons. Mary B. Spaulding (Mrs. Lucius Hartshorn), daughter of Samuel F. Spaulding, managed the Tip-Top House for three seasons. In a letter written a few years ago she gives a vivid description of the difficulty of managing a hotel on the Mountain at that day. Everything had to be brought on horses' backs from the Glen House, and fresh meat, potatoes, milk, and cream were absent from the menu. Among the supplies kept on hand were bacon, ham, tripe, tongue, eggs, and rice, and pancakes, johnnycake, fried cakes, and varieties of hot bread and biscuit were served. The number of guests for dinner was very uncertain and could be roughly estimated only from the number of visitors at the foot of the Mountain and

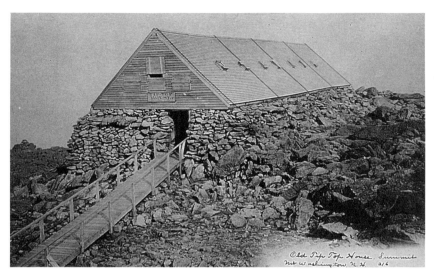

The old Tip-Top House on the summit of Mount Washington
was built in 1853 by Samuel F. Spaulding.

from the weather conditions. Among her guests she names Jefferson Davis,
Charles Sumner, Horace Greeley, and William H. Seward.

C.H.V. Cavis, engineer for the carriage road, was for one year manager
of the Tip-Top House. In his day, according to Mrs. Cavis, in order to estimate the number of guests for dinner, some one went to what is known as
Point Lookoff, overlooking the Lakes of the Clouds, and counted the ponies
in the cavalcade coming along the bridle path from Crawford's. Others
came from the Glen and Fabyan's. Landlord Cavis kept some cows on the
plateau, since known as the "Cow Pasture," near the seven-mile post of the
carriage road.

The first woman to sleep in the house after its opening in August, 1853,
was a Mrs. Duhring, of Philadelphia, who came up on horseback from the
Crawford House and walked down. Twenty-four years later she revisited
the Mountain.

From 1892 to 1872, the lessee of the Tip-Top House and Summit House
was Colonel John R. Hitchcock, who was also the proprietor of the Alpine
House in Gorham. He paid a rent of two thousand dollars a year after the
first year. Colonel Hitchcock connected the two houses, and, after the completion of the carriage road, an upper story containing seventeen little bed-
rooms was added to the Tip-Top House. Mrs. Atwood, the housekeeper of
the Alpine House, has charge of the Summit hotels, visiting them twice a

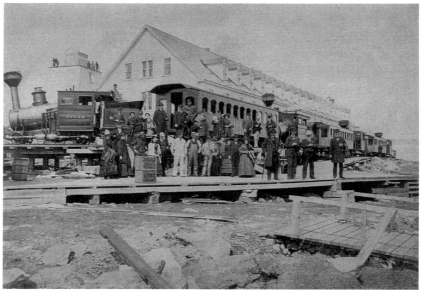

COURTESY LITTLETON AREA HISTORICAL SOCIETY

Cog Railway passengers and trains line up for a photograph
in front of the Summit House.

week in a specially constructed light two-horse carriage. During the Hitchcock regime, in which baked beans, brown bread, and other simple dishes
were chief features of the bill-of-fare, the business, especially after the building of the railway, far outgrew the accommodations. After the building of
the new Summit House, the Tip-Tip House was used by hotel and railway
employees for a few years. From 1877 to 1884, the printing office of *Among
the Clouds* was in the old hotel, its front room being equipped for that purpose in the former year. After that use of it ceased, the building, owing to
dampness, fell somewhat into decay and came to be visited only as a curiosity. In 1898, an observatory was constructed at the western end to afford a
good place from which to watch the sunsets.

But this ancient landmark was not destined to remain a curiosity only. As
the sole survivor of the fire which devastated the Summit just before the
opening of the season of 1908, the venerable structure had necessarily to
be restored to its original purpose of a place of entertainment and shelter.
As such it continued to be used until the opening of a new Summit House
in 1915.

The next structure to be built on the Summit after the erection of the

Tip-Top House was an observatory. Built in 1854, by Timothy Estus,[2] of Jefferson, it was a framework forty feet high supported by iron braces at the corners. It was provided with a sort of elevator operated by a crank and gearing and capable of accommodating eight persons at a time. This observatory, which cost about six hundred dollars, was abandoned as a complete failure after being used a part of the first season. It stood until the summer of 1856, when it was torn down.

No further buildings were erected on Mount Washington until after the building of the carriage road and of the railway, when the necessary structures for carrying on the operation of these means of visiting the Summit were erected. Soon the increase of business due to these agencies for making the peak more accessible necessitated the provision of greater accommodations for the shelter of visitors. From time to time, also, buildings for various other uses were added to the Summit settlement. The recording of the history of the later hotel and of the other structures referred to, however, properly follows the stories of the carriage road and the railway, and will be set down in due course after the latter have been related.

The construction of the first-named means of access to the summit of Mount Washington is a work which bears eloquent witness to the enterprise, courage, and persistence of its projector and builders. The road, which extends from the Pinkham Notch Road, near the site of the Glen House, to the Summit, is eight miles long and makes an ascent of forty-six hundred feet, the average grade being one foot in eight and the steepest, one foot in six. To General David O. Macomber, of Middletown, Connecticut, belongs the credit for originating this undertaking. The Mount Washington Road Company was chartered July 1, 1853, with a capital of fifty thousand dollars. The company was organized at the Alpine House, in Gorham, on August 31 of that year, General Macomber being chosen president. The road was surveyed by Engineers C.H.V. Cavis and Ricker. Two incidents of the surveying period have been preserved by John H. Spaulding. One is the measurement of the height of the Mountain by actual survey made by the engineers in 1854, who arrived at 6284 feet as a result. The other incident was the dining, on July 16 of that year, of President Macomber, Engineer Cavis, and Mr. Spaulding in the snow arch. It was then two hundred and sixty-six feet long, eighty-four feet wide, and forty feet high to the roof. Mr. Spaulding records that, during the time spent in this somewhat rash action, icy cold water constantly dripped down around them and a heavy thunderstorm passed over them.

2. So Spaulding. Professor Hitchcock, in *Mount Washington in Winter*, gives the builder's name as Timothy Eaton.

Construction was begun by Contractors Rich and Myers in or about the year 1855,[3] and within a year two miles were completed and further construction was under way. The section ending at the Ledge just above the Halfway House, a total distance of four miles from the beginning, was finished in 1856. Then the pioneer company failed, because of the great cost of construction. A new company, the Mount Washington Summit Road Company, was, however, incorporated two or three years later, and this company finished the road in 1861. Joseph S. Hall, one of the builders of the Tip-Top House, was the contractor for this work, and John P. Rich, the first contractor, was the superintendent. The road, which is splendidly built and which winds up the Mountain in long gradual lines of ascent, places where there are steep grades being rendered safe by stone walls on the lower side, was opened for travel on August 8, 1861.

The first passenger vehicle which arrived at the Summit—an old-fashioned Concord stage-coach with eight horses—was driven by George W. Lane, for many years in charge of the Fabyan House stables.[4]

The memory of Mr. Rich, who had so much to do with the construction of the road and who died in California in 1863, has been preserved by a tablet set in a rock by the roadside near the Glen and bearing a suitable inscription. Witness to the excellence of the engineering and construction work on the road, as well as of the care with which it has been maintained, is borne by its use for now more than fifty years and its well-preserved condition.

Striking as was this achievement in rendering the top of New England's highest mountain more accessible, it was soon to be surpassed in boldness of conception and skill and successfulness of execution by another undertaking directed to the same end. I refer to the building of the Mount Washington Railway, the first railway of its kind in the world. The projector of this enterprise was Sylvester Marsh, a native son of New Hampshire and a Yankee genius. The idea that it was wholly practicable to apply the principle of the cog rail to a mountain railroad and the carrying out of the conception was only one of this ingenious New Englander's services to the world. Having gone West in the winter of 1833–34, when thirty years old, Mr. Marsh became one of the founders of Chicago, prominent in the promotion of every public enterprise there. He was the originator of meat-packing in that city and the inventor of many of the appliances used in that

3. Mr. Spaulding notes that in June, 1855, the road is "in rapid progress towards completion."

4. Landlord Thompson, of the Glen House, drove to the Summit in a light wagon with one horse, just before the road was completed, thus beating his rival for the honor, Colonel Hitchcock. Two men assisted in keeping the wagon right side up as he drove over the uncompleted last section of the road. Landlord Thompson was also in the first coach driven up.

Sylvester Marsh, builder of
the "Railway to the Moon."

process, especially those connected with the employment of steam. The dried-meal process was another of his inventions.

When on a visit to his native State in 1852, he one day made an ascent of Mount Washington with a friend, the Reverend A. C. Thompson, of Roxbury. It was while struggling up the mountain, or perhaps a little later, that the idea came to him that a railway to the Summit was feasible and could be made profitable. Very soon he set to work and invented the mountain-climbing mechanism, and then with characteristic energy and perseverance he fought his project through to completion against much opposition and ridicule. In 1858, he exhibited a model of the line to the State Legislature and asked for a charter to build steam railways up Mount Washington and Mount Lafayette. The charter was granted on June 25 of that year, one legislator, it is said, suggesting the satirical amendment that the gentlemen should also receive permission to build a railway to the moon. Pecuniary support for so apparently ridiculous a proposal was difficult to obtain, and before anything could be done the breaking-out of the Civil War postponed action for several more years. Finally a company was formed, the necessary capital being furnished by the railroads connecting the White Mountain region with Boston and New York. At the outset, however, Mr. Marsh had to rely chiefly on his own resources, but little encouragement being received until an engine was actually running over a part of the route. Construction of the railway was at length begun in May, 1866, nearly eight years after the granting of the charter. In order to render its starting-point accessible, a turnpike from Fabyan's to the Base was begun in April of that same year.

As the railway is so important in the history of mountain railways a brief description of its mechanical features may not be out of order. The road is of the type known as the "cog road," or the rack and pinion railroad. The indispensable peculiarity of the invention is the heavy central rail, which consists of two parallel pieces of steel connected by numerous strong cross-pins or bolts, into the spaces between which the teeth of the cog wheels on the locomotive play. As the driving wheel revolves, the engine ascends or descends, resting on the outer rails, which are of the ordinary pattern and which are four feet seven inches apart.

The first locomotive, which was designed by Mr. Marsh and was built by Campbell and Whittier, of Boston, was used until entirely worn out. Exhibited at the World's Fair in Chicago in 1893, it is now in the Field Museum of Natural History. It had a vertical boiler and no cab, and thus resembled a hoisting engine in appearance. The present type of locomotive was designed by Walter Aiken,[5] of Franklin, New Hampshire, who was the man to work out the practical details of Mr. Marsh's idea and who supervised the construction of the road. The engine is furnished with two pairs of cylinders and driving gears, thus guaranteeing ample security in case of accident. The car is provided with similar cog wheels to those on the engine and with brakes of its own, insuring safety independent of the engine. There are separate brakes on each axle of the car and an additional safety device on both it and the engine in the form of a toothed wheel and ratchet. This latter mechanism affords the greatest protection against accident, as it prevents the wheels of the car or of the engine from turning backward. It is, of course, raised during the ascent, but it can be dropped instantly into place in an emergency. The car is pushed up the Mountain and descends behind the lo-

5. From an article by Mr. Aiken in *Among the Clouds* for September 1, 1877, it appears that Herrick Aiken, of Franklin, about 1850 conceived the idea of ascending Mount Washington by means of a cog railroad. He went so far as to build a model of a roadbed and track with the cog rail and to make two ascents of the Mountain on horseback for the purpose of determining the feasibility of the route, etc.; but he was dissuaded from undertaking the project by prominent railroad men whom he consulted and who thought it impracticable and unlikely to be profitable.

comotive, and is not fastened to it. The train moves very slowly, so slowly, indeed, that a person can easily, if necessary, step on or off while it is under full headway. Seventy minutes are required to make the trip up. The safety appliances, the powerfully constructed locomotive, the moderate speed, the constant inspection, and the experienced men concerned in the operation of the road have eliminated the element of danger from the trip. No passenger has yet been injured in all the years since the road's opening.

The route was surveyed and located by Colonel Orville E. Freeman, of Lancaster, New Hampshire, a son-in-law of the pioneer, Ethan Allen Crawford. Very appropriately, the course of the railway is substantially that of the latter's early path to the Summit. The length of the road is about three and one third miles, and the elevation overcome is about three thousand seven hundred feet. The average grade is one foot in four and the maximum thirteen and one half inches in three feet, or one thousand nine hundred and eight feet to the mile. With the exception of the railway up Mount Pilatus in Switzerland, the Mount Washington railway is the steepest in the world of the type of which it is the pioneer. The road is built on a wooden trestle all the way except a short distance near the Base, where the track lies on the surface of the ground.

But to return to its history. The first quarter of a mile was finished in 1866, and a test was made which demonstrated the practicability of the invention. A half-mile more was completed in 1867, and on August 14, 1868, the railway was opened to Jacob's Ladder.[6] Before work on it stopped that year, construction was carried to the Lizzie Bourne monument. The road was finished the following year, being opened to the Summit for business in July. The cost of construction and equipment was $139,500.

At the time of its completion, the nearest railroad station was at Littleton, twenty-five miles distant. Every piece of material for the construction of the railway and the locomotive and cars, had to be hauled through the woods, it should be remembered, by ox teams.

I have spoken of the beginning of the construction of the turnpike to the Base. This was completed in 1869, and for many years afforded the only means of access to the railway, passengers being brought by stage over it from Fabyan's. It was owned for some years by the Boston and Maine Railroad, but has recently been turned over to the State.

A word more as to the railway's projector and inventor. Leaving Chicago, he returned to live in New Hampshire, settling at Littleton in 1864. He

---

6. This name was transferred to the railroad from the path, having been given to the steep crag at this place, many years before the building of the railway.

passed the closing years of his life in Concord, where he removed in 1879 and where he died in December, 1884, at the age of eighty-one, a public-spirited and highly respected citizen. He was asked to build the railway up Rigi in Switzerland, which is patterned to some extent after the Mount Washington Railway, but he declined.

During the latter's construction, a Swiss engineer[7] visited the American railroad, and he was allowed to take back with him drawings of the machinery and track.

After the Swiss railroad was completed (1871), Mr. Marsh said of it, "They have made a much better road than mine. Mine was an experiment. When proved to be a success, they went ahead with confidence and built a permanent road."

A noteworthy incident of the first season of the Mount Washington Railway was the visit of President Grant, whose first term had begun the previous March. His trip up Mount Washington was made in the course of a tour through the Mountains that summer with Mrs. Grant and some of their children. Another episode of this excursion has been preserved.[8] The general, as is well known, was a great lover of horses. One can imagine, therefore, his keen enjoyment, as he sat on the box with the driver, Edmund Cox, of a stage-coach which traveled, drawn by six horses, from the Sinclair House in Bethlehem to the Profile House, more than eleven miles, in fifty-eight minutes.

Accidents on the carriage road, so strong are the vehicles and horses used and so careful and reliable the drivers employed, have been few. The first by which any passengers were injured, and the only serious one I have found recorded, occurred on July 3, 1880, about a mile below the Halfway House. A company of excursionists from Michigan had been visiting the Summit

7. This was Mr. Nicholas Riggenbach, then superintendent of the Central Swiss Railway, who took the first steam locomotive into Switzerland in 1847, and who appears to have independently conceived the idea of a new system of track and locomotives for the ascent of mountains. On August 12, 1863, he took out a patent for a rack railway and a locomotive for operating the same, but nothing further seems to have been done with the idea by him until after the visit to America mentioned in the text. On his return he associated himself with two others, got a concession, and built the road up the Rigi. The rack rail designed by Riggenbach is a distinct improvement upon that used by Marsh. Instead of a round tooth, it employs a taper tooth, which experience has shown to be preferable, inasmuch as it not only insures safe locking of the gear at different depths, but resists more efficiently the tendency of the gear-wheel to climb the rack—a further security against derailment. Riggenbach's type of tooth, with modifications, is that now used on rack railways. (From F. A. Talbot's *Railway Wonders of the World*, 1913.)

8. Recorded by Alice Bartlett Stevens in the *Granite Monthly* for February, 1903.

that day, and the last party of them to descend, consisting of nine persons, were thrown violently into the woods and on the rocks by the overturning of the six-horse mountain wagon in which they were riding. One woman was instantly killed and several other occupants were more or less injured. The husband of the dead woman was riding at her side and escaped with a few bruises.

It seems that the driver, one of the oldest and most experienced on the road and one who had himself uttered the warning, "There should be no fooling, no chaffing, and no drinking on that road," had failed to practice what he preached, and, while waiting for his party at the Summit, had indulged in liquor. This lapse, most serious under the circumstances, was discovered shortly after starting, and the passengers thereupon left the wagon and walked to the Halfway House, four miles down. There, on being assured by one of the employees of the Carriage Road Company that there was no dangerous place below that point, and on his telling them further that he thought it would be safe for them to ride the remainder of the way with the same driver, they resumed their seats, only to meet, a few minutes later, in rounding a curve at too great a speed, with the sad mishap that has been described.

As has been already stated, no passenger has ever been even injured on the Railway. The only mishap of any consequence, and a most peculiar one, occurred about the middle of July, 1897, when a train consisting of a locomotive, passenger car, and baggage car was wrecked. A heavy gust of wind struck the train, which was standing near the Summit, with such force as to start it off down the line. It was found that about a quarter of a mile down the engine and baggage car had jumped the track, had turned over and over while falling a hundred feet or more into the gulf, and had become total wrecks. The man sent out to investigate on a slide-board reported that he saw nothing of the passenger car, but it was later discovered that this had left the track at a curve near Jacob's Ladder, had turned over, and had been completely demolished. Fortunately no one was on board.

Mention has just been made of the slide-board. This interesting contrivance was invented to meet the need of rapid transit for the workmen employed in track repairing and the like. By this means an experienced rider can go from the Summit to the Base in three minutes. The slide-board is about three feet long, rests lengthwise on the center rail, and is grooved so as to slide on it. The braking mechanism, by which the board is kept under such perfect control that it can be stopped almost instantly whenever necessary, is very simple. On either side of the board is pivoted to it a handle, to which is attached, near the pivot, a piece of iron bent in a peculiar form

A Boston, Concord, and Montreal train (bottom) delivers passengers to the Cog Railway base area and waiting Cog engines and passenger cars.

so as to project underneath the rail. By pulling up the handle this piece of iron is made to grip the flange of the rail very tightly.

It was formerly the practice for the roadmaster or his assistant to descend on a slide-board before the noon train every day, going slowly enough to make a careful inspection of the track. The death of an employee in performing this hazardous act a few years ago, which accident cost the Railway Company several thousand dollars in damages and made evident the liability to mishaps of this kind, has caused the discontinuance of the use of this dangerous means of conveyance.

A picturesque employment of the slide-boards in former days was as a "newspaper train." This novel enterprise was carried on in the early nineties, when the coaching parades at Bethlehem and North Conway were at their height, and there was thereby created a great demand for the issues of *Among the Clouds,* which contained accounts of the festivities. So that readers of those towns might have copies of the paper at their breakfast tables, some of the skillful coasters used to transport the morning edition down the Mountain before daylight.

After the completion of the railway, steps had immediately to be taken to remedy the woefully inadequate provisions for feeding and sheltering visitors, and, accordingly, in 1872, was begun the building of the second "Summit House," the famous structure which for thirty-five summers entertained so many people of various walks in life, — guides, trampers, railroad officials, scientific and literary men and women, clergymen, and just ordinary persons, — and which had a wealth of associations connected with it, and especially clustered about its office stove. The undertaking was financed by Walter Aiken, manager of the Mount Washington Railway, whose tall, stalwart form and sterling manhood is one of the memories of the early days, and President John E. Lyon, of the Boston, Concord, and Montreal Railroad, whose contributions to the development of the Mountains have already been mentioned. The hotel, which was completed early in 1873 and opened in July of that year, was of plain outward appearance, but of the most rigid and solid construction possible of a wooden building. The difficulties of erecting so large a structure—it could accommodate one hundred and fifty guests—on a site where severe weather often prevails, are obvious as well as are the necessities for strong construction and for anchorage by bolts and cables. Two hundred and fifty freight trains were required to carry up the lumber, and the cost of the hotel, exclusive of the expense for freight (estimated at $10,000) was $56,599.57.

The excellence of the construction is evidenced by the fact that the solid frame withstood gales of one hundred and eighty-six miles an hour by actual record by the anemometer and very likely of higher unrecorded rates when no instrument or observer was there to tell the tale. Its cheerful office, with its great stove, was a welcome place to many a traveler arriving by railway, by carriage road, or by trail. Many a day weather conditions were such that visitors were marooned in the office during their entire stay on the Summit and were devoutly grateful for the hostel's hospitable shelter. Almost every evening of the season found a group of travelers whiling away the time enjoying the genial warmth of the stove and exchanging experiences of their mountain trips.

Notables who made longer or shorter stays there at various times, as recalled by Editor F. H. Burt of *Among the Clouds*, were Lucy Larcom, the poet; William C. Prime, editor, traveler, author, and angler; his sister-in-law, Annie Trumbull Slosson, entomologist and author, who came year after year for longer and longer sojourns and who latterly regarded the hotel as her home; the botanist, Edward Faxon; the entomologist, J. H. Emerton; E. C. and W. H. Pickering, the astronomers; the naturalist and author, Bradford Torrey; and among the cloth, Rev. Dr. W. R. Richards and Rev. Dr. Harry P. Nichols.

Day visitors of prominence were legion. Some names of such, culled from the pages of *Among the Clouds* in 1877, are those of President Hayes[9] and Mrs. Hayes, who, accompanied by William M. Evarts, Charles Devens, and D. M. Key, of the Cabinet, made their visit to the Summit on August 20; the Reverend and Mrs. Henry Ward Beecher on the same day; Vice-President Wheeler, on August 29, and in September, Sir Lyon Playfair, the eminent British statesman and scientist. Other noted visitors whose names are found in the records of later years were P. T. Barnum, General Joseph Hooker, General McClellan, Lord Chief Justice Coleridge, of England, who came on August 30, 1883, Phillips Brooks, Speaker Cannon, Lieutenant Peary, and Señor Romero, the Mexican Minister. In 1880, the eminent Scottish professor, William Garden Blaikie, spent "a night on Mount Washington," an account of which experience he gave in a typically British article with this title, published in *Good Words* in June, 1881. He went up by train and walked down the carriage road. As there was a cloud on top when he arrived, he walked down below to see the view and the sunset. "Nothing could be finer," he declared, than the dawn he witnessed.

The versatile English writer and scientist of Canadian birth, Grant Allen, was another foreign visitor to Mount Washington who deserves a passing mention. From his graphic and often facetious account of his brief

9. This was President Hayes's fifth visit to the summit.

visit to the Mountains in 1886, written for *Longman's Magazine*, we learn that he made the ascent by train and that he was much interested in the botany—his specialty—and the gastronomy of the region.

The first proprietor of this new Summit House was Captain John W. Dodge, of Hampton Falls, New Hampshire, who also became postmaster by Government appointment when the Mount Washington post-office was established July 1, 1874, and who died in June of the following year. For nine seasons, a period ending with 1883, his widow, Harriet D. Dodge, successfully managed the house. Charles G. Emmons, had charge for the two following seasons, and from 1886 to the end, the hotel was leased to the Barron, Merrill, and Barron Company by the railway company into whose hands, after the deaths of Mr. Aiken and Mr. Lyon, their interest passed. The Summit House was enlarged by the addition of an ell in 1874 and extensive improvements were made in 1895, 1901, and 1905.

From time to time, as need arose or circumstances required, buildings for various uses were erected on the Summit until a considerable summer settlement had been created. Besides such essential structures as the train shed, built in 1870 and subsequently blown down in a winter gale and rebuilt,[10] and the stage office, erected in 1878 by the owners of the carriage road for the accommodation of the agents and drivers of the stage line and sometimes used as sleeping quarters by trampers, several buildings came into existence for special purposes, which structures demand more attention than mere mention, either because of their uses or because of their associations.

When in May, 1871, the Government took up the work of maintaining weather-bureau service on the Summit, the observers, who were at that period detailed for this duty year round by the Signal Service of the Army, were quartered in the old railway station, but in 1874 a wooden building, one and a half stories high, the so-called "Signal Station," was erected for their use.

At the beginning of 1880, the buildings on the Summit were the old Summit House, which, as has been stated, was then used as a dormitory for the hotel employees, the old Tip-Top House, the front room of which then served as the printing-office of *Among the Clouds*, the stage office, the train shed, the Signal Station, and the Summit House. Two more buildings were added to the group during the years soon following, to stand with the others until the fateful evening in June, 1908, when the results of so many years' development were reduced in a few hours to ashes and blackened ruins.

In the year first named the railway company erected a strong wooden

10. A third train shed—the one burned—was built about 1890. The second one, having become disused and dilapidated, was taken down in 1904.

tower, twenty-seven feet high and of pyramidal shape, on high ground near the southwest corner of the Summit House. It overlooked all the buildings and became a favorite observatory. For several summers it was used by the United States Coast and Geodetic Survey in the triangulation of the region. In 1892, the tower was carried up another story and, during that season only, a powerful searchlight was operated on it. Having fallen into decay and having become unsafe, this, the second observatory built on the Mountain, was pulled down in 1902.

Four years after the erection of the tower came the last addition to the group of buildings. This was a home for the Mountain newspaper, *Among the Clouds*, which had outgrown its headquarters in the old Tip-Top House. In the autumn of 1884 was built the compact and cozy little office so well known to visitors for nearly twenty-five years. It contained a fully-equipped printing plant, with a Hoe cylinder press and a steam engine (superseded a short time before the great fire by a seven horse-power gasoline engine). Many a tourist here saw for the first time a newspaper plant in operation.

The same year saw another change in the Mountain buildings, for, as has been recorded before, the old Summit House was that year taken down, a wooden cottage being erected in its stead. Mention having just been made of the printing-office of *Among the Clouds*, and the establishment of that newspaper belonging chronologically to the period now under review, accounts of this unique journalistic enterprise and also of another similar undertaking may perhaps be interjected at this point.

The distinction of being the first and for many years the only newspaper printed regularly on the top of a mountain, and the further distinction of being the oldest summer-resort newspaper in America, belong to Mount Washington's daily journal. In was founded in 1877 by Mr. Henry M. Burt, of Springfield, Massachusetts, who had been connected with the *Springfield Republican* and various other papers, among them the *New England Homestead,* which he founded. In 1866, Mr. Burt published "Burt's Guide to the Connecticut Valley and the White Mountains," the preparation of which brought him first to Mount Washington. While spending a stormy day at the Summit House, in 1874, the thought of printing a newspaper on top of the Mountain came to him, resulting in the starting of *Among the Clouds* three years later, the first issue appearing on July 18, 1877. This unique and daring undertaking gained the admiration of all visitors, and the paper with so peculiarly appropriate a name soon filled a recognized position in White Mountain life. For eight summers it was printed in the old Tip-Top House. Thereafter until 1908, it was published in its own building, the erection of which in 1884 has been recorded. The genial editor, during the twenty-two years in which he conducted the paper, gained a host of personal friends among those frequenting the White Mountains and those carrying on business in the region. Since his death in March, 1899, his son, Frank H. Burt, has been its editor and publisher.

Before the great fire of 1908 deprived *Among the Clouds* of its well-equipped and appropriately located home, two editions were printed daily, the principal one being issued in the early morning. At 1 P.M. the noon edition, containing a list of names of visitors arriving by the morning train, was ready for purchase as a souvenir by the traveler before the train departed on the downward trip.

Besides recording all events of interest relating to Mount Washington, together with news of the leading Mountain resorts, many articles of historical and scientific value have appeared in its columns, all of which contents have combined to make a complete file of *Among the Clouds* at any time, and now especially after the fire, a treasure indeed.

In view of the staggering blow that the paper received in the loss of its home and equipment before the opening of the season of 1908, it was thought best to omit for that summer the daily edition, which was done. Thus, for the first time in a generation the history of the summer's events had to go untold. The enterprising editors, however, far from being discouraged and from giving up all for lost even that season, showed their quality by preparing a "magazine number," containing a very complete and interesting record of the fire by pen and camera, and many facts and reminiscences concerning Mount Washington.

The failure to rebuild the settlement upon the Summit is responsible for *Among the Clouds* not being able to regain its ancient and proper seat, but publication was resumed on July 5, 1910, and the paper is now temporarily established at the base.

The other journalistic enterprise referred to is that of a newspaper long widely known among Mountain visitors, *The White Mountain Echo and Tourists' Register*, the founding of which is almost contemporary with that of *Among the Clouds*. It was in 1878, in Bethlehem, that *The Echo* was started, the date of the first issue being July 13, and it has continued to be published there since. It is not, however, a local paper, but is devoted to the interests of the entire White Mountain region. Its founder and editor for twenty years, Mr. Markinfield Addey, had an interesting career. He was an Englishman, who, after serving in the publishing house of Chapman and Hall, had become a publisher on his own account. In 1857, when he was thirty-nine years old, his eyesight failed and he retired from business. The following year he came to America, where his eyesight improved. Twenty years later he founded *The White Mountain Echo*. Having entirely lost his sight in 1898, he gave up the editorship of *The Echo*, and returned to England, settling in Louth, in Lincolnshire. There he lived twelve years longer, dying November 18, 1910, at the age of ninety-two. He was a "bright, cheerful little man, of a very sanguine nature," always active in promoting by his pen and his influence the good of the Mountain region he had come to love so well. He lived to know of the carrying-out of many of the improvements he so earnestly and so long before advocated.

The only White Mountain summit other than Mount Washington, upon which anything more than a temporary shelter exists to-day, is Mount Moosilauke. The beautiful Mount Kearsarge[11] of the Bartlett-Conway region formerly bore upon its top a small hotel, in 1848 or 1849,[12] by Caleb Frye, Nathaniel Frye, John C. Davis, and Moses Chandler, which was kept open for several years and then fell into disuse. Andrew Dinsmore bought it in 1868 or 1869, put it in thorough repair, and reopened it. The weather-beaten old structure was blown down in a tempest in November, 1883. Mr. Dinsmore collected the fragments and rebuilt the structure on a smaller scale. This has been abandoned of late years and is rapidly falling into decay. It is now the property of the Appalachian Mountain Club, the building and ten acres on the summit having been given to the Club in 1902 by Mrs. C. E. Clay, of Chatham, New Hampshire. A small one-room house of logs and poles was built on Mount Moriah by Colonel Hitchcock, of the Alpine House, probably in 1854. A road up having been constructed under his auspices, that mountain for a time rivaled Mount Washington in popularity. In the sixties a rude house for the protection of climbers stood on the crest of Mount Lafayette, but, except for the low stone walls, it had disappeared by 1875.[13]

11. Now to be called, in accordance with a decision (1915) of the United States Board of Geographic Names, "Mount Pequawket."

12. So Mrs. Mason. Sweetser says, "built in 1845."

13. The substantial Peak House on Mount Chocorua, which was built in the early nineties, was not located on the summit, but at the base of the cone. This house was blown down on September 26, 1915.

June 1936

First to Die on
Mount Washington

Frank H. Burt

From *Appalachia*

*An Appalachian Mountain Club member for 66 years, and a frequent contributor
to the club's journal,* Appalachia, *Frank Burt (1861–1946) was as connected to
Mount Washington and the White Mountains as his father, Henry Burt, founder
of the summit newspaper,* Among the Clouds. *The younger Burt assumed editorship of the paper in the summer of 1899 following his father's unexpected death.
He ran the paper for the next eight seasons, or until the great summit fire of 1908
destroyed the paper's mountaintop office. During his long tenure with AMC, Burt
held down several important positions within the club, including Councilor of
Topography and Councilor of Publications.*

THE STORY of Mount Washington's first tragedy, the death in 1849 of
Frederick Strickland, second son of sir George Strickland, Bart., M.P., at
the age of twenty-nine, has been told many times but never in full and usually with much inaccuracy.

On a day now fixed as Friday, October 19, 1849 (but usually given as 1851),
Strickland and another Englishman set out with guide and saddle horses
from the Notch House, against advice, to climb Mount Washington. They
found the snow so deep that when Mount Pleasant was reached the guide
refused to risk himself and his horses further. Despite the urgent appeals of
his companions Strickland left them, intending to continue alone to the
summit of Mount Washington and go down by the Fabyan path to the
Mount Washington Hotel, near the site of the present Fabyan House. The

Fabyan path, originally located by Ethan Allen Crawford in 1820, was improved for horses soon after 1840 by Horace Fabyan, who had succeeded Crawford as landlord of the latter's hotel. The cog railway follows the same general course as this path.

Strickland reached the top of Washington safely and passed over the most dangerous parts of the descent, only to lose his path in the woods. Two days later his frightfully bruised body was found in the rocky bed of the Ammonoosuc. Unaccompanied, climbing a strange path, he had made the first recorded ascent of Mount Washington under winter conditions, but, like the first aviator to fly over the Alps, he died almost within reach of safety.

Students of the tragedy have heretofore relied for information upon two books published in 1855: *Incidents in White Mountain History* by Rev. Benjamin Willey, once minister of the North Conway Congregational Church and brother of Samuel Willey Jr., who perished in the famous slide in the Crawford Notch; and *"Historic Relics" of the White Mountains* by John H. Spaulding, then of Lancaster, landlord for many years of the Tiptop House. Either book might well have passed as absolute authority. Yet they differ by eleven years as to the date of the event, Spaulding putting it in 1851 and Willey setting it back, perhaps by a slip of the pen or a printer's error, to 1840. Spaulding omits to mention the name of the victim, incorrectly calling him "an English baronet".

Beside the doubt as to the date, several other questions occurred to me as I studied the stories. How came Strickland to be in the mountains at a season so unusual for tourists? Where did he lose the path? Where was he found? Where buried? What was his early history? The British *Who's Who* revealed a Major Frederick Strickland, World War hero, heir to a baronetcy and residing in Yorkshire; Burke's *Peerage* proved that he was nephew to the Frederick lost on Mount Washington and gave the date of death of the latter as October 13, 1849. A letter to the nephew brought a most cordial response but the admission that he knew practically nothing of his uncle's death except that he had been "lost in the snow in America". A search of the files of New England newspapers, made practicable as soon as the correct year was known, revealed a surprising wealth of material[1] from which it was easy to reconstruct a fairly full story.

Frederick Strickland and both his brothers, Sir Charles and Henry, were

---

1. The first story appeared in the *Daily Evening Transcript* of Boston on Wednesday, October 24, based largely upon a letter from "Thomas J. Crawford, Esq., the popular proprietor of the Notch House." The next day the *Herald* printed a letter from Horace Fabyan, who, with Mr. Crawford, led the searching party that found the body. This is a full and clear account.

graduates of Trinity College, Cambridge.[2] With his brother Henry, Frederick arrived in Boston about the first of October, 1949, after travelling for several months in this country, and they stayed about two weeks at the Tremont House. Coming, in the quaint phrase of the *Boston Advertiser*, "most respectably introduced," Frederick, "had become known to a considerable number of persons in this city and vicinity, by whom he was highly respected as a gentleman of amiable character, ardently devoted to literary and scientific pursuits." "He brought letters to some of our most distinguished citizens," says the *Transcript*, "and was advised to visit the White Mountains by several gentlemen of science and taste in our community." No newspaper that I have seen gives the names of any of Strickland's Boston friends, but a possible clue to their identity has come into my hands. The register of the Granite House, an old-time hotel in Littleton, New Hampshire, for the years 1842–50, a long cherished possession of Mr. George C. Furber, who for many years published the *White Mountain Republic* in Littleton, shows on July 30, 1849, the arrival of the following party, nearly all of whom were members of the Harvard faculty and pursuing the scientific study of the White Mountains: Louis Agassiz and his thirteen-year-old son, Alexander, Arnold Guyot, then lecturing at Harvard, Benjamin Pierce, professor of mathematics and astronomy, C. C. Felton, afterwards president of the college, George P. Bond, then connected with Harvard observatory and author of one of the first maps of the White Mountains, Ernest Sandos, Franklin E. Felton, and S. M. Felton. On August 2 there are again registered Agassiz, father and son, the three Feltons, Pierce, and Bond, also W. W. Gould of Boston. Such men as these the young Englishman would naturally have sought out, and it is a fair guess that among this group were those who advised him to visit the White Mountains and who later saw that proper honor was paid to his memory.

Henry Strickland left for home by the steamer Canada from New York, leaving Frederick to make the White Mountain trip alone. The latter travelled by stage via North Conway[3] and Crawford Notch, stopping on the way at the Mount Crawford House, kept by Abel Crawford, near the present Notchland Inn.

On arrival at the Notch House on Thursday, October 18, Strickland expressed his wish to ascend Mount Washington. There must have been a very heavy snowfall throughout the region a few days before, for we read in the Dover (New Hampshire) *Gazette* of the same week:

---

2. Trinity College Admissions, 1801–50, p. 465.
3. *Portland Daily Advertiser*, October 26, 1849.

"*White Mountains.* We learn by a gentleman from that neighborhood, that the mountains were covered with snow 3 feet deep. The tops of Gilford Mountains" [the Belknaps] "were covered with snow on Monday morning, 15th instant."

Thomas Crawford assured him it could not be done; the snow was too deep for horses to get through. "I can walk where no horse could go" was the substance of the young traveller's reply. Crawford finally consented to let him have a horse and guide, and seems to have advised him, in case he did proceed to the top of Washington on foot, to go down by the Fabyan path. "He at first refused to take any provision with him," says the Portland *Advertiser*, "stating that he should return before night—and it was only by earnest entreaty that he finally received a couple of crackers." Another Englishman joined him, probably a chance acquaintance, for he drops out of the picture before Strickland's death was discovered. The party started out by the Crawford bridle path on Friday morning, the 19th of October, and Strickland's guide and the other traveller were fully justified in turning back and urging him to return with them.

The weather must have been fine on the 19th to lure Strickland onward and there could have been no snowfall the day following, or his tracks would have been hopelessly buried.

Mr. Crawford, learning that Strickland was to go down to Fabyan's hotel, sent his trunk thither the same night. Driving over the next morning, he learned that he had not been seen. Fearing the worst, he ordered a searching party sent up his own path, while he and Fabyan, with others to aid, hastened to the foot of the mountain and started up a path by which Frederick was to have come down. A mile up the mountain they found his tracks, which showed that he had lost the path and after various wanderings had turned southerly and probably followed a little brook until it joined the Ammonoosuc River.

The *Transcript* account states that at a spot where the stream, normally not over two feet wide and six inches deep, spread out in a pool two or three feet deep, were found Strickland's trousers and drawers. Why did he discard them? Similar strange acts have been performed by others lost in the woods who have become hysterical and even temporarily insane on realizing their plight. It may have been that he fell into the stream and the garments having frozen to his legs he tore them off in desperation, a trail of blood marking the rest of his agonized movements.

Nightfall interrupted the search. On Sunday morning, with a much larger group, Fabyan and Crawford made an early start and about ten o'clock "found the body," says the *Transcript*, "about one mile from the spot where the clothes were discovered. The body bore many bruises and the legs were terribly lacerated. Mr. Strickland must have fallen several times and it was evident that when he fell for the last time, he made no effort to rise. . . . He did not walk more than seven miles," continues the account, "and a greater portion of that distance, the walking was tolerably good. His overcoat and gloves were not found."

Several important details are supplied by the *New Hampshire Patriot and State Gazette* (Concord, N.H.) for November 1, 1849, in which, after quoting an account of the tragedy from the *Boston Post*, the editor proceeds:

> "We have a letter from a gentleman living in the vicinity of the Mountains, giving a particular account of this occurrence. He states that the guide left Mr. S. on the top of Mount Washington [*sic*]. The snow was in many places very deep, and in his wanderings he crossed the road twice, and also crossed his own track, leaving blood upon the rocks and ground where he dragged himself along, and having crawled through a 'brush pile' and down a steep ledge of rocks, he appeared to have fallen, and was found with his face wedged in between two rocks, his legs, face and hands being much scratched and bruised. He was buried, with appropriate funeral exercises by Rev. B. D. Brewster, which were attended by a large number of people from the neighboring towns.
>
> "Our correspondent speaks highly of the conduct of Mr. Fabyan in the search for the lost man, &c., and says that he furnished gratuitously a splendid supper to those who attended the funeral. He says this is the second hunt this season for a lost man. The other was found alive, about midnight, in a tree where he had climbed for safety; and he advises persons unacquainted with the country there to procure guides to accompany them in their ramblings."

Strickland's Boston friends at once sent for the body and on its arrival a thorough surgical examination was made.[4] On Monday, the 29th, a second funeral was held in Trinity Church on Summer Street, the structure which went down in the great fire of 1872. The Right Reverend Manton Eastburn, D.D., Bishop of Massachusetts, officiated, with George F. Hayter at the organ. The British Consul, Mr. (afterwards Sir) Edmund Arnout Grattan, and the vice-consul, with Mayor John P. Bigelow and many of Strickland's friends, formed the procession to the vault under the chapel, where the body was laid to await instructions from the father in England.

4. *Transcript*, October 29, 1849: "The body was subjected to a minute surgical examination on Saturday, and all suspicions of a self-inflicted death were removed thereby. . . he had thrown off the clothes glued to his skin by the frost, excoriating his legs in the act."

The circumstances attending Sir George's decision are unknown, but on May 8, 1850, Frederick was buried in Mount Auburn Cemetery, Cambridge,[5] off Green Briar Path, a few moments' walk west of the main gateway and close by the monument to William Ellery Channing. A tall, square, cross-topped monument of brownstone, beautifully wrought, is inscribed:

SACRED
to the memory of
FREDERICK STRICKLAND
an English traveller,
who lost his life
October 20, 1849,
While walking upon the
White Mountains.
He was the second son of
Sir George Strickland, Bart.,
A member of Parliament
In England.

The name of the maker, "A. Cary," appears below in small letters. The date of Frederick's ascent is fixed beyond all question as Friday, the 19th, and it seems improbable that he could have survived even until midnight; possibly Sir George was misinformed as to the date of his son's death.

In an effort to located the point where Strickland lost the path, an Appalachian party comprising Messrs. Paul R. Jenks, Charles W. and Henry Blood, and the writer made an exploring trip on August 7, 1943, and succeeded in following a long session of the Fabyan path near the cog railway, between Waumbek Tank and Jacob's Ladder. Overgrown with grass, weeds and wild flowers, it was easy to identify a deep trench once travelled by sad-

---

5. The problem of Strickland's place of burial baffled me for months. Public records in New Hampshire and Massachusetts were silent. Finally came word from the family that he was doubtless buried in America. But where? The answer dawned upon me—there was but one place which his Harvard friends would have chosen. I telephoned Mount Auburn Cemetery. To my question there came in a moment the reply: "Yes; Lot 1747, Green Briar Path; date of death, October, 1849; interment, May 8, 1850; lot stands in the name of Sir George Strickland." Within an hour I had found and photographed the monument.

Such heartfelt interest did Major Strickland express in my research that I was grieved to learn of his sudden death before my studies were finished. In his last letter to me he related the surprising fact that his uncle Henry, Frederick's companion in America, died at the age of 89 in consequence of a fall from his horse when hunting—another instance of the indomitable Strickland spirit.

dle horses from Fabyan's Mount Washington Hotel. Near the so-called Cold Spring (which supplies a faucet for drinking water at the Waumbek Tank) was found a small brook, fitting the *Transcript's* description of the stream in which Strickland's garments were found:

> "It appears from his track that he followed the Ammonoosuc River some distance. His pants and drawers were found in a hole in the river. The stream at this point is not more than two feet wide and six inches deep, but occasionally there will be a little pond formed where the water will be two or three feet deep. In one of these ponds the clothes were found."

Messrs. Blood and Jenks, who have long been familiar with the Ammonoosuc, state that its volume is too great to conform to this description, which probably refers to some tributary stream. The brook we discovered lies in part of the track of a landslide dating from 1912 or 1913 and flows into the Ammonoosuc a little above the tablet marking the place where Herbert J. Young died December 1, 1925.

The party studied the entire terrain from the ridge at the foot of the steep and winding portion of the path once known as Jacob's Ladder (south of the railway trestle to which the same name was later given) to the Ammonoosuc River and thence to the Marshfield station. They were satisfied that Strickland would not have lost the path in the higher section, because (unless he lost it exactly at the foot of Jacob's Ladder) to reach the river he would then have had to climb up a steep ridge at the left of the trail, when the obviously easier way was to keep to the path as it swung northerly toward Burt Ravine, at his right. It seems clear that he stuck to the path until well below timber line and finally lost it in the woods, whereupon he followed the brook to the Ammonoosuc, where, overtaken by darkness and suffering repeated falls, he at last succumbed.

This theory received support from the discovery, later, of the article in the *New Hampshire Patriot* (*supra*) which stated that "in his wanderings he crossed the road twice, and also crossed his own track." This could not have happened on the sharp ridge above timber line, but where the ridge spreads out above the Waumbek Tank there was ample space for a lost traveller to go around in circles. A clearing has been made there recently by the men of the C.C.C., through which can be seen the Southern Peaks and other parts of the range; but Strickland could have had no such aid to orient himself.

It is pathetic that such a tragedy as that of Frederick Strickland,—young, scholarly, brilliant, the heir of a noble race—should have been so nearly forgotten. In writing these pages it has been my hope that his prophecy expressed in the *Transcript* (Oct. 26, 1849) may be fulfilled:

"This is the first instance, we believe, that a death has occurred among the visitors to those mountains, and the circumstances attending this calamity will doubtless be rehearsed to thousands upon thousands of those who will visit the region in coming years. The exalted station, accomplishments, and personal history of the deceased, will afford ample scope for the imagination to invest the story with romantic interests; and many a traveller will silently sigh over the interesting incidents connected with the last hours of him who was

"'By strangers honor'd and by strangers mourn'd.'"

1994

A Melancholy Occurrence on Mount Washington

Floyd W. Ramsey

From *Shrouded Memories*

Retired English teacher Floyd W. Ramsey (1931–   ) is a northern New Hamp-shire native who has been writing about true historic events of the North Country for more than a decade and a half. The 65-year-old Ramsey, who lives in Little-ton, self-published a collection of 20 such historical pieces in the popular book, Shrouded Memories, *which debuted in late 1994. Two selections from that book, including the one you are about to read, appear in this volume.*

ON TUESDAY, September 18, 1855, the funeral planned for beautiful twenty-three-year-old Elizabeth Greene Bourne of Kennebunk, Maine, had to be canceled for one day due to heavy rain. Five days earlier she had died on the summit of Mount Washington under circumstances that also played a role in the death of her well-known uncle, George Bourne, fifteen months later.

Prior to the tragedy, George Bourne had been highly successful in the Bourne family shipbuilding firm. Financially secure, he had retired in 1852, while only in his early fifties. From that time, until the death of his niece, he had shared his zest for life with his family, friends, community and church. He was also an active and influential member of the local Sons of Temperance, a group that favored complete abstinence from intoxicating beverages.

Following the tragedy, he was a broken man.

Today Elizabeth Bourne is remembered as the first person to perish on the summit of New England's highest peak. But, just what were the cir-

Lizzie Bourne, as portrayed in this painting done several years after her tragic death in 1855.

cumstances surrounding her death there on the night of Thursday, September 13, 1855, that so deeply affected her genial Uncle George?

On the date in question, George Bourne, accompanied by his wife Jane, his twenty-five-year-old daughter Lucy, and his niece Elizabeth, checked in at the Glen House at the base of the mountain. It was early afternoon, and they had just completed their 120 mile journey from Kennebunk.

Elizabeth, or "Lizzie" as she was affectionately called, possessed a playful, coaxing manner. Despite her father Edward's concern for her fragile health, which was caused by a heart defect, she was able to obtain his permission to share in the holiday trip. He knew that, like her uncle, she possessed a love for the outdoors. Adding to her enthusiasm for going was also the prospect that a climb up Mount Washington in those days provided unparalleled adventure.

Though Lizzie knew that food and lodging could be obtained on the summit at both the Tip Top House and the Summit House, her primary purpose for making the climb was to witness the spectacle of sunrise from the top of New England's highest peak. This was a spectacle that she had heard a great deal about from friends, so she did not want to miss out on the opportunity to see it for herself.

With the carriage road still under construction, hikers had to use either existing footpaths or the bridle path. For a fragile girl like Lizzie Bourne, these choices posed a daunting challenge. However, she evidently felt equal to it because she talked her Uncle George and Cousin Lucy into making the climb that very afternoon instead of waiting until the following morning.

When the trio began the eight-mile ascent at about 2 p.m., tragically none of them recognized the need for a guide. Their plan was to spend a warm, comfortable night at the Summit House, and be up at daybreak so that Lizzie could see the sunrise from the top of the 6,288-foot peak. As fate would have it, they were rushing to keep a rendezvous with death.

Within two hours of their departure, they reached the end of the Carriage Road construction. Soon after leaving it, they came to the "Camp House at the Ledge," which is now known as the Halfway House. At this point they were 3840 feet above sea level. Because Lizzie was showing signs of tiredness, they stopped for a brief rest.

While visiting with workmen who were staying at the camp, they were told word had just been received from the summit that there were signs of a storm brewing. With the mountain's reputation for sudden, arctic-like storms, they were advised to turn back.

Unfortunately, because the weather was mild at that particular level, the girls insisted on continuing. With the best of intentions, George yielded to their arguments. This set the final stage for the tragedy that was soon to follow.

As they continued to use the remaining daylight to work their way up the bridle path, the late hour soon brought them to the "point of no return." Then when they were two miles below the summit, a strong wind suddenly whipped up that made further climbing extremely difficult.

With the mountain now wrapped in twilight, the wind reached gale proportions and the temperature dropped dangerously low. To make matters worse, Lizzie was also showing signs of exhaustion. George and Lucy were struggling to keep her moving. While assisting her up what they thought was the last steep slope, a thick cloud settled over the summit and created the illusion of an even higher climb. Momentarily discouraged, they halted.

Nine days later George would write of this experience: "To our sorrow another mountain stood before us, whose summit was far above the clouds."

And so it was, without the guide that they so badly needed they had no idea of where they were. The next day, when they found out, it was a shock from which George never recovered.

Before long they started upward again, but what little progress they were making ceased altogether as they became enveloped by the dark of the night and the wind's paralyzing cold.

Fighting back panic, George had the shivering girls stop and lie down on the path while he feverishly built a rock wall from the life-threatening cold. Occasionally he laid down to rest, and to share his body warmth.

Sometime later, when the wall was finally completed, it gave him the encouraging feeling that now they would all survive. Clinging to this hope, periodically he left the shelter to restore his body warmth by thrashing his arms and by stamping his feet.

However, whenever he was outside the wall, the roaring wind and bitter cold quickly engulfed him. Minutes later, gasping for breath, he would be forced to crawl back to the girls. At no time throughout the entire ordeal did he leave them alone for more than ten minutes.

As the hours passed slowly, he began to suffer miserably. Then around ten o'clock, as he lay down next to Lizzie, he reached for one of her hands. It was icy cold! Trembling, he touched her forehead. That was cold, too! He shouted to her. She did not respond.

When he wrote about this moment, he simply said, "She was dead. She had uttered no complaint, expressed no regret or fear, but had passed silently away."

Driven by grief, over the next eight hours George spared no effort to keep his daughter alive.

At dawn the two survivors left the shelter to seek help. And this was made when they found the soul-shattering discovery that they had spent the night only one hundred yards from the Tip Top House. What an agonizing moment this must have been for George Bourne.

Immediately after the owners and guests had been awakened and alerted to the tragedy, two men and two women rushed down to the rock sanctuary to retrieve Lizzie's body. On returning to the house, for four hours they tried every method imaginable to restore life to her. In George's words, "For four hours they labored with hot rocks, hot baths, and used every exertion to call back her spirit, but all in vain."

Just before noon Lizzie's body was placed in an open, shallow pine box which was slung from a long pole. She was then carried off the mountain by two men, with two others acting as relief. Brokenhearted, George and Lucy traveled with them.

At the Glen House, while the grief-stricken Bournes were completing final arrangements for the journey home, early newspaper accounts of the tragedy were heralding the fact that Lizzie's persistent eagerness to view the

COURTESY FLOYD W. RAMSEY

The stone monument marking the spot where Lizzie Bourne died is shown alongside the Cog Railway tracks, just a few hundred yards from the summit.

"splendid sunrise" produced a "Melancholy Occurrence" which left her in a pine box and destroyed her uncle's health.

Before the story ran its course, it was a tragedy that stunned all of New England.

On Saturday evening, September 15, George, Jane, and Lucy Bourne somberly arrived back in Kennebunk, and Lizzie's body was delivered to her father's house.

The day after the delayed funeral, Edward Bourne wrote a letter to the

A modest wooden sign marks the site of Lizzie Bourne's
Mount Washington deathbed.

Summit House proprietors expressing his wish "that no material change be made to the wall thrown up by my brother as I hope to place there some more enduring monument to the memory of my daughter."

To this day, this "more enduring monument" has never reached Mount Washington's summit. The Mount Washington Road Company suffered financial failure after constructing the first four miles of the Carriage Road, and this bankruptcy removed the only route by which the marker could have been hauled to the site of the tragedy. Having no other alternative, Edward Bourne had the stone placed at Lizzie's grave in Kennebunk's Hope Cemetery. It is still there.

As evidence of the family's unwillingness to accept Lizzie's death, they had four portraits done of her by 1858 from daguerreotypes that she had sat for in the early 1850s. Three of them graced the walls of the Bourne Mansion for more than 109 years. As for George Bourne, following the funeral his health continued to deteriorate. Within fifteen months he became the second victim of that terrible night on the mountain. Referring to that fact, his brother Edward wrote, "The suffering of that night, both mental and bodily, without doubt, very seriously impaired George's physical constitution so that it became more accessible to attacks and ravages of disease."

Which it did. Thirteen months after the tragedy George was stricken with typhoid fever. Following two months of almost continuous bed confinement, he died on December 7, 1856. His grotesque nightmare that started on New England's highest peak was finally over.

1994

The Short Adventurous Life of Dr. Benjamin Ball

Floyd W. Ramsey

From *Shrouded Memories*

DESCRIBED AS a man of unfaltering courage and singular coolness of head in the face of extreme difficulty, Dr. Benjamin Lincoln Ball of Boston, Massachusetts, was about to prove the truth of that description as he stepped from the train in Gorham, New Hampshire, on Wednesday morning, October 24, 1855.

Following his return from Europe more than a year earlier, he dreamed of making an excursion to the White Mountains to compare some of the finest American scenery with that which he had seen while abroad. However, various engagements interfered with his plans for such a trip, and the season passed when it was safe to make such a journey that year. Then, as the following summer advanced and passed as well, his time was further taken up by preparations for the publication of his book, *Rambles in Eastern Asia*.

Early that October, while conversing with friends who had visited the White Mountains, he learned that even though it was late in the season the scenery there was still worth the visit. Accordingly, he resolved to go as soon as he possibly could.

As fate would have it, on the evening of October 22 while he was visiting at the house of a friend, he met the Reverend Thomas Starr King. King, who was well known for his love of the White Mountains, spoke to him of the grandeur and beauty of the scenery to be seen from the summit of Mount Washington. He also remarked that he himself would most certainly like to see the surrounding mountains in their gray costume of late autumn as well as their white robe of snow.

Agreeably impressed by King's remarks, Dr. Ball was now determined to visit the White Mountains immediately.

The next afternoon the sun shone clear and warm in Boston, and it held out the promise of continued fair weather. This was all Dr. Ball needed to call on his friend, Dr. A. B. Hall, to see if he wished to join him on his trip to the White Mountains. Unfortunately Dr. Hall's engagements prevented him from leaving Boston at that time. Consequently, Dr. Ball returned home with the resolve to go alone.

Picking up a small valise which he had already packed, he made haste to reach the Eastern Railroad Station in order to catch the 2:30 p.m. train north. Following his arrival in Portland, Maine, a little after dark, he was disappointed to learn that there were no trains to Gorham, New Hampshire, before the next day. Since he had no other choice, he rented a room for the night at the Commercial House.

The following morning he arose early only to learn that the day was wet, gloomy, and cold. His first impulse was to return to Boston, but then he decided to proceed on to Gorham on the chance that the sun would come out.

As Dr. Ball disembarked from the train shortly after 11:00 a.m. the rain continued to fall in torrents, and since the area was shrouded in fog, there were no mountains to be seen. Following the conductor to the Alpine House, he asked him, "Could you please tell me, just where are the White Mountains?"

"Oh," the conductor replied, pointing toward the front of the hotel, "they are off there seven or eight miles. You will not be able to see them short of the Glen House unless the fog clears away."

"Very well," Dr. Ball said, "I will go to them and endeavor to get a view of them. I thought before this, that if I succeeded in seeing them from this place, and the weather continued stormy, that I should return home."

Hiring a horse, at noon he set off for the Glen House with his valise in front of him and with his umbrella raised to shield him from the continuing downpour. Little did he realize how important that umbrella would be to him in the days just ahead.

Arriving at the Glen House, he observed that the mountains were still concealed by the dense fog. While housing the horse at the stable, he decided to stop for only a half hour and then return to Gorham for the trip back to Boston.

In the months ahead he had every reason to wish that he had stuck by that decision.

COURTESY FLOYD W. RAMSEY

Dr. Benjamin Lincoln Ball

On entering the hotel, Dr. Ball met the proprietor, Colonel Joseph M. Thompson. While standing by the fire drying his clothes, he asked him, "The mountains are not now to be seen, I presume?"

Thompson answered, "No sir, you will not probably be able to see them today. At all events, not till after the weather has cleared up."

When Thompson mentioned that a new road was presently being constructed that Ball might walk up, his dwindling interest was immediately rekindled. "The new road," he asked, "what is that?"

Thompson answered, "It is the carriage road which is being built by a New York company so that people may ride all the way up Mount Washington on a smooth Macadamized road to the summit."

"I suppose I can follow the road easily enough?" Dr. Ball replied.

Thompson said, "Oh, yes. There is no difficulty about that. You can see it from the window there. It crosses the bridge, and enters the woods a little beyond. If there was no fog it could be seen to the Camp House and the Ledge, which is as far as it extends at present."

Dr. Ball then asked, "What am I to understand by the Camp House? The Ledge, I presume, is a ledge of rocks?"

Dr. Thompson told him, "The Camp House is a small one-story building for the use of the workmen on the road. It is about four miles from here, or about halfway to the summit. It is situated at the foot of the Ledge. The

Ledge is a kind of high bluff with a steep and somewhat precipitous face. At one point a path leads up and over the top. This is called the bridle path and is the one used by visitors in making the ascent to the summit either in walking or on horseback."

Dr. Ball replied, "I think I will take a walk up the carriage road, and be satisfied with a survey of that."

By way of warning, Thompson told him. "I would by no means attempt to go to the summit. It is too late in the day. Besides, you could see nothing for the clouds."

Because the wind had now started blowing, before leaving the Glen House Dr. Ball exchanged his top hat for a cloth cap which he saw hanging in the room. And, since it was raining, he also took along his umbrella.

Shortly after crossing the bridge he came upon the new road. Though he found the walking wet and rough, the pure cold air invigorated him. Walking quickly, in less than two hours he reached the Camp House. Without stopping, he went past it and scrambled up the Ledge. Reaching the top without too much difficulty, he still found the view limited by the fog. However, not one to admit defeat, he headed for the higher ground that he could see before him.

As he climbed higher, the cold wind penetrated his clothes and the rain formed a crust on the snow that continuously broke under his weight. Walking for an hour, he found it very tiring to continue stepping on the collapsing snow which now measured a depth of twelve inches. Not seeming to gain any distance, he turned to retrace his steps. As darkness closed in on him, he panicked a little and began running downhill.

Falling frequently, the darkness made it difficult for him to see his tracks. He made his way by feeling the indentures in the broken crust. Just as he began to fear he had lost his way, the Ledge suddenly appeared beneath his feet.

Virtually sliding from one rock to another, he arrived at the Camp House completely encased in ice and chilled through from the cold. Admitted into the building by Mr. J. D. Myers, his coat was immediately hung up to dry and his shoes were taken off and his stockings rung out. Given a dry pair, he then sat down and enjoyed the warmth of a blazing fire.

Following a welcome cup of hot coffee and a hearty supper, he accepted Mr. Myers' invitation to spend the night. However, as tired as he was, because his mind was so full of thoughts he spent the entire night listening to the wind howl and the rain pelt the roof. When the morning light appeared, he was still wide awake.

That morning, as he stood outside the Camp House with Mr. Myers, he

The Camp House, halfway up the mountain from the Glen House, was used
by Dr. Ball during his first night on the mountain. It was also here that
he was welcomed "back from the dead" three days later.

saw that the rain had freed the bridle path of snow. Unfortunately this led
him to believe that if nothing stood in his way he could easily reach the summit and be back at the Glen House by noon. In addition, he also thought
he could then take the night train to Portland and be back in Boston no later
than noon of the next day.

When he shared these thoughts with Mr. Myers, Myers proceeded to tell
him of the tragedy that had occurred there just a month earlier.

Dr. Ball interrupted him asking, "I presume you are referring to Miss
Lizzie Bourne?"

Myers replied, "Yes, Miss Bourne from Kennebunk. She was a beautiful
lady. I saw the party when they passed here. They were all in such good spirits. I knew it was too late in the afternoon for them to go. I tried to prevail
upon them to stop here overnight, but they were determined to go on. It
was a sad sight when they brought her over the Ledge. To see her form so
lifeless, and all so changed and sorrowful. I pitied the whole party from the
bottom of my heart."

He concluded, "I later learned that she did not die from the cold, but
from fatigue and general exhaustion. I believe they also said she had some

difficulty of the chest. It seemed hard that they could not find the Summit House when they were so near it."

In preparation for the ascent, Dr. Ball drank a bowl of coffee and ate lightly since he had little appetite. He also exchanged his shoes for a pair of Myers' stout thick boots which were much too large for him. And, since it continued to sprinkle, he took his umbrella along with a cane that Myers gave him as a present.

As he departed, Myers told him, "Should you see any bears in your way let me know and I will come up with my gun."

Ascending the Ledge with little fatigue, Dr. Ball reached the top of it within a half hour. From there he could see that the ground climbed gradually. Beyond a quarter of a mile, however, the landscape was obscured by misty clouds.

Starting upward, he was soon surprised to find the large footprints of a bear. The animal had apparently followed behind him during his descent the night before. Returning to the Ledge, he shouted this information down to Mr. Myers.

Returning to the climb, a mile further on he lost the path altogether as the snow depth mounted up to ten inches. He then recalled that he had heard that the mountain between Camp House and the summit was made up of four peaks, and that Mount Washington constituted the fourth and last peak.

As he passed the first peak, his trek became more difficult. His feet broke through the crust at each step, and this caused a great deal of pain to his ankles. Occasionally his feet caught between hidden rocks, and he sometimes experienced rough going in extricating them.

Whenever the way of his climb became too difficult he would retrace his steps or make a circuit until he found a way around the obstacle. At times, when the clouds broke away, he saw blue sky. Tragically, he allowed this encouragement to lure him on.

Somewhere between the second and third peaks the air turned disagreeably cold. The rain then turned from hail to sleet, and finally to heavy snow. When the wind increased, he closed his umbrella and used it as a walking stick along with the cane. Once, while disengaging his feet from among the rocks, he thought of turning back but at that moment the clouds opened again and drew him on.

As the landscape quickly became obscured once more by the clouds, he thought, "There is the third peak, and not more than fifteen minutes walk from here. I will keep along yet and reach it."

Struggling in that direction through the heavily falling snow, he again found that he could not travel in a straight line due to the rise and fall of the rocks. This misled him into believing that he was at least three-fourths of the way to the summit of Mount Washington. Whatever the situation, he felt certain that he could follow his footsteps back when he chose to return. He was pleased that he had taken the extra precaution of occasionally placing two stones together upon the large rocks in the event that he had to use them as guide marks.

Leaving the top of the third peak, he made his way down a gradual slope. During the descent he noticed again that the air was piercing cold. As the wind grew more violent, the snow whirled around him like a thick blanket. Convincing himself that the storm would dissipate within a half hour, he also believed that he would reach the Summit House where he would find comfortable shelter from the storm.

Walking as fast as his weary limbs would carry him, he climbed piles of craggy rocks until he found himself on more regular rising ground. It was at this point that he finally noticed his feet, hands, and face ached from a cold air that he estimated to be not less then ten degrees below zero. Despite his discomfort he pressed on, going first in one direction and then another as he was buffeted about by the ferocity of the storm.

As the day wore on he found it necessary to stop, face away from the wind, and thrash his arms around himself in order to restore some warmth to his body. Because his hands were now swollen, he sought to protect them by alternately placing them in his pockets. And because he was more and more being thrown to the ground by the force of the wind, in order to have the use of his hands he tied the umbrella to a button on his coat.

As he secured the umbrella, he concluded that this was the toughest storm that he had ever encountered, and that the cold was the most severe he had yet endured.

As he toiled on he experienced an unusual pain in the bones of his face. Placing a hand to his face, he found that it was totally encased in ice. On further inspection he also discovered that a row of icicles two inches in length had formed around the visor of his cap. His eyelashes were also riddled with ice, and he frequently had to remove it in order to see.

To fortify his flagging spirit he told himself, "The summit must be near. I will not turn back yet. At the Summit House I can make myself comfortable. The storm is too violent to continue long, especially so early in the season as October."

Facing into the wind, he shouted, "I will still try for the Summit House!"

Struggling on with the hope that he was on some part of the fourth peak, he found that with each step forward often there were several steps lost backward. Also, the intensity of the storm appeared to increase. Sheets of snow now descended on him in hard crystallized grains that struck his eyes with painful intensity.

At length he suddenly came upon comparatively level ground. With his whole frame shaking from the debilitating cold he cried out, "Mount Washington at last! And here is the summit!"

His feeling of victory was shortlived. The storm grew more violent than ever.

Continuing on with the rise of the land as his only guide, at length he saw a dark shape ahead of him. Thinking it was the Summit House, after suffering several falls he succeeded in reaching it. He was disappointed to learn that it was nothing more than a large rock.

As he groped in different directions, the cold grew even more intense and his breathing became extremely labored. He finally concluded that he had to descend. When he attempted to follow his tracks back, though, he discovered that they were nowhere to be found. By chance he happened upon one of the stakes which marked the route of the Carriage Road. When he attempted to follow succeeding stakes downward, in time he lost them altogether in a thick patch of stunted brushwood.

While searching for others in the deep snow, he was soon startled by the realization that night was coming on. Forced to face the fact that he was hopelessly lost, he was now determined to continue downward even though he did not know which side of the mountain he was on.

While hurrying over and around the rocks, the violent wind at times drove him forward. When he stopped for a moment of reflection, he cried, "My God! Am I to pass the night here?"

Exhausted and trembling from the cold, he began to wonder if he was going to survive. Then a sudden gust of wind threw him to the ground. Springing back up, he looked around for anything that would give him shelter. Stepping onto a flat rock, he saw a small recess between it and a patch of low firs. Detaching his umbrella, he opened it and then thrust a hand into the snow looking for something that he could attach it to. He came in contact with a strong upturned root. Resting the handle of the umbrella against it, he fastened it to the root with the cord tied to his coat button.

Following a brief rest, he set to work pulling up bushes. He piled them on the umbrella to protect it from the wind. Next he battened in the sides of his little camp with crusts of snow, and with the tops of small firs that he struggled to twist off. The work was slow and painful, but was somewhat successful despite the fact that he could not use his penknife because of the condition of his fingers.

The Glen House, where Dr. Ball started and ended his
near-tragic adventure up Mount Washington.

Then he next attempted to build a fire using paper from his wallet. He knew that ten-dollar bills were among the papers he burned. When his matches were nearly exhausted he quit because the wood would not kindle.

Having done all he could, he dragged himself under the umbrella. He was now prepared to spend the night shivering and chattering five-thousand feet above any human habitation.

During the long night the storm continued to howl down the mountain with such violence that he often clutched the handle of the umbrella for fear that his only form of shelter would be blown away. And, to prevent sleep, he took strained positions that would force him to stay awake. First he leaned on one elbow, and then on another. Next he changed from side to side, and then he would bend forward and then backward.

To keep his mind active and alert, he thought of the Summit House, the comforts of the Camp House, his room at the Glen House and the accommodations available at the Alpine House where other beds awaited him. Then he thought of each member of his family, and of all his friends and acquaintances. He knew that each of them would offer him a place to stay could they but be made aware of his exposed situation.

In this manner he survived into the second day, which was Friday, October 26.

As the first rays of the morning light found their way beneath his umbrella, he was surprised that the night had passed as quickly as it did. When he attempted to move out from under the umbrella, he found that both his feet and hands were "more or less frozen." This forced him to creep out into the open on his hands and knees.

Supporting himself by placing his hands on the flat rock, for a long period of time he remained there stamping his feet in order to get the circulation restored so that he could walk. Once this was accomplished, he ascended the slope a short distance to try and determine the direction he wanted to take.

Though the snowstorm had stopped for the moment, the cold wind still blew hard against him and low clouds limited his view. Finding himself standing near the brush patch where he had lost the road stakes, he hoped that he could find where they led and to be able to follow them. Toward that end he once again fastened the umbrella to his coat, and with the aid of his cane he began a lengthy search.

Failing to find any other stakes, throughout that day he wandered aimlessly looking for an outlet that would lead him in the right direction. At nearly every step his frozen feet broke through the hard crust that had formed over the new snow. Periodically he cracked the ice off rocks desperately seeking water that would quench the burning thirst he had developed.

Toward noon he found himself staring down into a great ravine which became lost to view in a sea of low clouds. Turning around, he retraced his steps and headed back in the same direction that he had traveled for the past four hours. As he stumbled along, he became more aware of his hunger, weakened body, and frozen limbs. The lumps of snow and ice that he consumed from time to time afforded him only a temporary relief. Finally, at one spot, when he broke the ice he found a small trickling of water. This became his only luxury that day.

As he approached the area where he had spent the night, he heard a strange clinking sound coming from above him. Looking toward the top of a high bluff, he could see two men outlined against the sky. Again hearing the noise he concluded they were doing some type of work. Though he shouted repeatedly to them against the howling wind, they failed to hear him. Soon they disappeared from view. In his weakened condition he knew it would be futile to make any attempts to reach them. Later he learned they were two guides whom Colonel Thompson of the Glen House had sent out to search for him.

Cruelly disappointed by this strange experience, he returned to where he had encamped. Upon reaching the flat rock, he observed that the sun would soon disappear from sight and that darkness would once again be upon him.

While he sat on the rock and pondered his next move, thick clouds gathered overhead which indicated another snowstorm was brewing. Looking at them, he shuddered to think that he had to lie on the cold ground through another long night.

Thinking that he might find a better place where he would suffer less than he had the previous night, he went searching for it. During this time he once again found himself engulfed by heavy swirling snow as the fury of the next snowstorm intensified. It was only with some difficulty that he descended the short distance back to the flat rock that was necessary to his survival.

Fastening his umbrella to the same upturned root, he tried to enclose it better than he had previously. However, because of his swollen and almost useless hands he accomplished very little. Also, before he could crawl in for the night he knew that he had to get some form of water to ease the intolerable thirst that made his throat and stomach feel as though they were on fire.

Gathering up large crusts of snow, he placed them in front of him on the ground and pushed them under the umbrella. He then crawled in and passed the second night much as he had the first.

In the hours ahead he suffered a great deal for a want of water. Every few minutes he bit off a piece of the crust, but it only alleviated his distress while he was swallowing it. He quickly learned that it would not melt fast enough to quench his thirst.

He was also now distressed by being unable to take a full breath. His breathing came in short gasps, and his lungs appeared to only inflate to about half of their natural capacity. He attributed this weakness to the contracting action of the extreme cold on his chest.

In addition to this problem, he experienced a severe pain in his left side which felt as if there was a heavy weight resting there. Due to his deteriorating physical condition, he busied himself periodically by taking his pulse. He accomplished this by pressing his left hand against his right wrist. He found it to be nearly a third less than was natural for him. Despite his circumstances, this told him that if he did not fall asleep he would live to see another day.

As before, he fought off sleep by a constant variation in strained positions and by a multiplicity of thoughts. First he thought of the many agreeable acquaintances he had made in various parts of the world. This was followed by thoughts of friends at home and abroad from whom he had received favors, kindnesses, and many different types of hospitality. Then, as his frail covering quivered and bent from the strength of the wind that was screeching just over his head, he thought of the important part his umbrella had played in his preservation. He then realized how different everything would have been had the rain ceased before he began his climb, and if he had left it behind.

As the night wore on he also came to realize that his body had become so numb that he was no longer subject to the tremblings he had suffered earlier. In fact, the sensation of cold was now succeeded by a kind of soothing glow which was working its way through every nerve and fibre of his being. Recognizing the danger this posed, he fought off his desire to sleep by making extra exertions.

The long night once again passed, and with the coming of daylight he at first resisted leaving his shelter in order to rest a little longer on his cold hard bed. Before long he gave up that idea, and crawled out from under the umbrella. As he emerged out in the open, he was amazed to see a building off in the distance below him.

Crawling to the front of the rock, he sat on it to ponder what house could be seen on this side of the mountain. Without realizing it, he was actually looking down on the Glen House where his painful journey had begun three days earlier.

Next, as he had done the day before, he supported himself against the rock and began to stamp his feet to restore the circulation. However, because his weakness was now much greater, he had to stop every few minutes to rest. Finally, after two draining hours, he was finally able to walk.

Tottering and slipping, he climbed a short distance looking for a clear view that would help determine the direction he would take on this day. He knew that there was no longer any room for further error.

Since the house he was seeing was several miles off and on the far end of a large forest, he decided to go in the opposite direction to avoid getting lost in the woods. Starting off, he walked slowly and unsteadily while bracing himself against nearby rocks until he could gain better use of his frozen feet and hands. He frequently stopped to break off pieces of ice from the rocks to ease the pain of his unending thirst.

As he stumbled along he found that it was difficult to hold his body erect, and that he was inclined to stoop forward like a man who was bowed down by age. Though he often raised himself upright, soon he was back in the same bent posture. He then thought of how long he had been without food, drink, or sleep, and the fact that he had constantly been exposed to extreme cold.

With the aid of the cane, and by placing his left hand on the rocks, he hobbled on hoping that each step was bringing him to the outlet.

Toward the middle of the day he rested upon a large flat rock to plot his next direction. He had just decided to move up a hundred feet higher in order to keep the house below in view, when to his joy and astonishment he saw a party of men coming into sight around the angle of a nearby bluff.

As six of them came into view he could see that they were carrying long poles. They appeared to be looking for something. Not realizing that they were searching for his body, Dr. Ball shouted to them. They stopped and stared at him in amazement and disbelief.

Joseph S. Hall, who only a month earlier had helped to carry Lizzie Bourne's body to the Glen House, was the first to approach him. In a tone of doubt he asked, "Is this Dr. Ball?"

When Dr. Ball answered that he was, Hall further asked, "Are you the person who left the Glen House Wednesday afternoon to walk up the new road?"

Dr. Ball again answered him in the affirmative.

Realizing that the whole situation was incredible, Hall also asked him, "And you have been out on the Mountain since that time?"

Dr. Ball assured him that he had.

Hall then exclaimed, "It is very wonderful! Why, how could you preserve yourself all this time? You had nothing to eat and nothing to drink! And you can stand!"

Dr. Ball was then told that men had been out looking for him since the day before. Hall informed him that the men with him were all experienced guides who were now out in search of him, and that they were Francis Smith, J. J. Davis, Thomas Culhane, Patrick Culhane and an Irishman named Thomas.

Dr. Ball inquired if anyone had been looking for him on the high bluff the previous afternoon. Francis Smith told him that he and another man had been there, and that the wind had been blowing very hard. This confirmed Dr. Ball's belief that this was why they did not respond to his shouts.

Unable to endure his thirst any longer, he then asked them for a drink. He was distressed to learn that they were not carrying liquid in any form. With the best of intentions, one man handed him a piece of gingerbread. However, it was impossible for him to swallow it. Besides, he had little desire for food.

After wretching from what little gingerbread he had placed in his dry mouth, Dr. Ball threw his arms around the necks of two of the men and he was helped along the path toward the Camp House. When they came to a rock that had a small hollow in the top, he got some relief from the two swallows of water that it provided.

Since the party was able to work its way down the mountain at a good pace, they soon arrived at the Camp House. After Mr. Myers welcomed Dr. Ball "back from the dead," he told him, "I know that you have had a severe trial. During your first night out, the water in a bowl here was frozen thick in a room adjoining one which had a fire going."

He also told him, "Towards night of that first day I went up on the Ledge, and while standing and looking to see if you were not yet coming I froze both of my heels. And such a night of anxiety I never wish to pass again! All night long the storm beat down upon the house. Since I could not sleep I spent the night walking to and fro and looking out the door. And how, I thought, must it be for you on the mountain, and during the whole of that long night?"

A short time later, when Dr. Ball's boots were removed, both feet were found to be frozen. They were immediately plunged into cold water until the frost was removed. At this time he also attempted to drink a cup of warm tea, but his stomach rejected it. Cold water, which he craved, was the only liquid that he could retain.

After his feet and badly swollen hands were wrapped in flannel, he was placed on a gentle horse named Tom. With a man walking on each side, he was brought down the Carriage Road to Colonel Thompson who was waiting for him with horses and a carriage. Thompson had been notified by means of signal flags that Dr. Ball had been found. He watched the descent by telescope.

Welcoming Dr. Ball back, he said, "You have been through what no other person has, or probably will again in a thousand years."

After the party arrived at the Glen House at about five o'clock that afternoon, Dr. Ball was made as comfortable as possible. When asked what he would like first for nourishment, he asked for a little hot cordial. Next he drank a small quantity of gruel to which milk was added. This was fed to him in intervals of an hour along with occasional swallows of water.

A short time later, when Colonel Thompson was about to send an errand boy to Gorham for the mail, he asked Dr. Ball if he had any communication he would like to make. Dr. Ball requested that a few lines be sent to his brothers in Boston informing them of his accident and of his improving condition.

Through the first few hours following his return, though he was strengthened by the care he was receiving, his hands and feet remained greatly swollen and turned a sickly black. Their appearance led his caregivers to conclude that all vitality in them was lost. The sense of feeling was also gone, and they seemed to be no more than cold clay attached to his limbs. Both his right foot and right hand were also found to be more severely frozen than their opposite counterpart.

Dr. Ball suggested that his hosts apply a poultice of flaxseed meal along with oil and charcoal, but Joseph Hall, who had experience with frozen limbs, recommended a poultice of charred hickory leaves that were pulverized and simmered with fresh lard. Since Dr. Ball had no objection to this treatment, once the poultice was cooled it was laid on his hands and feet and enclosed with large cloths.

Since Dr. Ball had now been without sleep for close to eighty hours, toward nine o'clock that evening he began to experience a strong desire to do just that. Hall remained in the room with him, and during the night he aroused him from an extremely deep slumber several times as a precautionary measure.

For the first few days following his rescue, Dr. Ball's sufferings were comparatively light. Dr. Wardwell of Gorham attended him, as did his brother, Dr. A. Ball of Boston. At this time he ran a slight fever, and his severe dehydration required that he be given water often during the day and every half hour at night. Then, beginning at his feet, slight chills frequently ran through his body causing his whole nervous system to vibrate. His feet, still without feeling, remained distorted by swelling and became covered with water blisters. About the ankles, and just above his injuries, the pain grew quite severe. When cramps finally set in, for the first few minutes he found the pain quite excruciating. Though his hands ached and burned day and night, under the circumstances he still felt that he was comfortably well off.

After remaining at the Glen House for a week, he then made preparations to return home. By means of a sofa placed in the carriage, on the day of his departure he was able to ride comfortably to Gorham. Once aboard the train he reclined all the way to Boston. Arriving there that evening, he was met by his brothers and conveyed to the American House.

Four months after his ordeal he was remarkably recovered from it. His hands were nearly well, with no loss except for a single nail from one finger. As for his feet, he was able to use them in moderation. With the coming of cold weather, however, he found them to be much more sensitive to the cold than they had been previously.

Tragically, having survived this ordeal, he died four years later on December 11, 1859, at the age of 39 in the Chiriquy region of Panama. According to the news account detailing his death, he had not enjoyed vigorous health following his dramatic exposure to the elements on Mount Washington. In this respect, the account stated, "In order to avoid the rigors of our New England climate this past winter, he made a visit to Central America. He intended to return early next spring, and to establish a medical practice in Brooklyn, New York."

The account further noted, "While in Central America he made explorations amid the striking volcanic scenery of Chiriquy Province. During the temporary absence of his traveling companions he started from Bocas del Toro in a canoe with a Spanish sailor. He wanted to examine a stream that was rich with fish. Unfortunately they were exposed all night to a sudden rain which induced a severe bilious fever in Dr. Ball. Faithfully attended in a neighboring village by the sailor, he was in full possession of his faculties almost to the hour of his death which occurred some ten days after the attack began."

A sad irony, to say the least, this is how the short adventurous life of Dr. Benjamin Lincoln Ball ended. And, as Joseph Hall once wrote to Dr. Ball's brother in Boston following his rescue on Mount Washington, "There is nothing in the history of the White Mountains to compare with this case of your brother; and I am sure its parallel will not be known in time to come."

To this day it remains a truly unique experience.

1859

A Mountaintop Spectacle

Thomas Starr King

From *The White Hills: Their Legends, Landscape, and Poetry*

Long regarded as one of the "classics" in White Mountain literature, The White Hills: Their Legends, Landscape, and Poetry, *was written by Unitarian minister and inveterate mountain explorer Rev. Thomas Starr King (1824–1864). The book, which primarily features a collection of dispatches previously published in the* Boston Evening Transcript, *was first published in 1859 and is credited with attracting many thousands of first-time visitors to the Whites. Starr King was among the first group of trampers to explore the great ravine north of Mount Adams in the Presidential Range, back in 1854. This ravine, long known as King Ravine, and Mount Starr King in the nearby Pliny Range, are named for Rev. King. Similarly, a mountain in the Yosemite Valley of his adopted state of California also bears his name.*

THERE ARE three paths for the ascent of Mount Washington, — one from the Crawford House at the Notch, one from the White Mountain House, five miles beyond the Notch, and one from the Glen.

The path from the White Mountain House requires the shortest horseback ride. Parties are carried by wagons up the side of Mount Washington to a point less than three miles from the summit. The bridle-path, however, is quite steep, and no time is gained by this ascent. The rival routes are those from the Notch and the Glen. Each of these has some decided advantages over the other. The Glen route is the shortest. For the first four miles the horses keep the wide and hard track, with a regular ascent of one foot in eight, which was laid out for a carriage road to the summit, but never completed. This is a great gain over the corduroy and mud through the forests of Mount Clinton, which belong to the ascent from the Notch.

When we rise up into this region where the real mountain scenery opens, the views from the two paths are entirely different in character, and it is difficult to decide which is grander. From the Notch, as soon as we ride out of the forest, we are on a mountain top. We have scaled Mount Clinton, which is 4,200 feet high. Then the path follows the line of the White Mountain ridge. We descend a little, and soon mount the beautiful dome of Mount Pleasant, which is five hundred feet higher. Descending this to the narrow line of the ridge again, we come to Mount Franklin, a little more than a hundred feet higher than Pleasant, less marked in landscape, but very difficult to climb. Beyond this, five hundred feet higher still, are the double peaks of Mount Monroe; and then winding down to the Lakes of the Clouds, from whence the Ammonoosuc issues, we stand before the cone of Mount Washington, which springs more than a thousand feet above us. The views of the ravines all along this route, as we pass over the sharpest portions of the ridge, are very exciting. And there is great advantage in this approach to be noted, that if Mount Washington is clouded, and the other summits are clear, travellers do not lose the sensations and the effects produced by standing for the first time on a mountain peak.

Sometimes on the path from the Notch over the ridge, the cloud-effects add unspeakable interest to the journey. We have in mind, as we write, an attempt which we once made with a small party to gain the summit of Mount Washington, on a day when the ridge was clouded, though the wind was fair. We started in hope, and were attended by sunshine nearly all the way through the forest. But on the top of Clinton there is rain and shoreless fog. Compelled to descend, we return after reaching the lower sunshine, in the belief that the squall has passed. But it is raining more furiously; yet this time we press on, although unable to see a rod ahead, assured by the guide that it will clear within an hour. A slow and chilling ride for half a mile on the rocky ridge has begun to dishearten us. We think of returning. But what is this? How has this huge cone leaped out of the gray, wet waste, and whence can it catch this flush of sunlight that sweeps over it? It is the dome of Mount Pleasant which our horses' feet had just begun to climb. Hardly can we swing our hats and scream our cheers, when it is hidden. The frolicsome west wind tears open the curtain at our left, and shows Fabyan's, so snug in its nest of green. But see, on the right the vapors melt under our feet, and the unbroken forests start up as if created that instant in those vast valleys. They are concealed as soon as shown; but the dull cloud about our heads is smitten with sunshine, and we are dazzled with silver dust. Now look up, — the whole sky is unveiled, and we stand in an ocean of vapor overarched by a canopy of blazing blue. The bright wind breaks the clouds in a

The southern peaks of the Presidential Range as seen from the summit. The large round peak seen in the upper middle is today known as Mount Eisenhower. In Moses Sweetser's time, it was called Mount Pleasant.

hundred places, scatters them, rolls them off, rolls them up, chases them far towards the horizon, mixes them with the azure, shows us billow after billow of land, from the Green Mountains to Katahdin, and at last sweeps off the mist from the pale green dome of Washington, and invites us to climb where the eye will traverse a circuit of six hundred miles.

By the Glen route we cross no subordinate peaks, and do not follow a ridge line from which we see summits towering here and there, but steadily ascend Mount Washington itself. In this way a more adequate conception is gained of its immense mass and majestic architecture. After we pass above the line of the carriage road to the barren portion of the mountain, there are grand pictures at the south and east of the Androscoggin Valley, and the long, heavily wooded Carter Range. Indeed, nothing which the day can show will give more astonishment than the spectacle which opens after passing through the spectral forest, made up of acres of trees, leafless, peeled, and bleached, and riding out upon the ledge. Those who make thus their first acquaintance with a mountain height will feel, in looking down into the immense hollow in which the Glen House is a dot, and off upon the vast green breastwork of Mount Carter, that language must be stretched and intensified to answer for the new sense awakened. Splendid, glorious, amazing, sublime, with liberal supplies of interjections, are the words that usually gush to the lips; but seldom is an adjective or exclamation uttered that interprets the scene, or coins the excitement and surge of feeling. We shall never forget the phrase which a friend once used,—an artist in expression as in feeling, and not given under strong stimulant to superlatives,—as he looked, for the first time, from the ledge upon square miles of undulating wilderness. "See the tumultuous bombast of the landscape!" Yet the glory of the view is, after all, the four highest companion mountains of the range, Clay, Jefferson, Adams, Madison, that show themselves in a bending line beyond the tremendous gorge at the right of the path, absurdly called the "Gulf of Mexico," and are visible from their roots to their summits. These mountains are not seen on the ascent from the Notch, being hidden by the dome of Mount Washington itself. On the Glen path these grand forms tower so near that it seems as though a strong arm might throw a stone across the Gulf and hit them. There should be a resting-place near the edge of the ravine, where parties could dismount and study these forms at leisure. Except by climbing to the ridge through the unbroken wilderness of the northern side, there is no such view to be had east of the Mississippi of mountain architecture and sublimity. They do not seem to be rocky institutions. Their lines have so much life that they appear to have just leaped from the deeps beneath the soil. We say to ourselves, these peaks are nature's struggles against petrifaction, the earth's cry for air. If the day is not entirely clear, if great white clouds

> Are wandering in thick flock among the mountains,
> Shepherded by the slow, unwilling wind

the shadows that leisurely trail along the sides of these Titans, or waver down their slopes, extinguish their color, as it blots the dim green of their peaks, then their tawny shoulders, then the purple and gray of their bare ledges, and at last dulls the verdure of their lower forests,—thus playing in perpetual frolic with the light,—are more fascinating than anything which can be seen from the summit of Mount Washington itself, on the landscape below.

But let us not begin by disparaging at all what is to be seen on the summit. Suppose that we could be lifted suddenly a mile and a quarter above the sea level in the air, and could be sustained their without exertion. That is the privilege we have in standing on the summit of Mount Washington, about sixty-three hundred feet above the ocean. Only the view is vastly more splendid than any that could be presented to us if we could hang poised on wings at the same elevation above a level country, or should see nothing

GUY SHOREY

Looking north into the Great Gulf and toward the northern peaks
of the Presidential Range.

beneath us but "the wrinkled sea." For we are not only upheld at such a
height, but we stand in close fellowship with the noblest forms which the
substance of the world has assumed under our northern skies. We estimate
our height from the ocean level, and it is on a wave that we are lifted, — a
tremendous ground-swell fifteen miles long, which stiffened before it could
subside, or fling its boiling mass upon the bubbling plain. We are perched
on the tip of a jet in the centre of it, tossed up five hundred feet higher than
any other spout from its tremendous surge, and which was arrested and is
now fixed forever as a witness of the passions that have heaved more furiously in the earth's bosum than any which the sea has felt, and as a "tower
of observance" for sweeping with the eye the beauty that overlays the globe.

It may be that this billow of land was cooled by the sea when it first arose,
and that these highest peaks around us were the first portions of New England that saw the light. On a clear morning or evening the silvery gleam of
the Atlantic is seen on the southeastern horizon. The waves, that form only
a transitory flash in the landscape which the mountain shows its guests, once
broke in foam over the rocks that now are beaten only by the winds which
the Atlantic conjures, and covered by the snows that mimic the whiteness
of the Atlantic surf, out of which their substance may have been drawn.
And, since the retreat of the sea, what forces have been patiently at work to
cover the stalwart monarchs near us with the beauty which they reveal! We
call them barren, but there is a richer display of the creative power and art
on Mount Adams yonder than on any number of square miles in the lowlands of New England equal to the whole surface of that mountain. The noblest trees of New England are around its base, and there are firs on the ledge
from which its peak springs that are not more than two inches high. Alpine

and Lapland plants grow in the crevices of its rocks, and adorn the edges of its ravines. Since the sea-wave washed its cone, the light and the frosts have been gnawing the shingly schist, to give room and sustenance for the lichens that have tinted every foot of its loosely-shingled slopes with stains whose origin is more mysterious than any colors which a painter combines,—as mysterious as the painter's genius itself. The storms of untold thousands of years have chiselled lines of expression in the mountain, whose grace and charm no landscape gardening on a lowland can rival; and the bloom of the richest conservatory would look feeble in contrast with the hues that often in morning and evening, or in the pomp of autumn and the winter desolation, have glowed upon it, as though the whole art of God was concentrated in making it outblush the rose, or dim the sapphire with its flame.

The first effect of standing on the summit of Mount Washington is a bewildering of the senses at the extent and lawlessness of the spectacle. It is as though we were looking upon a chaos. The land is tossed into a tempest. But in a few minutes we become accustomed to this, and begin to feel the joy of turning round and sweeping a horizon line that in parts is drawn outside of New England. Then we can begin to inquire into the particulars of the stupendous diorama. Northward, if the air is not thick with haze, we look beyond the Canada line. Southward, the "parded land" stretches across the borders of Massachusetts, before it melts into the horizon. Do you see a dim blue pyramid on the far northeast, looking scarcely more substantial than gossamer, but keeping its place stubbornly, and cutting the yellowish horizon with the hue of Damascus steel? It is Katahdin looming out of the central wilderness of Maine. Almost in the same line on the southwest, and nearly as far away, do you see another filmy angle in the base of the sky? It is Monadnoc, which would feel prouder than Mont Blanc, or the frost-sheeted Chimborazo, or the topmost spire of the Himalaya, if it could know that the genius of Mr. Emerson has made it the noblest mountain in literature. The nearer range of the Green Mountains are plainly visible; and behind them Camel's Hump and Mansfield tower in the direction of Lake Champlain. The silvery patch on the north, that looks at first like a small pond, is Umbagog; a little farther away due south a section of the mirror of Winnipiseogee glistens. Sebago flashes on the southeast, and a little nearer, the twin Lovell lakes, that lie more prominently on the map of our history than on the landscape. Next, the monotony of the scene is broken by observing the various forms of the mountains that are thick as "meadow-mole hills,"—the great wedge of Lafayette, the long, thin crater of Carter, the broad-based and solid Mount Pleasant, the serrated summit of Chocorua, the beautiful cone of Kiarsarge, the cream-colored Stratford peaks, as near alike in size and shape as two Dromios. Then the pathways of the rivers interest us. The line of the Connecticut we can follow from its birth near Canada to the point where it is hidden by the great Franconia wall. Its water is not visible, but often in the morning a line of fog lies for miles over the low land, counterfeiting the serpentine path of its blue water that bounds two states. Two large curves of the Androscoggin we can see. Broken portions of the Saco lie like lumps of light upon the open valley to the west of Kiarsarge. The sources of the Merrimack are on the farther slope of a mountain that seems to be not more than the distance of a rifle-shot. Directly under our feet lies the cold Lake of the Clouds, whose water plunges down the wild path of the Ammonoosuc, and falls more than a mile before the ocean drinks it at New Haven. And in the sides of the mountain every wrinkle east or west that is searched by the sunbeams, or cooled by shadows, is the channel of a bounty that swells one of the three great streams of New England.

> Fast abides this constant giver,
> Pouring many a cheerful river.

And lastly, we notice the various beauty of the valleys that slope off from the central range. No two of them are articulated with the mountain by the same angles and curves. Stairways of charming slope and bend lead down into their sweet and many-colored loveliness and bounty.

1867

The Ascent from the Crawford House

From *Eastman's White Mountain Guide*

Concord, N.H., native Samuel Coffin Eastman (1837–1917), a well-known attorney with degrees from Brown University and Harvard Law School, provided White Mountain tourists with one of the earliest and most successful guides to the region. The White Mountain Guide Book, *first published in 1858, was edited annually by Eastman. The handy guide provided information not only on the finer natural wonders of the Whites, but also on area tourist accommodations. That should come as no surprise, however, as Eastman served as a director on the board of the Profile and Flume Hotel Company, operators of two of the region's finest hotels, both in the Franconia Notch area.* The White Mountain Guide Book *went through 15 different editions between 1858 and 1879.*

DURING THE height of the season the excursion is made every day, when the weather will allow, and generally occupies about ten hours. It can be made, however, in a somewhat shorter time if necessary. The distance to the summit is, according to the guideboard at the entrance to the path, only seven miles, but if you have a pleasant day you will be by no means sorry to find it nine, which is commonly supposed to be nearer the truth. The entire distance is accomplished on the backs of well trained horses, with the attendance of two or three experienced mountain guides, who will be always at hand to mend a failing girth. If you do not like so long a ride on horseback, you can be conveyed round in a carriage by a longer route over Fabyan's Path to the foot of Mt. Washington, and can then take the horses for the last three or four miles. By this course, however, you lose all the beautiful views from the four mountains passed over on the other path. These are the most satisfactory to be obtained, when, as is often the case, the summit of Mt. Washington is clothed in mist. Sometimes the ascent is made on foot, but on account of the unparalleled roughness and steepness of these mountain paths, this method is to most persons too wearisome for enjoyment, unless they spend a long time in the ascent, and pass the night on the mountain. A flask of brandy is frequently considered indispensable for pedestrians, as persons often faint from fatigue. Whatever path or method you select, it is never advisable to attempt the ascent, for the first time, without a guide. Many accidents and inconveniences arise every year from the neglect of this precaution. Often you pass from the brightest sunshine below into impenetrable mists upon the summits of the mountains.

The clothing for this excursion should be of the commonest description at your command, but must be as warm as any required for winter wear. The temperature below cannot be taken as a criterion of that at the height of four thousand feet or more, where it is almost without cessation severely cold. Thick woolen mountain jackets can be obtained of the porter at the hotel at a charge of twenty-five cents; but you will be more independent if you have garments of your own suitable for the purpose. Sacks and jackets are generally worn, even by ladies, rather than shawls or cloaks, on account of their greater convenience in the strong winds, which blow incessantly across the tops of the mountains. Close caps or hats, secured very firmly on the head by strings, are indispensable for the same reason. Half the pleasure of the excursion is often lost on account of the annoyance arising from a loose hat continually blowing off, or from the troublesome shawl or cloak incessantly flapping in the wind, and, threatening to burst every fastening. The horses are brought to the door immediately after breakfast, and, when the weather is promising, the party does not generally consist of less than twenty-five. The greater part of the guests at the hotel commonly come down to the piazza at the north-eastern end of the house to see these strange-looking cavaliers, in all their grotesque costumes, set out for the mountains. The path passes directly into the forest on the east.

General View of the Range.

The first mountain which we ascend on this path is Mt. Clinton. It belongs to the great range, which extends from the Notch north-easterly to Mt. Madison, a distance of fourteen miles. The whole mountain region of New Hampshire is about forty miles square, but the name, "White Mountains," is sometimes applied, for the sake of distinction, only to this particular group, of which Mt. Washington is the culminating point. The following list gives the name and height of each mountain of the range, in its order, commencing at the Notch:—

Mt. Webster,	4,000 ft.	Mt. Washington,	6,285 ft.
Mt. Jackson,	4,100 "	Mt. Clay,	5,400 "
Mt. Clinton,	4,200 "	Mt. Jefferson,	5,700 "
Mt. Pleasant,	4,800 "	Mt. Adams,	5,800 "
Mt. Franklin,	4,900 "	Mt. Madison,	5,400 "
Mt. Monroe,	5,400 "		

One of the Indian names of these mountains was "Agiocochook," which signifies "the place of the Spirit of the Great Forest," or, according to Judge Potter, "the place of the Storm Spirit," and another, "Waumbekketmethna," alluding to the whiteness of the mountains. The distinctive title of "White" has always been applied to them on account of their peaks being white with snow during ten months of the year.

Even in July and August the bare rocks have a grayish cast, when seen from a distance, which almost entitles them to the name of white. These noble hills were first visited in 1732, by a man named Darby Field.

The great advantage of this route to the summit of Mount Washington consists in the passage over separate mountain peaks, from each of which views of great beauty are obtained. It often happens, too, that when the summit of Washington is wrapped in an impenetrable mantle of mist, these lower summits, and all the surrounding landscape, are in clear light, and often, indeed, bathed in sunshine. When this is the case, those who ascend by this route have the pleasure of enjoying the peculiar excitement of standing on the clear mountain top. Neither should one regret an occasional cloud or shower. No mountain effect can be finer than that produced by the dense masses of boiling vapor, as they gather in the valleys, now all on fire from the rays of the sun, shading off into golden tints, and now a dark sombre gray, needing only a little less light to become the "l'aer perso" of Dante's Inferno, slowly yet steadily rolling up the mountain side, concealing the depths of the ravine, and at last enveloping you with its penetrating moisture. Then the mist leaves you as suddenly as it came, and opens to your vision an abyss yawning at your very feet and reaching to the mountain's base. Such sights as these are ample compensation for the passing shower. Then at another time, both here and on the summit, you may often see the light fleecy clouds floating about the ravines, climbing the slopes, or hurrying over the valleys, casting long shadows over the green mountain sides, and spotting the fields with a deeper color. We shall see these clouds

"Lie couched around us like a flock of sheep,"

when the haze has been swept from the horizon, immediately after a rainstorm. This is unquestionably the pleasantest time to ascend the mountains.

The fatigue of the long horseback ride is greater to those not accustomed to it than the ascent in a carriage. But there is more romance attending this mode of conveyance; there is a different class of views to be obtained, and perhaps more which will be pleasant to look back upon when passed. Mr. Taylor calls it "by far the most compensating road to the summit."

Ascent of Mt. Clinton.

At a few rods' distance from the Crawford House is the base of Mt. Clinton, which we continue to ascend for two or three miles, until at its summit we are more than two thousand feet above the point of starting, and more than four thousand above the sea. The path lies all the way through a wild forest, and is so steep and winding that we often see the more advanced of the party through the trees almost directly above our heads. Now and then we pass a long piece of corduroy, made of logs laid closely together across the way, and forming a hard but quite rough path. When wet with rain, this portion of the way is quite dangerous in the descent. It should be improved if possible. At some points are cool springs of water issuing from the sides of the path, where the horses are accustomed to rest for a moment, and quench their thirst. Occasionally the way lies through a wet gully three or four feet deep, which has the appearance of being the bed of a small mountain stream, and, after a rain, spatters our garments with a plentiful quantity of mud. It is most interesting on this ascent to watch the everchanging character of the trees and shrubs in their transition from beech, and yellow birch, and sugar maple, and mountain ash, and aspen poplar, and striped maple below, to white pine, and hemlock, and white birch, and spruce, and balsam fir, hung with festoons of hair-like moss high up, every sort giving way near the top to a kind of dwarf fir, often so intertangled that it is possible to walk over the tops of the trees as over moss. Beneath the trees—a strange union of the arctics with the tropics—the ground is covered with a dense growth of ferns. Just before reaching the summit of Mt. Clinton we pass through a region of dead trees, which are supposed to have been killed by the intense cold of 1812, and the seasons which followed until 1816, when, it is asserted, they remained frozen throughout the year, even in summer.

Their trunks and branches have been bleached by the rains and the winds, and they stand like weird giants stretching out their ghost-like arms to guard the approach to the enchanted regions above. At the height of 4,000 feet we emerge from the forest, and find above nothing but scattered firs hiding here and there in the crevices of the rocks.

View from Mt. Clinton.

The path lies a little to the north of the summit of Mt. Clinton, and as we wind around it over the bare rocks, the first noble mountain view bursts upon our sight. Almost directly before us, towards the east, is the conical summit of Kearsarge, and apparently near it some little silver lakes, with a blue setting of many mountains; and behind we can discern Willard, and the other mountains around the Notch, mottled here and there with the shadows of passing clouds.

As we begin to descend to the narrow ridge, which joins this mountain to the next, we gain a view of the nearer objects beneath us. On the right, at a depth of 2,000 feet, is a vast forest, through which winds the Mt. Washington River, and beyond is a long range of giant hills, which, like these we are on, seem marching in solemn procession towards the great central shrine. On the left, at a similar depth, the Ammonoosuc is seen threading the forest, and at last finding its way to the open country in the distance. The first experience of real mountain travel is gained as we slide down the rocks, and wind along the bleak ridge, which connects Mt. Clinton with

Mt. Pleasant.

The path generally pursued passes around the southern side of this mountain several hundred feet below its summit, although there is one directly over, which the horses by no means fancy, and can very seldom be induced to take. A guide-board should be erected here, as the descent on the other side of Mt. Pleasant is very difficult, and parties, in advance of the guide, sometimes take the wrong road. As we pass along the narrow path, we come to a delightful spring, where we can, if we choose, drink from a glass kept there for the purpose. It is remarkable that both men and horses always drink more upon the mountains than they do below, perhaps on account of the increased rapidity of evaporation. In the vicinity of this spring, as at other sheltered sunny spots along the path, exquisite little spring flowers, such as anemones and bluebells, are found just opening in August. The season here resembles the arctic summer, the snow not disappearing till July,

The dome of Mount Pleasant (now called Mt. Eisenhower) as seen
along the Crawford Path near Mount Franklin.

and coming early again in September. During two months vegetation comes
on with wonderful speed, and the whole cycle of growth and fructification
is completed. You must not allow your horse to turn out of the beaten path
to crop the tender grass, as he desires, for often serious accidents are the result of such yielding. Here, if he should lose his foothold, you would be pre-
cipitated a great distance down the side of the mountain. Neither, if you
dismount, should you allow your bridle to leave your hand, with the expec-
tation that your horse will patiently await your return. Especially if you lead
the line are you liable to serious disappointment if you do. Mt. Pleasant has
a peculiarly rounded top, and presents a beautiful appearance at a distance,
whence, probably, its name, somewhat incongruous when compared with
those of all the others of the patriot group. On the northern side are immense slides, which are supposed to have occurred, like most of those among
the mountains, in the memorable storm of 1826. After passing around Mt.
Pleasant, we come to an extended sort of plain lying at the foot of

Mt. Franklin.

This is a very irregular, flattened peak, about a hundred feet higher than the
last. The arduous ascent to its summit is an excellent preparation for the

ascent of Mt. Washington, by which alone it is surpassed in difficulty. It is almost fearful to look up at the more advanced of our party winding along the lofty crags far above our heads, but we soon climb the rocks in safety, and look down in turn upon those below. The path passes a short distance to the north-west of the summit, but there is no danger in turning out a little way to the right, and attaining the highest point. The view thence towards the south-east is extremely grand. Far to the south appear the four beautiful peaks of Chocorua (*Cho-cor-u-ay*), the one to the right being higher and more conical than the rest. Thousands of feet below us stretches the interminable forest, like a carpeting of rich, dark grass. The mountain on the eastern side is almost perpendicular, and, as we leave it behind, we can see the long scar left by a slide, which occurred one stormy night in the summer of 1857.

Mt. Monroe.

We are now approaching the two majestic peaks of Mt. Monroe, which is inferior to Mt. Washington in height rather than in symmetrical beauty. We pass around the south-eastern side, several hundred feet below the summit, over what we are now prepared to consider an easy path. Far down to the right is the frightful abyss known as "Oakes's Gulf." The other side of this ravine is formed by the same range of mountains, which, farther back, we observed across the wide valley, approaching the central cluster. As we gaze down into the dizzy depths, and see huge rocks scattered in confusion on the bottom, and perpendicular craggy precipices forming the sides, we cannot help being impressed with a feeling of awe. Sometimes clouds are entrapped in this fathomless gulf, and whirl round and round in vain attempts to escape. On the northern side of Mt. Washington is a similar ravine called the "Great Gulf."

Approach to Mt. Washington.

Winding around Monroe, we gain our first view of Mt. Washington, towering nearly fifteen hundred feet above us. It appears to consist of an irregular pyramidal pile of shattered grayish brown stones, standing as steep as they can without rolling down. Too often this long-expected view is lost on account of the almost perpetual mists which surround the summit. Before reaching the foot of the cone, we must pass over an extended plateau, which is at first quite smooth, and allows the horse to trot for a short distance. Nearer the mountain, however, it is scattered with innumerable bowlders,

A modern-day hiker makes his way along the Crawford Path
with the summit of Mount Washington rearing up in the distance
between Mount Monroe's double peaks.

which appear to have been deposited here at the same time that the pyramid of similar stones before us was thrown up. The path winds among these rocks, and is occasionally pointed out by small heaps of stones piled up for that purpose many years ago. This plain extends a long way to the right, and is nearly a mile above the sea. Little patches of coarse grass and small ponds are found here and there upon it. In the western part is a beautiful sheet of water, called the "Lake of the Clouds," from which the Ammonoosuc issues. Leaving the path, and passing along the plain towards the east, we should come to the most wonderful of all the gorges in this region, — Tuckerman's Ravine.

Ascent of the Last Peak

The ascent of the cone of Mt. Washington is made by parties from the Crawford House, on the south-western side, where the rocks appear to stand almost perpendicular, although in reality less steep than on the southern side. The path appears to have been formed by rolling the great blocks and slabs of stone on each side, leaving a partially clear way between. Up this we wind slowly to the very summit. The rocks are of the most uninteresting character, consisting principally of a dull-brown mica slate. During the first part of the way a great abundance of a delicate Alpine plant, with small white flowers, is observed among the rocks. It is curious to discuss the manner in which the seeds of the plant were first brought here, for it is entirely unlike any other plant found in this part of the world. But at any rate it is here, and relieves the scene of much of its gloominess. Higher up there is nothing but bleak, bare rock. If you propose to pass the night on the mountain, and wish to ride down, you must have another horse sent up, when you are ready to return. The few steps which separate us from the top are easily passed over on foot, the horses being left here merely for the convenience of the guides, so that they shall not become mingled with those from other paths. A finger on a guide-board, elevated upon a pile of stones, points out the path, and buildings on the summit being as yet hidden from view.

The Summit.

The acre of comparatively level surface on the top of the mountain is so completely covered with irregular angular rocks, that one can scarcely find a smooth place to stand upon. The building which first appears in sight is the Tip-Top House. This is used at present as a dining-room. A little to the east, and somewhat below, is the Summit House, the first building ever erected on the mountain. Both of these have thick walls of the native rock, and are very low, with roofs nearly flat, so as to present as little surface as possible to the fierce winds. The Summit House was erected in 1852, by the united efforts of Mr. Hall and Mr. Rosebrook, two farmers of Jefferson. It was commenced in June, and sufficiently completed towards the close of July to form a comfortable shelter. It was bound down to the mountain by several large cables, which passed over the top of the roof. The interior is divided into two principal rooms, each of which is heated by a stove. Around these fires the shivering guests crowd, and present about the same appearance as travellers in January stopping to warm themselves at a country inn. The thermometer does not perhaps indicate a temperature below 50°, but the constant wind produces the effect of even thirty degrees below that point. In the rear of the main rooms are narrow dormitories, furnished since the opening of the carriage road with comfortable beds and other appliances for a good night's rest. Above are also other "sleeping-places," separated from the rooms below by wooden slats. Every inch of space within the building appears to be turned to some account. The tops of the lower rooms are ceiled with cotton cloth, and the sides, formed of rough stone walls, well pointed with mortar, like a common cellar wall, are now ceiled with boards and papered, adding to the comfort and dryness of the room. In deep recesses are good glass windows increasing very materially the comfort of the place. This, and the Tip-Top House, erected some years afterwards, together form a hotel, at which we can stop as long as we choose. Neither does it seem by any means a bad one, when we consider that every foot of board and every article of furniture was originally brought several miles up these steep paths on the backs either of men or of horses. Stone and water are the only material to be obtained on the Summit, a never failing spring of the latter being found a few rods north of the Summit House, a little down the mountain. The expense of transportation has been, of course, considerably diminished by the completion of the carriage road, but still one must readily see the cost of supplying the house is much greater than within a short distance of goods markets. We must not, therefore, be surprised at a somewhat higher charge than the prices established by the hotels at the base, if we choose to stay a while. If the tourist wishes to devote his whole time to the view, a luncheon taken at the hotel will make an excellent substitute for the dinner in the Summit House.

There are generally three parties arriving on the Summit every day, one from the Crawford House, one over Fabyan's Path, and one from the Glen House. Quite a large number is generally stopping here, so that it is not unusual to meet a hundred people on the top of the mountain in the middle of the day. One of the pleasantest elements of the excursion is the manner in which so many persons are thrown for a time into one family, sympathizing in their common elevation above the rest of mankind.

The View.

Although the view from the Summit has already been described in connection with the ascent from the Glen, the following enumeration, from Oakes's White Mountain Scenery, of the objects of interest, visible on a clear day, may be of use to the tourist. "In the west, though the blue haze, are seen in the distance the ranges of the Green Mountains; the remarkable outlines of the summits of Camel's Hump and Mansfield Mountain being easily distinguished when the atmosphere is clear. To the north-west, under your feet, are the clearings and settlements of Jefferson, the waters of Cherry Pond, and, farther distant, the village of Lancaster, with the waters of Israel's River. The Connecticut is not visible, but often, at morning and evening, its appearance is counterfeited by the fog rising from its surface. To the north and north-east, only a few miles distant, rise up boldly the great north-eastern peaks of the White Mountain range, — Jefferson, Adams and

Madison,—with their ragged tops of loose, dark rocks. A little farther to the east are seen the numerous and distant summits of Maine. On the south-east, close at hand, are the dark and crowded ridges of the mountains in Jackson; and beyond, the conical summit of Kearsarge, standing by itself on the outskirts of the mountains; and farther, over the low country of Maine, Sebago Pond, near Portland. Still farther, it is said, the ocean itself has sometimes been distinctly visible. The White Mountains are often seen from the sea, even at thirty miles' distance from the shore, and nothing can prevent the sea from being seen from the mountains but the difficulty of distinguishing its appearance from that of the sky near the horizon. Farther to the south are the intervals of the Saco, and the settlements of Bartlett and Conway, the sister ponds of Lovwell, in Fryeburg, and still farther, the remarkable four-toothed summit of Chocorua, the peak to the right much the largest and sharply pyramidal. Almost exactly south are the shining waters of the beautiful Winnipesaukee, seen with the greatest distinctness in a favorable day. To the south-west, near at hand, are the peaks of the southwestern range of the White Mountains; Monroe, with its two little Alpine ponds sleeping under its rocky and pointed summit; the flat surface of Franklin, and the rounded tops of Mt. Pleasant, with their ridges and spurs. Beyond these the Willey Mountain, with its high, ridged summit; and beyond that several parallel ranges of high, wooded mountains. Father west, and over all, is seen the high, bare summit of Mt. Lafayette, in Franconia.

"At your feet is the broad valley surrounded by mountains, through which wind deviously the sources of the Ammonoosuc, with its clearing at its farther extremity, and the Mt. Washington House; and beyond this, at twenty miles' distance, the little village of Bethlehem is dimly visible."

In spite of the assertion of Mr. Oakes, the host of the Tip-Top House will point you out two places in which, he will assure you, the shining waters visible are parts of the Connecticut.

The Descent.

Returning to the spot where the ponies were left, we find each one looking for his steed, and mounting with as much speed as the chilly wind and the rough rock will allow. The ladies generally walk down the first steep descent to the plain, as it is much more difficult than the ascent. There is really no danger, however, as the horses never take a step till they see where they are going. The view is also much finer going down, as our faces are now turned away from the steep side of the mountain. Especially is it beautiful on the right of Mt. Monroe, where we can trace the silver water of the Ammonoosuc in its windings through the forest far below. Soon after reaching the plain the party becomes scattered, and we wander on perhaps alone, greeting each solitary peak, like an old friend, as we pass it, and arrived at last at the summit of Clinton. The descent of this mountain becomes somewhat tiresome, with its interminable "corduroys," and its troublesome black flies, and we are not sorry at last to discover the white piazza of the Crawford House appearing through the trees.

1871

Life on the Summit

Joshua H. Huntington

From *Mt. Washington in Winter, Or the Experiences of a Scientific Expedition Upon the Highest Mountain in New England, 1870–71*

During the winter of 1870–71, a team of four men took up residency on top of Mount Washington for the purpose of observing and recording the weather on the summit of New England's highest mountain. This expedition, which found the observers living in a small mountaintop building just constructed that fall by the Mount Washington Railway, was the brainchild of state geologist Charles H. Hitchcock and his assistant, Joshua H. Huntington. The two had conceived the idea more than a decade earlier, but it took years before the expedition was economically feasible. Huntington had spent the previous winter atop another White Mountain summit, Mount Moosilauke, with fellow expedition member Amos F. Clough of Warren, a photographer. This 1869–70 venture served as a warm-up act for the following year's Mount Washington stay, which again saw Huntington and Clough take part, along with a Concord photographer, H. A. Kimball, and an extra observer, S. A. Nelson of Georgetown, Mass. Charles Hitchcock, meanwhile, monitored events of the winter occupation with a direct telegraph line from the summit to his Dartmouth College office in Hanover. Mount Washington in Winter, *first published in 1871, chronicles the experiences of the intrepid Mount Washington adventurers, with all four participants (plus Hitchcock) contributing pieces to the book. The following two excerpts were both written by Huntington, for whom the great glacial ravine on Mount Washington's eastern face is named.*

MOST PERSONS suppose life on Mount Washington in winter must be gloomy, and gloomy enough it would be, at times, when the summit is enveloped in dense clouds for weeks, if it were not for the cheering click of the telegraph instrument. They might suppose also that time would be extended indefinitely; that at night we should wish it is morning, and that in the morning we should long for night to come, and thus drag out a weary existence. If the time of any persons in excellent health is wholly occupied in a pursuit that is congenial they are rarely gloomy, and are almost unconscious of the flight of time. But here, besides good health and time occupied, there is an excitement found nowhere else.

The Excitement of Living on a Mountain Summit.

One gorgeous sunrise throwing a flood of light across a sea of clouds, one glorious sunset tingeing the clouds with crimson and gold, and as the sun descends leaving the blush of day upon these snowy summits, or a storm unprecedented at lower elevations, infuse into our life enough that is grand and sublime to occupy the thoughts for weeks. With such surroundings, a person, on account of the intense excitement, may live too fast to have life extended to full threescore years and ten; but there is a pleasure in it that would fully compensate for as few days cut off from the number to which life might be lengthened if passed in some quiet retreat, undisturbed by anything that arouses the whole being, and carries the mind into ecstasies of delight. So days and weeks pass, and we are almost unconscious of time.

Our Arrangements for Comfort and Convenience.

But this record would not be complete without something specific being said of our habitation and our daily life, and it cannot be told better than in the language of "Ranger," the excellent correspondent of the "Boston Journal."

"As the lessee of the Tip-top and Summit houses raised objections to the occupancy of either of those buildings, Mr. Huntington and his companions obtained permission from the Railway Company to set up their lonely habitation in the newly erected depot. The depot was built last summer, and occupies a site of the same elevation as the Tip-top and Summit houses, northeasterly of these structures, upon the verge of the little plateau forming the summit of the mountain. The building, unlike the two diminutive public houses, whose sides are of stone, is constructed wholly of wood. It is sixty feet long by twenty-two feet wide, and stands nearly north and south. It has eleven-feet posts, and the elevation of the ridge-pole is twenty-five feet, the roof being of the same form as the roofs of ordinary buildings. The apartment inhabited by the party is situated in the southwest corner of this edifice. It is a room about twenty feet long, eleven feet wide, and eight feet high. The larger portion of the depot forms a sort of vestibule to this room and is wholly inclosed except at the easterly end of the northern face, where the outer door is situated. The little room was formed in the following manner: 1st, there was the thick plank floor of the depot itself, which constituted a good foundation to build upon; 2d, a course of sheathing paper was laid over the original floor; 3d, an additional floor of close-fitting boards was then laid down; 4th, two thicknesses of sheathing paper were placed on the top of the second floor; 5th, a layer of carpet lining was added; 6th, a thick woolen carpet was made the uppermost layer of all. The inside of the outer walls was covered first with tarred paper, then with boards, a layer of sheathing paper was added, and wall paper was spread upon this. The ceiling is formed of two thicknesses of boards with sheathing paper between, and the inner walls consist of single thicknesses of boards, sheathing paper, and wall paper. There are two double windows—or rather half windows—on the westerly side of the room, and these are protected by strips of board without. The door of the room is of ordinary size, but the outer door is nothing but a little opening two feet square, some two feet from the floor. After the last observation is taken at ten o'clock P.M., the little aperture is closed by means of two sliding boards, but at all other times is left open. Very little additional cold finds its way into the building through this aperture, and its elevation from the floor prevents the snow from blowing in to any great extent. More snow finds its way through the crevices between the boards upon the sides of the building than through this hole. Contrary to what ordinary experience would seem to teach, the north side of the building is less exposed to the fury of the elements than any other.

"We have thus far described none of the precaution taken to prevent the building from being torn to pieces by terrible winter tempests, or from being blown away altogether. The frame-work is of the strongest possible kind, and is fitted together in the best manner. The sills extend beyond the walls eight or ten feet, and every means are taken to fasten the whole structure down to its rocky base. Within, bolts, iron rods, and wooden braces add strength to the walls, and three strong iron chains, securely fastened to the rocks, pass over the roof. Notwithstanding all these provisions the building rocks and bends before a furious wind-storm in a manner well-calculated to create consternation and dismay. An ordinary house would stand no longer before such terrific blasts than would a house of cards before an ordinary wind. The great gale in December awakened the fears of the party for the safety of the depot, but as the structure stood that frightful assault it was thought no further danger on that score need be apprehended. It was nevertheless thought best to strengthen the walls with additional braces and supports.

"Young couples about to enter upon the responsibilities of housekeeping might learn some useful hints from these dwellers of the clouds. The little snuggery is made to serve not only as a kitchen, dining-room, sleeping-room, sitting-room, parlor, library, and study, but also as an observatory and telegraph office. Every inch of space is utilized. The telegraph instrument, battery, and other appurtenances of lightning communication with the outside world, are in one corner of the cozy apartment, beneath one of the windows. At the same end of the room is a bedstead, while above it is a wide bank, arranged after the manner of an upper berth in a steamboat. The most prominent objects that greet one upon entering the door are two stoves, which occupy the middle of the floor. One is an ordinary cook-stove, and the other a Magee parlor stove. The latter is prized very highly on account of its marvelous heating properties. A story was published not long since to the effect that it required seven dampers to regulate the draft, and also that considerably more than one half of the coal was already consumed. Neither of these statements are true. The stoves are easily enough governed by single dampers, and as for fuel, Mr. Huntington has enough on hand to last until next summer. The dining-table, which is generally covered with books, papers, and writing materials when not otherwise in use, occupies one corner of the room, while between it and the telegraph instrument is a well-filled book-case and several shelves. Shelves, in fact, appear everywhere, and they contain a general assortment of everything, while clothing, and at least an hundred articles of utility, hang suspended from pegs and nails. A writing tablet is hung upon the wall near the head of the bed, and upon this the observations are bulletined until they can be telegraphed, copied into the record books, or placed in the blank forms provided by the Smithsonian Institution. Beside it are two barometers, from one of which observations are made, and further on is a formidable row of smoking pipes. Some waggish member of the party has hung the tin sign of the old telegraph office over Sergeant Smith's seat, and also inscribed something of similar import on the door without. During the early part of the winter the corner of the room now occupied in part by the telegraph was used by Messrs. Clough and Kimball as a 'dark room' in their photographic operations. The anemometer—the curious little instrument for measuring the velocity of the wind—is in a state of quietude on a shelf over the table. Beside the book-case, upon a projecting beam, is a coffee-mill, affording a striking exhibition of the combination of the scientific and practical. Among the other wall ornaments are a pair of snow-shoes, a hand-saw and other mechanical implements, an infinitude of tin dishes, a map of Paris and its fortifications, the photograph of a young lady, etc. The floor is made the receptacle of numberless articles which cannot be put anywhere else. There seems to be, in short, 'a place for everything,' but it not always happens, I believe, that everything is found in its place. In the absence of the female element of a well-regulated house-hold, the scientific gentlemen content themselves with following out one half of the apothegm. They all complain that it is the easiest place to lose anything in they ever saw. In justice, however, it should be said that the apartment in general is in a very neat and tidy condition. A rocking-chair and three or four common chairs and stools, together with the table and beds, comprise all the movable furniture, while an ingenious member of the party has constructed a reclining seat upon one of the wooden braces. Most of the provisions are kept in the open part of the depot without,—about all, in fact, that freezing does not affect. Frozen pieces of fresh meat and of salt pork are suspended from the roof of this commodious refrigerator."

1871

Frost-Work and Clouds

Joshua H. Huntington

From *Mt. Washington in Winter*

THE FROST-WORK is one of the most remarkable phenomena of this high altitude. It is difficult to convey in words any idea of its wonderful form and beauty. It was not easy at first to understand how it could be formed, but from the study given to it last winter, and the opportunities we have had observing its formation this, we are able to give a plausible, if not a correct theory to account for this, the most plastic of all the handiwork of nature.

How Formed

At our first observation, we see that it forms only when the wind is north-ward, *i.e.* at some point between north and west or north and east, and never when the wind is southward. It begins with mere points, on everything the wind reaches: on the rocks, on the snow, on the railway, and on every part of the buildings, even on the glass. On the south side of the buildings and the high rocks it is very slight, as the wind reaches there only in eddying gusts. When the surface is rough, the points, as they begin are an inch or more apart; when smooth it almost entirely covers the surface at the very be-ginning, but soon only a few points elongate, so that on whatever surface it begins to form, it has very soon the same general appearance, presenting everywhere the same beautiful, feathery-like forms.

> "Thus Nature works, as if defying art;
>   And in defiance of her rival powers,
>   Performing such inimitable feats,
>   As she with all her rules can never reach."

Mount Washington's second Summit House wears a coating of rime ice
in this late 19th-century stereo view.

When the ice which has formed on the rocks is transparent and the frost-work forms on this, we can often see in the interstices of the frost-work, which is purely white, the gray rocks and the many colored lichens, the whole making a picture of rare beauty. In going up the mountain we do not see the frost-work until we get some distance above the limit of the trees; it is nearly a mile before it is seen in its characteristic forms, and it is only immediately about the summit that it presents its most attractive features. We notice also, that it always forms toward the wind, never from it, and the rapidity with which it forms, and the great length of the horizontal masses, is truly wonderful. We placed a round stick, an inch in diameter, in a vertical position, where it was exposed to the full force of the wind, and in less than two days some of the horizontal icicles—we call them icicles for the want of a more appropriate name—were two feet in length and scarcely any thicker than the stick itself. They formed on every part of the stick that was exposed, but of course some points were much longer than others. They remained there several days, but with a change of wind they were blown off. On the piles of stones south of the house, these horizontal masses are sometimes five or six feet in length. Although these masses are often as hard as the hardest ice, yet throughout they are as white as the purest snow.

On the southern exposures, instead of the frost-work—especially on the telegraph poles along the railway,—there are only masses of pure ice, which have always a peculiar hue of greenish blue, which is in striking contrast with the pure white of the frost-work on the opposite side.

In the early part of December, when the thermometer ranged from 25° to 29°, and the wind was southward, the ice formed to the thickness of a foot or more on the telegraph poles near the house. These icy masses are formed evidently by the condensation of the vapor of the atmosphere, as it is not uncommon for the air to be above the point of saturation. The frost-work is also formed by the condensation of the vapor, but besides the vapor, the air must be filled with minute spiculae of ice. As the vapor condenses these are caught, and thus the horizontal, feathery masses are formed. This accounts for the facts that we have observed, namely, that it forms when the wind is northward and always toward the wind.

The Clouds.

Mountains without clouds are spiritless and tame. It is true, that on high summits even under a noon-day sun, when there is some haze in the atmosphere, we get an idea of immensity that we could not before comprehend, but on the same heights with clouds floating gracefully around the distant peaks or their shadows flitting across illimitable forests, we have besides, a beauty and a grandeur, of which one who has never looked upon a cloud-scene from a mountain-summit "has little imagination or understanding as he has of the scenery of another planet than his own." I suppose we might stay here a lifetime and not see a single cloud effect repeated; we might see something similar, but in its details each would be unlike that which preceded it. Hence the attraction is ever new, and each succeeding day reveals new glories not seen before. In summer, often in the morning, the fogs lie along the valleys, over the lakes and streams. When the sun warms the air, these fogs rise and form clouds that pass over the summits

ROBERT KOZLOW

Rime ice coats the tower of the present-day summit observatory.

and float away to be dissolved as they meet the warmer currents of the air, or to be augmented, when they meet the cooler currents. In winter the cloud effects are quite different from those of summer. Often we stand on the summit and look forth upon an illimitable sea of mist glittering in the bright sunlight, while every peak, except that on which we stand, is concealed by clouds. So it is not uncommon for it to be a dark day in the valleys while on the summit we are in the bright sunlight. Sometimes the clouds are two thousand feet below the summit of Mount Washington; in that case innumerable mountain peaks protrude and seem like islands in an ocean bounded only by the sky. In winter these cloud-effects continue often a whole day almost unchanged.

At times the whole country westward is covered with clouds which are moving eastward, but when they pass the ridge that runs south to the Notch they are redissolved as they meet the warmer currents, and the air is then as transparent as if there was but a single cloud westward. It has not, to my knowledge, ever rained or snowed in the valleys when there was only a single stratum of cloud spread over the country at this low elevation. It has been noticed by aeronauts, "that when there is rain from a sky completely covered with clouds, there is always a similar range of clouds situated above at a certain height; and that on the contrary, when it does not rain, although the

As seen from the summit of Mount Washington, the peaks of the
nearby Southern Presidentials poke through the undercast skies.

sky presents below the same appearance, the space situated immediately
above, as a dominant character, has a great extent of clear sky, with a sun
unobstructed by a single cloud. This explains why a similar state of things
frequently exists,—a very cloudy overcast sky without a drop of rain."

Clouds from the Ocean.

It is one of the sublime scenes on Mount Washington, to watch clouds as
they come moving in solid phalanx from the ocean. The upper surface is
generally higher than Mount Pleasant in Maine, hardly as high as the summits of Pequawket, or the Carter Range. When lower than the Carter
Range it is frequently the case that the clouds come into the deep ravines
between Mount Washington and the Carter Range, both from the north
and the south. In every instance when the clouds have come in thus from
the sea, there has been a storm the same day or the day following, not only
on the mountain but throughout New England. When the clouds have
come thus from the eastward, the wind on Mount Washington has been
west or southwest. The clouds, when a storm has approached from the
south, have always been at a high elevation, and they seem to be continually
augmented as they come northward, extending over the high mountain

summits; although far above them, a column would be formed from each summit to the mass above. The gradual formation of the cloud is easily explained. The moisture-laden atmosphere from the south, coming in contact with the colder currents north, the vapor is condensed. In the vicinity of the snow-clad mountain summits, it is quite probable that there is a colder stratum of air, hence the column extending to the clouds above. Instead of a great sea of mist, or a storm gradually approaching, the clouds may be driven by fierce winds into "boiling heaps of illuminated mist, furrowed by a thousand colossal ravines," or dashed against the jutting cliffs and crags, being thrown like spray hundreds of feet into the air to be caught again by the wind and hurled down into the seething depths. No pen, no pencil, can portray the grandeur of the scene, when these clouds are touched with rose-tinted amber light, while into the depths of the chasms formed by the whirling mist, shadows fall dark as night, or when the sea of clouds with "mighty icebergs floating in it," extends as far as the eye can reach, or the forest-clad peaks protruding above its surface, the bosom of the sea apparently as smooth as polished marble, then perchance agitated by slightly undulating swells, or rolling in waves burnished with silver and tipped with gold.

1896

View From the Top

Moses F. Sweetser

From *Sweetser's White Mountains*

The first guidebook to contain route descriptions to many of the White Mountains'
major peaks first appeared in 1876 and was written by Moses F. Sweetser (1848–
1897). His trademark red, leather-bound guides provide the best information on
the hiking paths and routes used by late 19th century mountain explorers. Joshua
H. Huntington, who just a few years earlier had assisted in the state geological
survey led by Charles H. Hitchcock, assisted Sweetser in preparing the text for the
first edition of this guidebook. Sweetser's guides were issued in 15 different editions
between 1876 and 1896. Especially useful for trampers were the foldout panoramic
view guides included in the guidebook. An inferior, watered-down version of his
guide was also published in 1918, more than 20 years after his death.

The View from Mt. Washington

has justly been called "an epic landscape." The English alpestrian, Latrobe,
said that it is magnificent, but gloomy. The view-line sweeps around a cir-
cumference of nearly 1,000 M., embracing parts of five states and the Province of Quebec. Within this vast circle are seen scores of villages and hamlets
and hundreds of mountains, with the widening valleys of the chief rivers of
New England. If the peak was 5,000 feet higher, the beauty of the view would
be seriously impaired by the indistinctness caused by the greater distance.

The first mood of the visitor (unless he is one of the dull and improvi-
dent souls who herd by the hotel-stove) is of wonder and amazement at the
vastness of the prospect. Everything appears confused and chaotic for scores
of leagues around, and the undulations of the land seem scarcely more

characteristic than would so many suddenly arrested waves of a mighty sea. But the deeply innate topographical instinct of the world-encircling Anglo-American race soon asserts itself, and from the recognizable villages or peaks a curiosity is excited as to the others on all sides. In the hope of gratifying this feeling, the following analysis of the view has been prepared with great care, and after thorough investigations. The Editor stayed six days on the summit of Mt. Washington, and Prof. Huntington remained there more than ten days, preparing notes for this description; and the last-named gentleman also passed fifteen days there in December, 1875, making fresh observations during the sharp clearness of the winter. Only a few who ascend the mountain carry compasses, and the description of the view has therefore been subdivided with reference to conspicuous peaks which are visible hence, rather than according to the cardinal points.

An experienced mountain-traveller, who has spent many summers at the Glen House, says that he has *always* secured clear days for his frequent visits to the summit of Mt. Washington, by waiting until the whole sky was absolutely free of clouds, and the wind was from the W. or. N.W. A high tower has been erected, back of the Summit House, overlooking all the buildings, and affording the best point from which to get the view. A small fee is charged for admission. Cold winds frequently blow over this airy perch. The need of warm wrappings will often be felt. Most of the transient visitors are on the mountain during the middle hours of the day, when the view is least interesting, being deadened by excess of light, and unrelieved by shadows. The clearest days are just after the close of long rain-storms, when the air is washed clean.

The View. — *From Mt. Adams to Mt. Moriah*

Directly N. of Mt. Washington is the noble peak of Mt. Adams, about 3 M. distant over the dark and profound depths of the Great Gulf. Its upper parts are covered with loose fragments, and form a fine spire, flanked by long ridges and spurs. Mt. Madison adjoins Adams on the r., and is lower and less imposing. Between Adams and Madison is a portion of the heavily wooded Crescent Range, beyond which the view-line traverses the wilderness of Berlin, and rests on the fair Androscoggin Valley, dotted with the farms and clearings of Milan and Dummer. Over the r. shoulder of Adams, touching the remote horizon, and marked by a precipitous slope on the E., is Mt. Carmel, on the border between Maine and New Hampshire, and within 7 M. of the Anglo-Canadian frontier. To the r. of this view-line, and nearer, is the forest-bound sheet of Head Pond, over which are the Milan

Hills; and before reaching Mt. Carmel the line passes over the rolling wilderness of the Magalloway Mts., with Mt. Pisgah in advance. Farther to the r., on the remote horizon, nearly over Head Pond, are several Canadian and border peaks, Saddleback, Mt. Gosford, Ben Durban, and Mt. Nicolet, with the distant speck of Mt. Megantic, which is on the l. of Mt. Adams. On this line, but nearer, are the wilderness highlands of Wentworth's Location and the Dartmouth-College Grant. Just on the l. of Madison the line passes over the white houses of Milan Corner and the forests of Cambridge and Erroll, beyond which is Mt. Dustan, lifting its sharp apex. N.W. of Lake Umbagog, with the Diamond peaks still farther out.

On the r. of Mt. Madison, over the farms on Randolph Hill, the view rests on the white hamlet of Berlin Falls, and the great booms in the river can be distinguished. The broad valley of the Androscoggin extends thence to the N., the Chickwolnepy Range being on the r. and the low black mound of Mt. Forist on the l. of the hamlet. The broad bright mirror of Lake Umbagog is then seen far away, with the ledge-crowned peak of Mt. Aziscoös near its N. shore, over a hummock on the S.E. spur of Madison. To the r. of Umbagog the lakes of Welokenebacook (Richardson), Mollychunkemunk, and Moosetocmaguntic are seen stretching away in a deep valley to the N.E., surrounded by lines of noble peaks, which tower out of the deep woods, and have never yet been visited or named.

To the right of the lakes is the dome-shaped Mt. Bigelow, in Flag-staff Plantation, with Saddleback to the l., N. 53° E. Farther to the right is the blue group of Mt. Abraham, on the S. of which rises the sharp apex of Mt. Blue. In the same line, 135 M. distant, N. 63° E., is Ebeme Mt., beyond Moosehead Lake, the farthest visible point from Mt. Washington.

> According to the best maps the air-line distance between Mt. Washington and Mt. Katahdin is 165 M., and it has therefore been doubted whether the latter is visible. No other theme in all the scenery of the White Mountains has drawn out such sharp and protracted discussions as this of the visibility of Katahdin, which is also asserted by the admirers of Mts. Kiarsarge and Osceola. During several remarkably clear days in December, 1875, Prof. Huntington, the foremost of the dissenters, recognized Katahdin from Washington, and thereafter withdrew his opposition. But his later researches, and those of eminent Appalachians, prove that Katahdin is surely invisible.

The view now returns from its distant flight and rests on the Chandler Ridge, which is a part of Mt. Washington, running N.E. from the summit, and appearing like a long terrace below, with the Nelson Crag further down, near the great cliffs of Huntington's Ravine. Over the Chandler Ridge, and

GEORGE MITCHELL

Mount Jefferson and the Northern Presidentials provide the dramatic backdrop
for a Cog Railway train descending to the base station.

across the mouth of the Great Gulf, is Pine Mt., which hides the village of
Gorham; over which and N.E. of the Androscoggin is Mt. Hayes, a low and
ledgy mountain, with the ravine of the Lead-mine Brook on the E., on
whose r. is the dark mass of Baldcap. Over the r. part of Mt. Hayes is the
blue and pointed peak of Parlin Pond Bald Mt., over 100 M. away, in the
solemn wilderness of Maine. On the l. of and beyond Goose-Eye (through
the Mahoosuc Notch) are Speckled Mt. and Bear-River White Cap, enclosing the Grafton Notch; and close on its r. is the Sunday-River White
Cap, over which rise the many mountains of Andover and Byron. Nearer at
hand is a section of the Peabody Glen, over which is the hardly perceptible
knoll of Mt. Surprise, on the long flank of Moriah. A beautiful vista is now
gained down the Androscoggin Valley, over which, between Baldcap and
the nearer Moriah, is the crest of Mt. Ingalls. Farther away in this direction
are tall peaks of Maine, rising from the settled townships, Black and Puzzle
Mts., the Rumford White Cap, and Mt. Blue, the latter of which cuts the
horizon to the r. of the Nelson Crag. In this direction the graceful curves of
the Androscoggin are followed through the valleys of Shelburne, and several
of its islands are seen. The Grand Trunk Railway is also plainly visible, and
the head-lights of its locomotives appear on clear evenings. The lower course
of the Peabody River is distinguishable on account of its deep wash-outs.

Mt. Moriah to Mt. Baldface.

Mt. Moriah is 5–6 M. E.N.E. of Washington, and is seen over the heading cliffs of Huntington's Ravine, being at the angle of the eastern range as it bends to the N.E. It has no distinct or well-marked peak, and over its r. are the hills of Bethel. To the r. is the indistinct peak of the Imp, whence a ridge with high cliffs descends to the Peabody Glen. A little to the r. are the long white walls of the Glen House, diminished by distance to a mere dot of light among the shadowy forests. To the right of Imp and beyond is the more distant Mt. Calabo, in Maine. Toward the E., across the adjacent Pinkham Notch, are the massive and imposing Mt. Carter and Carter Dome, which have two convex peaks, on the S. of which is a hollow, into which fall two white slides.

> The mountains on the island of Mt. Desert are due E., 145 M. distant, over the Carter Range. It is claimed that the White Mts. are seen thence, and some people think that the island is visible from Mt. Washington, with a powerful glass and on a clear day. A trifle to the r., one or two degrees S. of E., the high-placed village of Paris Hill is visible, 42 M. distant, with Streaked Mt. beyond; over which, 115 M. distant, it is claimed that Mts. Megunticook and Battie, of the Camden Mts., on the shore of Penobscot Bay, are seen from Mt. Washington.

The view now enters more certain ground and falls on the dark and adjacent Mt. Wild-Cat, covered with forests and separated from the Carter Dome by the invisible Carter Notch. The distant highlands of Waterford, Norway, and Hebron are beyond. Over its highest point is Mt. Baldface, with its N. peak bare on the apex, and the S. peak showing white ledges.

Mt. Baldface to Mt. Kiarsarge.

On the r. of the white crest of Baldface are the round and wooded summits of Mts. Sable, Eastman, and Slope, over which are sections of the Upper Kezar Pond and of Long Pond, beyond Bridgton. Between the higher part of Wild-Cat and Sable is the long and partially cleared ridge of Black Mt. in Jackson. Close over these pastured slopes are the similar summits of Double-Head, massive and symmetrical, above which are the sharp twin crests of Mt. Gemini, on the ridge running N. from Kiarsarge. To the L. of Double-Head is the long rampart of Mt. Pleasant, rising from the sandy plains beyond Fryeburg, and forming several low crests. A white hotel is on the central peak, and is readily seen in the afternoon, when the sunlight is reflected from its walls. On the left of Pleasant are the Kezar, Upper Moose and Long Ponds; and on the r. are Pleasant Pond and the square-shaped sheet of Lovewell's Pond, renowned in early border-history for the desperate battle on its shore. To the right of Pleasant, over and on either side of Peaked Mt., in the town of Sebago, are the broad, bright waters of Sebago Lake, far beyond which, and a little to the r., is the city of Portland, on Casco Bay. Farther out is the ocean, which is seen for leagues on the l. and r., but is so nearly the color of the sky as to be discerned with difficulty. In clearest weather vessels can be seen off shore all the way through the broad bight of the sea which was formerly known as the Gulf of Maine.

Mt. Kiarsarge to Mt. Chocorua.

Kiarsarge is nearly S.E. and about 15 M. distant. It is a graceful mountain, of conical shape. On this side of Kiarsarge are Tin and Thorn Mts., on the same ridge, the latter being the highest and farther to the r. In the foreground is the long valley of the Ellis River, with its upper part densely wooded, and farms appearing as it extends to the S. The valley over and beyond the Ellis is that of the Wild-Cat Brook, and between the two are the Spruce and Eagle Mts. At the end of the Ellis Valley is Thorn Hill, over which opens the rich and beautiful Saco Valley, wherein the white hamlets of Lower Bartlett, N. Conway, and Conway are seen in succession. The Green Hills appear E. of No. Conway and from behind Kiarsarge; and on the r. is the flashing mirror of Walker's Pond. Over the Green Hills are the Frost and Burnt-Meadow Mts., in Brownfield; Saddleback, in Baldwin; and the rolling highlands of Hiram, Cornish, and Limington. It is said that Prout's Neck and Old-Orchard Beach are seen in this direction, nearly over Mt. Cutler, in Hiram.

The great gorge near at hand in Mt. Washington is Tuckerman's Ravine, whose S. wall is seen, striped with light-colored slices. Over the S. wall are the high and massive crags of Boot's Spur (2 M. S.S.E.), above which is the rounded summit of Iron Mt., falling sharply on the N. to a cultivated plateau, and braced on the S.E. by a ledgy spur. Farther away in this direction are the highlands of Madison and Eaton, with the long ridge of the Green Mt. in Effingham still more remote. Over the l. flank of the latter, down by the sea-shore, is the low round swell of Mt. Agamenticus, the landmark for sailors. Over the r. of Iron Mt. is the ridge of Mt. Attitash, overlooked by the two rocky peaks of Moat Mt., uplifted above the forests. Over Moat are the distant waters of Silver Lake and Ossipee Lake, and the line over their centre crosses the bold hills about N. Wolfeborough, and rests on

Copple Crown and Big Moose Mts., in Brookfield, with the Frost Mts. in Farmington, near the birthplace of Henry Wilson, far beyond. Mt. Pawtuccaway, in Nottingham, is still more distant. On the r. of Moat is Mt. Langdon.

Mt. Chocorua to Mt. Carrigain.

Mt. Chocorua is S. by E., 22 M. distant, and appears on the r. of and beyond Table Mt. It is the sharpest peak in all the view from Mt. Washington, and lifts its white pyramidal ledges far, flanked by bare supporting ridges. On the r. of Langdon is the cone of Mt. Parker, beyond which is the long dark ridge of Bear Mt., with the curving and ledgy top of Mt. Paugus beyond, and on the r. of Chocorua. Still farther out in this direction is the long blue line of the Ossipee Range, on whose r. are the island-strewn waters of Lake Winnepesaukee, seen directly over Paugus and in several places to the r.

The view in this direction should be taken from the U.S. Signal Station. Below is the alpine terrace of Bigelow's Lawn, over which the forest-crowned Montalban Ridge is seen, running down to the hardly distinguishable crest of Giant's Stairs, 8 M. distant. Far beyond, and a little to the l., is the double peak of Mt. Belknap, over the shining waters of Lake Winnepesaukee. Close to Giant's Stairs, on the r., is the flat top of Mt. Resolution, marked by ledges of reddish granite. Next to the r. is the lower peak of Mt. Crawford, which is in poor relief.

Over Resolution is the black top of the Bartlett Haystack; and over the r. of Crawford is the foreshortened ridge of Tremont, with its highest peak on the S., partly burnt over. Paugus and the blue Ossipee Mts. are l. of and beyond the Haystack. The high round dome of Passaconaway is over the main peak of Tremont, and under it is the singular white mound of Potash. On the r. of Passaconaway, and over the r. shoulder of Tremont, is the high cloven peak of Whiteface. The twin Uncanoonucs are far away on the l. of Passaconaway, near Manchester; and on the r.-hand side of Passaconaway is Joe-English Hill nearer, in New Boston. To the r. of Whiteface are the distant Temple Mts. and Crotched Mt., in Francestown.

On the r. of Tremont is the square-headed top of Green's Cliff, up the valley of the Sawyer's River. Over Green's Cliff is a round peak of Tripyramid, whose two other peaks, on the r., are sharp. The view now passes down the long valley of the Mt.-Washington River, which runs about S.S.W. from Bigelow's Lawn and opens into the Saco Valley 14 M. below. Down this long trough is the spur from Sawyer's River to the Nancy Range, overlooked by the N.E. ridge of Tripyramid, with the long curving crest-line of

Looking south from the summit toward the Lakes of the Clouds,
Mount Monroe, and AMC's Lakes of the Clouds Hut.

Sandwich Dome beyond, flanked by the Sachem Peak and Aceton Range. Far away in this direction is the top of Mt. Prospect, near Plymouth, just to the l. of the Sachem Peak; and the scarce distinguishable top of Mt. Weetamoo is on the r. of the Sachem.

Mt. Monadnock lifts its faint blue curve 104 M. away, nearly over Prospect, and about S.S.W. On its r., and nearly over Mt. Weetamoo, is the bold peak of Mt. Kearsarge, and on the r. of the mouth of the Mt. Washington River, is the Frankenstein Cliff, around which the lines of the Portland & Ogdensburg Railroad are visible. Below the Cliff is the Nancy Range, containing Mts. Nancy, Anderson, and Lowell, and the view then rests on Carrigain.

Mt. Carrigain to Mt. Lafayette.

Carrigain is a massive mountain, with a deep hollow turned to the E., and the rounded knoll of Vose's Spur on the E. It is one of the most striking and remarkable of the peaks which are seen from Mt. Washington, and is best viewed from the Signal Station. On its r., behind and close to it, is the wilderness peak of Mt. Hancock. Between and beyond Carrigain and Hancock is Osceola, with a precipitous slope to the E. and a bold secondary peak towards the Mad-River Notch. To the r. of Osceola, and far beyond, are the white rounded crests of Mt. Cardigan, with Sunapee Mt. still farther out and the dark Croydon Mt. on the r.

The view now falls on the S.W. peaks of the Presidential Range. From the Signal Station the Lakes of the Clouds are seen, 1,200 ft. below, over which are the dark and rugged battlements of Mt. Monroe, with the bridle-path winding along on the l. Beyond, and a little to the r., is the flat top of Franklin, marked by the serpentine trail of the Crawford-House Path, on whose r. is the high and rounded summit of Pleasant, with Clinton to the l. The bare ledge beyond is the crest of Jackson; and the wooded heights of Webster end the range. On the r. of Webster, across the Notch, is Mt. Willey, which is also nearly over Mt. Pleasant, and is marked by a sharp descent towards the S., and a bare exposure on the N. The low crest of Mt. Willard is over the r. flank of Clinton, and above it is the wooded ridge of Mt. Field, continuous with Willey. Over this range the view extends across Hancock's flank to the mountain-chain which runs from Osceola to the mouth of the Hancock Branch, whose peaks are surrounded by the wilderness and have no names. Beyond this range are the Loon-Pond Mts., marked by bare granite ledges. Far way over these ridges is the monotonous range of Mt. Carr, and still more distant is the dim blue peak of Ascutney, 80 M. distant.

Over Mts. Field and Willey, the view enters the Pemigewasset Forest, near whose lower end is the Potash Mt., 3 M. above Pollard's, over which are the highlands of Woodstock, a part of the Mt.-Carr range, and Smart's Mt. On the r. of Mt. Field is the ravine of Beecher's Cascade, which enters S. of Mt. Tom; and over this depression are the long and lofty ridges of Mts. Bond and Guyot, rising out of the central wilderness, and cut by a ravine in the N.E. slope. Over Bond's r. shoulder is Mt. Flume, on whose r. is the sharp peak of Mt. Liberty. Between Flume and Liberty, and directly over Beecher's Cascade, is the long crest of Moosilauke, crowned by a house. A short distance to the r. of Moosilauke is the sharp peak of Lincoln, beyond which rises the splendid serrated ridge of Lafayette, with its crest of gray rocks. Very far away between Moosilauke and Lafayette are the dim crests of the Killington and Shrewsbury Peaks, near Rutland.

It should be mentioned that one of the best topographers in New England (Prof. C. H. Hitchcock) has studied from Mt. Washington the line of the Green Mts. S. of the Killington Peaks, and by reason of previous familiarity with the Vermont and Massachusetts mountains has recognized (in succession to the l. from Killington Peaks) Mt. Aeolus and Equinox, Stratton Mt., and the remote Greylock, the chief of the Berkshire Hills. The latter is distinguished by its sharp apex, and is nearly over Mt. Carr. Farther to the l. he also recognized the dark disk of the Hoosac Mt., where the great tunnel is. Greylock is about 160 M. distant, a little S. of S.W. The latest Appalachian reports show that Greylock is not visible hence.

Mt. Lafayette to Cherry Mt. (Owl's Head).

In looking towards the high sierra of Lafayette the long ridge of the S. Twin Mt. is seen under it, with the N. Twin on the r., marked by a whitish slide. (This part of the view should be taken from beyond and above the old stone house back of the hotel.). On the r. of N. Twin, and lower, is Mt. Hale, flanked by the white-topped Sugar Loaves, near the Twin-Mountain House. The view now passes down the Ammonoosuc Valley, by Ammonoosuc Station, the square clearing of the Twin-River Farm, and the white walls of the Fabyan House, with the low curving summits of Mt. Agassiz and Round Hill apparently at its end, close to the clustered houses of Bethlehem. Between Mt. Tom and the Fabyan House are the bold hills called Mt. Andalusite and Mt. Rosebrook, the latter being near the Fabyan. Farther out, above Bethlehem, is the long Mt. Gardner range, over which are the Bread-Loaf Mt. and others of the Green Mts., with the lofty crest of Camel's Hump, N. 74° W. Just to the l. of Camel's Hump, and still more remote, is the dim group of the Adirondack Mts., beyond Lake Champlain, in the State of New York. Over the r. slope of Camel's Hump rises Whiteface, N. 73° W, 130 M. distant.

Nearer at hand, across the head of the Ammonoosuc Valley, and 6 M. distant, is Mt. Deception, to the r. of the Fabyan House, with light deciduous trees on the E. slope and dark evergreens on the summit, meeting on a well-defined line. Over its l. flank is Beech Hill, N. of the Ammonoosuc, above which is the white village of Littleton (with Camel's Hump on its l.). Far away on the horizon, a few degrees N. of Camel's Hump, is the conspicuous peak of Mt. Mansfield, the greatest of the Green Mts of Vermont. Before it is Mt. Elmore, with Worcester Mt. on the l. and Mt. Sterling on the r. These stately summits are nearly over Mann's Hill, N. of Littleton village. Over and to the r. of Deception, and but 2–3 M. from it, is the long dark mass of Cherry Mt., with three small peaks, of which the bare one, on the N., is called Owl's Head. Nearly over the middle of Cherry is the long ridge of Dalton Mt. (l. of which is Mt. Mansfield), and far away in the Green-Mt. line are the mountains of Belvidere.

From Cherry Mt. (Owl's Head) to Mt. Jefferson.

The Owl's-Head peak of Cherry Mt. is a bare hummock on the N. end of the ridge, about W.N.W. by N., 8–10 m. distant. On its r. is seen the clear sheet of Cherry Pond, above which is Mt. Niles, over the Lunenburg Heights, in Vermont, and far beyond and over the latter are the picturesque peaks of the Lowell Mts., in the N. part of the Green-Mt. chain. To the r. of Cherry Pond, a few miles further distant, and over Bray Hill, are the round-topped highlands of Lancaster, Mts. Prospect and Pleasant, and the Martin-Meadow Hills. The Martin-Meadow Pond is seen on their l.; and on their r., partly concealed by intervening highlands, is the fair white village of Lancaster, nestling down on its rich green meadows, near the winding Connecticut. It has been a theme of frequent arguments whether the waters of the Connecticut are visible from Mt. Washington, except during the spring inundations. However this may be, the white fog which lies over the course at morning is plainly seen, winding among the hills and over the lowlands for many leagues.

Far away on the horizon is the sharp apex of Jay Peak, in Northern Vermont, with the Lowell and Montgomery Mts. near it on the l. Much nearer, and on the same line of view, is the dark massive Burke Mt., with Mts. Tug and Umpire and the Victory Hills on the r.

The view now rests on Mt. Clay, close at hand and joined to Washington below, over which are the white hotels of Jefferson Hill. The valley of Israel's River lies in this direction, and is the broadest valley visible from Mt. Washington. The roads and farms are plainly seen for many miles; and the Mt.-Adams House is distinguished, of the right of Jefferson Hill. Back of the latter village rises Mt. Starr King, with no conspicuous peak, but recognized by a slide on the side of its ridge. Farther away, over Jefferson Hill, are the Cow and East-Haven Mts., in Vermont, beyond which are Mts. Hor and Annanance, at Willoughby Lake. The famous Willoughby Notch, between these two mountains, does not show to advantage from this point. Over the ridge which runs. S.W. from Starr King is the well-marked peak of Owl's Head, which rises from the shore of Lake Memphremagog. Farther to the r., nearly over Starr King, and beyond Mt. Burnside and the highlands of Guildhall and Ferdinand, is Mt. Orford, the chief peak in the Eastern Townships of Canada. Between Mt. Washington and Mt. Starr King are the wooded heights of the Pliny Range; and over Starr King is Cape Horn, rising out of the Northumberland plains. The view now rests on the distant ranges near Maidstone Lake and about the Smuggler's Notch, over the l. slope of Mt. Jefferson.

Mt. Jefferson to Mt. Adams.

Mt. Jefferson is a high and massive peak, across the upper part of the Great Gulf, and about 3 M. N. by W. from Mt. Washington. Over it and to the r. is the great assemblage of the Pilot Mts., stretching across the wilderness of Kilkenny. The South Peak of the Pilots is over the E. point of Jefferson, and shows a sharp apex. Over the r. shoulder of Jefferson, and beyond the Pilot Range, are the singular round domes of the Percy Peaks, drawing attention on account of their light color, which strongly contrasts with the surrounding forests and woody ridges. Back of the Percies are the Stratford and Sugar-Loaf Mts.; and the Long Mt. of Odell extends from the Peaks to the r. In the foreground, nearer to Jefferson, is the dark and well-wooded range of the Randolph Mts. A long reach of the Upper Ammonoosuc Valley is seen beyond, for the most part filled with forests and unbroken by clearings. The ridge which is on the r., is Green's Ledge, on whose l. are Hager's Peak and Deer Mt., the latter forming a long line of heights. Back of all these ranges which are seen between Jefferson and Adams are the distant peaks towards the Connecticut Lakes, most of which are in the Dixville, Crystal, and Magalloway Ranges. The upper Monadnock, in Lemington, Vermont, is on the extreme l. of this vista. Far beyond, and low down on the horizon, are two or three peaks in the Eastern Townships of Canada, including Mt. Megantic, 86 M. distant.

1887

The Mount Washington Carriage Road

Moses F. Sweetser

From *Chisholm's White Mountain Guide-Book*

STARTING OUT from the Glen House, across the meadows of the Peabody, the adventurous climber soon enters the dark and luxuriant woods which clothe the heavy eastern shoulder of the mountain, and so fares upward along the firm white road for nearly four miles, while the trees gradually dwindle until they become hardly more than shrubbery, and at last disappear altogether, leaving the mountain above the Half-Way House, four miles up, almost entirely bare, except for the dead white trees which cover considerable areas, and bear the name of buck's-horn, or bleached bones. A little way above is the Ledge, or the Cape of Good Hope, where the road suddenly doubles on itself, ever rising at a high grade, and revealing one of the most awe-inspiring views of the profound and shadowy depths of the Great Gulf, almost under foot, with the splendid peaks of Jefferson, Adams, and Madison looming high above, across the chasm. Downward, to the east, is the long green wall of the Carter Range, at whose base is a rectangular dot, in which the outlines of the Glen House are recognizable. The prospect continually varies, as higher levels are gained, and as the road turns from side to side, and faces now the south, and the Saco-Conway region, now the east, and the rising peaks and silvery lakes of Western Maine, and now the north, with dainty bits of distant landscape, plaided meadows and white villages, framed between the great dark peaks so near at hand. The grandeur of mountain architecture is more evident from this route than from the railroad, as the firm white highway ascends by the five great spurs to the east-

The Halfway House as it appeared in 1910.

ward, looking down into the dark ravines, and out along the little Labrador of the Alpine Garden. On one side or the other, the topographical map of Northern New England is continually outspread, basking in the vivid sunshine, or dappled with deep cloud-shadows. At last the panting horses, or the weary pedestrian, who has become all knees and lungs, clamber up the final high grade, and reach the top of the last cone,—the crest of Mount Washington.

The valleys toward the Androscoggin first meet the view, as the slow ascent is made; and when higher grades come, the Saco Valley and its tributary plains of Western Maine are unrolled like a vast map. When the ridges of Mount Clay are overlooked, from the upper reaches of the road, the Ammonoosuc Valley appears, on the west, opening away towards the distant Connecticut River, and girt with rolling highlands.

Routes to the Glen House

The routes to the Glen House are three: by stage from Gorham, 8 miles north; or from Glen Station, 14 miles south; or from the summit of Mount Washington, 8½ miles south-west. Without doubt, the stages, horses, and drivers of the Glen-House corps form the best establishment of the kind this side of the Rocky Mountains, affording transportation at once swift, sure, and safe. The ride upward from Glen Station, through Jackson City, and along the ascending grades of the Pinkham Notch, is full of interest; the mountain-road is altogether exciting; and the drive from Gorham is more beautiful than either,—leading up long glens, by the rushing stream, with the great mountains coming out, one by one, to be seen and admired of every clear eye.

The Glen House

About two-thirds of the way from North Conway to Gorham, by the Pinkham-Notch road, stands the Glen House, which ranks high among the mountain-hotels in the grandeur of the view from its verandas, and is one of the first in respect to the position of its guests. Let us also bluntly state a conspicuous fact, somewhat alien in kind to the *belles-lettres* of guide-books, in saying that the *menu* at the Glen House is one of the best and most wholesome in New Hampshire; and also that the tables are waited on by polite college-students, competent to take orders in the language of the Horatian odes, or of the sonnets of Petrach, or of the theses of Schleiermacher. This vast hotel, with its parlor covering more than an acre, its copious and peculiar water-supply, its book-and-picture shop, telegraph and post-offices, billiard and bowling-rooms, tennis-court, archery-lawn, and furlongs of piazzas, is able to accommodate five hundred guests at one time, and to satisfy them with aesthetic, social, and gastronomical luxuries.

But even such a Sybaris would fail on the Lynn marshes or the Newark meadows; and so the success of the Glen House must be attributed to its peerless situation, *vis-à-vis*, with the five noblest peaks east of Colorado, separated from them only by a narrow valley, and surrounded by many choice bits of scenery in ravine, peak, and waterfall. These things are sometimes casually alluded to by the summer-correspondence parasites; but let us look upon them as the reason for being of the Glen House.

The Glen, therefore, is an open square in the great street of the eastern hills, bounded on the north by the approaching ridges of Mount Carter and Mount Madison, on the south by Wild-Cat and Washington, on the east by the tangled and inaccessible Carter Range, and on the west by the great Presidential Range. It is 1,632 feet above the seas,—a height which is well above the hay-fever line, and within the domain of almost perpetual coolness,—with air perfumed by the surrounding forests, and made musical by the rushing streams, the sighing foliage, and the songs of countless birds, not less than by the merry waltzes of the hotel-band. Below the great inn are the verdant meadows of the Peabody River, with dark forests beyond, and over them the Great Gulf,—a vast bowl-like ravine opening deep into the heart of the Presidential Range, filled with curving forests and silent lakelets, and sheltering milliards of speckled trout in the dark pools of its mountain streams. (*En passant*, who that has visited the Glen House does not remember the great salmocide, Josh Billings, deep-eyed and hirsutely aureoled, and talking much of trout in language which, even in its spoken form, reveals how preciously distinct, subtle, and blessed its orthography must be?) Across the Great Gulf, then, rises the crown of New England,— the five-pointed star which is visible from Monhegan to the Adirondacks, and from Massachusetts to the St.-Lawrence Valley. Let us begin on the north, with the least and lowest of the group, and observe the rugged crest of Mount Madison, with its long slopes falling into the Androscoggin Valley; and then the clear and shapely pyramid of Mount Adams, cutting sharply into the blue sky, or repulsing the gray mists from its iron-bound shoulders, and in some way typifying the coldness and loftiness, the firmness and permanence, of the noble family from whose ancient head it was named. Next, to the left, is the ponderous rocky peak of Mount Jefferson, with the strength of Adams, but without its quality of fineness; and sustained on the south by the apparently low crags of Mount Clay, for which mountain-climbers have devised the name of "humps," as if the Sage of Ashland was represented as a petrified dromedary. Mount Washington is almost concealed by a huge foot-hill, almost an Alp in itself, over which spur after spur of the sovereign mountain is seen, falling away towards the eastern valleys, with the ultimate peak visible over all, and crowned—not by a temple to Apollo, or to St. Benedict, but—by the favorite American shrine, a spacious white hotel. If this prospect is not enough, you may climb Mount Wild-Cat, behind the Glen, by a path an hour-long, and look into the ravines under the peaks; or even take the new path up Mount Madison, four miles long, and trample over all the northern line of summits. Or, if you prefer figurines to these colossal statues of the immortals, descend the old Randolph road to Dolly Copp's, and see the Imp, carved in profile on the Carter Range; or study the Garnet Pools, a mile northward, on the Peabody River, where countless ages of falling waters have whirled the rounding stones on the submerged ledges, until they have worn deep circular basins, brimming with translucent mountain dew; or clamber up to Thompson's Falls, two miles to the southward, just off the North-Conway road, where one of the brightest of brooks falls down the steep side of Mount Wild-Cat, with infinite play of white foam, roaring plunges, and deep dimpling pools, stretching for a half-mile through the woods, and from its summit looking into the heart of Tuckerman's Ravine; or sit down by Emerald Pool, close by, and see the busy Peabody River, fresh from its dance among the boulders and ledges, idling for a moment in a broad deep basin, overhung by rich foliage, and reflecting delicious dark colors from its shadowy depths in the seclusion and tranquillity of the forest.

The Crystal Cascade

The lover of Nature will find it profitable to go down the North-Conway road for three miles, and then diverge to the right, by a convenient guide-board, for a half-hour's stroll up a woodland path, among grand old trees, mossy rocks, and the sights and sounds that were once heard "eastward in Eden," to the Crystal Cascade, the first-born daughter of Mount Washington, where the stream which flows out of Tuckerman's Ravine falls over a cliff of dark slate, 80 feet high, gracefully and merrily, filling the woods with the voice of its going. There is a little rustic bridge below, whereby one crosses to the right bank, and gains a vantage-ground of opposing cliff from which the whole sweep of the fall is charmingly visible.

The Glen-Ellis Falls

are about a mile beyond the Crystal Cascade, where another friendly guide-board indicates the divergence of a path to the left. These are the most beautiful and impressive falls in the State, and have been ardently admired by poets and painters and the rank and file of humanity for over half a century. The name *Glen Ellis* has much prettiness; but the ancient name, *Pitcher Falls*, was closely descriptive, and might well have been retained. It is thus that the water is gathered—the delicious frosty water from the Snow Arch—as if by the contracting edges of a great rocky pitcher, over which it pours in a solid and compressed column, 70 feet high, or twice the height of the Senate Hall at Washington. The grooves in the side of the cliff give a singular spiral twist to the water, and slightly deflect it from a direct downward course. Above are lapsing rapids; below, a deep dark pool gathering the white column of light, and wreathed with prismatic mists; overhead are the rugged slopes of Mount Wild-Cat; and all around are the forest-arches. So much for the details of mensuration, with which a volume of this kind must be content, leaving the soul of the scene, the Arethusa spirit, to be interpreted by Shelley and Coleridge, Bryant and Lovell, or the spark of poetic fire which lingers in every heart.

GLEN ELLIS FALL.

Tuckerman's Ravine

Cutting deep into the elephantine mass of Mount Washington, on its southeast side, and so marked a feature as to be visible even in Portland, on a clear day, is this vast gorge, which bears the name of one of the most honored early explorers of the White Mountains. The abrupt promontory of the Lion's Head, projecting from the Alpine Garden, enwalls one side; and the rocky plateau of Boott's Spur forms the other wall; while at the head is a line of formidable cliffs, from which descends the so-called Fall of a Thousand Streams. In the floor of this vast natural cathedral, paved with shattered rocks and perfumed by dwindling shrubbery, are the two dark and silent Hermit Lakes; and the chancel is fitly furnished with the glittering tracery of the Snow Arch, from which flows waters purer than those of the Sacramental Lake. Here the snows of winter accumulate to a depth of hundreds of feet, compacting into ice, and eaten away by the stream beneath until there is formed a deep cavern, whose sides and roof are of crystalline beauty. Although it vanishes by late August, this is a true glacier, showing (in small) all the phenomena of the *Mer de Glace*, the moraines, and the scratchings on the bed-rock.

There is a sort of path from the Crystal Cascade into the ravine, but the

best route is by a newly-cleared bridle path which leaves the Mount-Wash-
ington carriage-road about two miles up, and enters by Hermit Lake. One
may traverse the ravine, ascend its head-wall, and reach the top of Mount
Washington, in from five to seven hours from the Glen House. But the best
way to enjoy and comprehend the scene is to pass the night in the Appalachian camp near Hermit Lake, with good store of blankets and a roaring
fire. Then the sunset, the gloaming, the solemn starlight, even the red glare
of the camp-fire, and the swift sunrise, add infinite charms to the varying
hours. Solitude, a sense of strangeness, a feeling of amazing other-world-
ness, fill the soul; and the shop, the study, the boudoir, seem removed by
infinite eons and impassable spaces. Do not take merry men in there to
encamp under those majestic cliffs. Rabelais should not intrude in the Ho-
meric realm.

1881

A Scramble
in Tuckerman's

Samuel Adams Drake

From *The Heart of the White Mountains*

*An historian and Civil War veteran who frequently visited, then wrote about
many different areas of New England, Boston-born Samuel Adams Drake
(1833–1905) was the author of the 1881 book,* The Heart of the White Mountains, Their Legend and Scenery. *Significant portions of this book, which follows
Drake as he frequents many of the White Mountains' most popular and scenic
localities, originally appeared in Harper's Magazine in the June, July and August
1881 issues.*

AT THE MOUNTAINS the first look of every one is directed at the heavens, not in silent adoration or holy meditation, but in earnest scrutiny of the
weather. For here the weather governs with absolute sway; and nowhere is
it more capricious. Morning and evening skies are, therefore, consulted with
an interest the varied destinies of the day may be supposed to suggest. From
being a merely conventional topic, the weather becomes one of the first importance, and such salutations as "A fine day," or "A nice morning," are in
less danger of being coupled with a wet day or a scowling forenoon. To sum
up the whole question, where life in the open air is the common aim of all,
a rainy day is a lost day, and everybody knows that a lost day can never be
recovered. Sun worship is, therefore, universal.

The prospect being duly weighed and pronounced good, or fair, or fairly
good, *presto!* the hotel presents a scene of active preparation. Anglers, with
rod and basket, betake themselves to the neighboring trout brooks, artists

to the woods or the open. Mountain wagons clatter up to the door with an exhilarating spirit and dash. Amid much laughter and cracking of jokes, these strong, yet slight-looking vehicles are speedily filled with parties for the summit, the Crystal Cascade, or Glen Ellis; knots of pedestrians, picturesquely dressed, move off with elastic tread for some long-meditated climb among the hills or in the ravines; while the regular stages for Gorham or Glen Station depart amid hurried and hearty leave-takings, the flutter of handkerchiefs, and the sharp crack of the driver's whip. Now they are off, and quiet settles once more upon the long veranda.

My own plans included a trip in and out of Tuckerman's Ravine; in by the old Thompson path, out by the Crystal Cascade. It is necessary to depart a little from the order of time, as my first essay (during the first week of May) was frustrated by the deep snows then effectually blockading the way above Hermit Lake. The following July found me more fortunate, and it is this excursion that I shall now lay before the reader for his approval.

I chose a companion to whom I unfolded the scheme, while reconnoitering the ravine through my glass. He eagerly embraced my proposal, declaring his readiness to start on the instant. Upon a hint I let fall touching his ability to make this then fatiguing march, he observed, rather stiffly, "I went through one Wilderness with Grant; guess I can through this."

"Pack your knapsack, then, comrade, and you shall inscribe 'Tuckerman's' along with Spottsylvania, Cold Harbor, and Petersburg."

"Bless me! it is so very tough as all that? No matter, give me five minutes to settle my affairs, and I'm with you."

Let us improve these minutes by again directing the glass toward the ravine.

The upper section of this remarkable ravine—that portion lifted above the forest line—is finely observed from the neighborhood of the Crystal Cascade, but from the Glen House the curiously distorted rim and vertical wall of its south and west sides, the astonishing crag standing sentinel over its entrance, may be viewed at full leisure. It constitutes quite too important a feature of the landscape to escape notice. Dominated by the towering mass of the Dome, infolded by undulating slopes descending from opposite braces of Mount Washington, and resembling gigantic draperies, we see an enormous, funnel-shaped, hollow sunk in the very heart of the mountain. We see, also, that access is feasible only from the north-east, where the entrance is defended by the high crag spoken of. Behind these barriers, graven with a thousand lines and filled with a thousand shadows, the amphitheatre lifts its formidable walls into view.

For two miles our plain way led up the summit-road, but at this distance, where it suddenly changes direction to the right, we plunged into the forest. Our course now lay onward and upward over what had at some time been a path—now an untrodden one—encumbered at every few rods with fallen trees, soaked with rain, and grown up with moosewood. Time and again we found the way barred by these exasperating windfalls, and their thick *abatis* of branches, forcing us alternately to go down on all-fours and creep underneath, or to mount and dismount, like recruits, on the wooden horse of a calvary school.

But to any one loving the woods—and this day I loved not wisely, but too well—this walk is something to be taken, but not repeated, for fear of impairing the first and most abiding impressions. One cannot have such a revelation twice.

I recall no mountain-path that is so richly diversified with all the wildest forms of mountain beauty. At first our progress through primitive groves of pine, hemlock, and birch was impeded by nothing more remarkable than the giant trees stretching interminably, rank upon rank, tier upon tier. But these woods, these countless gray and black and white trunks, and outspread framework of branches, supported a canopy of thick foliage, filled with voices innumerable. Something stirred in the top of a lofty pine; and then, like an alguazil on a watch-tower, a crow, apparent sentinel of all the feathered colony, rose clumsily on his talons, flapped two sable winds, and thrice hoarsely challenged, "Caw! caw! caw!" What clamor, what a liliputian Babel ensued! Our ears fairly tingled with the calls, outcries, and objurgations apparently flung down at us by the multitudinous population overhead. Hark to the woodpecker's rat-tat-tat, the partridge's muffled drum! List to the bugle of the wood-thrush, sweet and clear! Now sounds the cat-bird's shrill alarm, the owl's hoot of indignant surprise. Then the squirrels, those little monkeys of our northern woods, grated their teeth sharply at us, and let fall nuts on our heads as we passed underneath. Never were visitors more unwelcome.

Before long we came to a brook, then to another. Their foaming waters shot past like a herd of wild horses. These we crossed. We now began to thread a region where the forest was more open. The moss we trampled underfoot, and which here replaces the grass of the valleys, was beating the tallest trees in the race for the mountain-top. It was the old story of the tortoise and the hare over again. But this moss: have you ever looked at it before your heel bruised the perfumed flowers springing from its velvet? Here are tufts exquisitely decorated with coral lichen; here the violet and anemone nestle lovingly together; here it creeps up the gray trunks, or hides the bare roots of old trees. Tread softly! This is the abode of elves and fairies. Step lightly! you expect to hear the crushed flowers cry out in pain.

These enchanting spots, where stones are couches and trees canopies, tempted us to sit down on a cushioned bowlder, or throw ourselves upon the thick carpet into which we sunk ankle-deep at every step. Even the bald, gray rocks were tapestried with mosses, lichens, and vines. All around, under the thick shade, hundreds of enormous trees lay rotting; yet exquisitely the prostrate trunks were overspread with robes of softest green, effectually concealing the repulsiveness, the suggestions of decay. Now and then the dead tree rose into new life through the sturdy roots of a young fir, or luxuriant, plumed ferns growing in its bark. This inexpressible fecundity, in the midst of inexpressible wastefulness, declared that for Nature there is no such thing as death. And they tell us the day of miracles has passed! Upon this dream of elf-land the cool morning light fell in oblique streams through the tree-trunks, as through grated windows, filling all the wood with a subdued twilight glimmer, leaving a portion of its own gleam on the moss-grown rocks, while the trees stretched their black shadows luxuriously along the thick-piled sward, like weary soldiers in a bivouac.

We proceeded thus from chamber to chamber, and from cloister to cloister, at times descending some spur of the mountain into a deep-shaded dell, and again climbing a swift and miry slope to better ground, until we crossed the stream coming from the high spur spoken of. From here the ground rapidly rose for half a mile more, when we suddenly came out of the low firs full upon the Lion's Head crag, rising above Hermit Lake, and visible from the vicinity of the Glen House. To be thus unexpectedly confronted by this wall of imperishable rock stirs one very deeply. For the moment it dominates *us*, even as it does the little tarn so unconsciously slumbering at its feet. It is horribly mutilated and defaced. Its sides are thickly sowed with stunted trees that bury their roots in its cracks and rents with a gripe of iron. In effect it is the barbican of the great ravine. Crouched underneath, by the shore of the lake, is a matted forest of firs and spruces, dwindled to half their usual size, grizzled with long lichens, and occupying, as if by stealth, the debatable ground between life and death. It is, in fact, more dead than alive. Deeply sunk beneath is the lake.

Hermit Lake—a pool nestling underneath a precipice—demands a word. Its solitary state, its waters green and profound, and the thick shades by which it was covered, seemed strangely at variance with the intense activity of the foaming torrents we had seen, and could still hear rushing down the mountain. It was too small for a lake, or else it was dwarfed by the immense mass of overshadowing rock towering above it, whose reflected light streamed across its still and glossy surface. Here we bid farewell to the forest.

Tuckerman Ravine as it appears most every year in late winter.

We had now gained a commanding post of observation, though there was yet rough work to do. We saw the whole magnificent sweep of the ravine, to where it terminates in a semicircle of stupendous cliffs that seem hewn perpendicularly a thousand feet down. Lying against the western wall we distinguished patches of snow; but they appeared of trifling extent. Great wooded mountain slopes stretched away from the depths of the gorge on either side, making the iron lineaments of the giant cliffs seem harder by their own softness and delicacy. Here and there these exquisite draperies were torn in long rents by land-slips. In the west rose the shattered peak of Monroe—a mass of splintered granite, conspicuous at every point for its irreclaimable deformity. It seemed as if the huge open maw of the ravine might swallow up this peak with ease. There was a Dantesque grandeur and solemnity everywhere. With our backs against the trees, we watched the bellying sails of a stray cloud which intercepted in its aerial voyage our view of the great summit; but it soon floated away, discovering the whitish-gray ledges to the very capstone of the dome itself. Looking down and over the thick woods beyond, we met again the burly Carter Mountains, pushed backward from the Pinkham Notch, and kept back by an invisible yet colossal strength.

From Hermit Lake the only practicable way was by clambering up the bed of the mountain brook that falls through the ravine. The whole expanse

GUY SHOREY

Hikers pose under the snow arch in Tuckerman Ravine.

that stretched on either side was a chaos of shattered granite, pitched about in awful confusion. Path there was none. No matter what way we turned, "no thoroughfare" was carved in solid stone. We tried to force a passage through the stunted cedars that are mistaken at a mile for greensward, but were beaten back, torn and bleeding, to the brook. We then turned to the great bowlders, to be equally buffeted and abused, and finally repulsed upon the brook, which seemed all the while mocking our efforts. Once, while forcing a route, inch by inch, through the scrub, I was held suspended over a deep crevice, by my belt, until extricated by my comrade. At another time he disappeared to the armpits in a hole, from which I drew him like a blade from a scabbard. At this moment we found ourselves unable either to advance or retreat. The dwarf trees squeezed us like a vise. Who would have thought there was so much life in them? At our wits' end, we looked at our bleeding hands, then at each other. The brook was the only clew to such a labyrinth, and to it, as from Scylla to Charybodis, we turned as soon as we recovered breath. But to reach it was no easy matter; we had literally to cut our way out of the jungle.

When we were there, and had rested awhile from the previous severe exertions, my companion, alternately mopping his forehead and feeling his bruises, looked up with a quizzical expression, and ejaculated, "Faith, I am almost as glad to get out of this wilderness as the other! In any case," he gayly added, "I have lost the most blood here; while in Virginia I did not receive a scratch."

After this rude initiation into the mysteries of the ravine, we advanced directly up the bed of the brook. But the brook is for half a mile nothing but a succession of leaps and plunges, its course choked with bowlders. We however toiled on, from rock to rock, first boosting, then hoisting each other up; one moment splashing in a pool, the next halting in dismay under a cascade, which we must either mount like a chamois or ascend like a trout. The climber here tastes the full enjoyment of an encounter with untamed nature, which calls every thew and sinew into action. At length the stream grew narrower, suddenly divided, and we stood at the mouth of the Snow Arch, confronted by the vertical upper wall of the ravine.

We stood in an arena "more majestic than the circus of a Titus or a Vespasian." The scene was one of awful desolation. A little way below us the gorge was heaped with the ruins of some unrecorded convulsion, by which the precipice had been cloven from base to summit, and the enormous fragments heaved into the chasm with a force the imagination is powerless to conceive. In the interstices among these blocks rose thickets of dwarf cedars, as stiff and unyielding as the livid rock itself. It was truly an arena which might have witnessed the gladiatorial combats of immortals.

We did not at first look at the Snow Arch. The eye was irresistibly fascinated by the tremendous mass of the precipice above. From top to bottom its tawny front was covered with countless little streams, that clung to its polished walls without once quitting their hold. They twined and twisted in their downward course, like a brood of young serpents escaping from their lair; nor could I banish the idea of the ghastly head of a Gorgon clothed with tresses of serpents. A poetic imagination has named this tangled knot of mountain rills, "The fall of a thousand streams." At the foot of the cliff the scattered waters unite, before entering the Snow Arch, in a single stream. Turning now to the right, the narrowing gorge, ascending by a steep slope as high as the upper edge of the precipice, points out the only practicable way to the summit of Mount Washington in this direction. But we have had enough of such climbing, for one day, at least.

Partial recovery from the stupefaction which seizes and holds one fast is doubtless signalized in every case by an effort to account for the overwhelming disaster of which these ruins are the mute yet speaking evidence. We need go no further in the search than the innocent-looking little rills, first dripping from the Alpine mosses, then percolating through the rocks of the high plateau, and falling over its edge in a thousand streams. Puny as they look, before their inroads the plateau line has doubtless receded, like the great wall of rock over which Niagara pours the water of four seas. With their combined forces—how long ago cannot be guessed; and what, indeed, does it signify?—knitted together by frost into Herculean strength, they assailed the granite cliffs that were older than the sun, older than the moon or the stars, mined and countermined year by year, inch by inch, drop by drop, until—honey-combed, riddled, and pierced to its centre, and all was ready for its final overthrow—winter gave the signal. In a twinkling, yielding to the stroke, and shattered into a thousand fragments, the cliffs laid their haughty heads low in the dust. Afterward the accumulated waters tranquilly continued the process of demolition, and of removing the soil from the deep excavation they had made, until the floor of the ravine had sunk to its present level. In California a man with a hose washes away mountains to get at the gold deposits. This principle of hydraulic force is borrowed, pure and simple, from a mountain cataract.

Osgood, the experienced guide, who had visited the ravine oftener than anybody else, assured me that never within his remembrance had this forgement of winter, the Snow Arch, been seen to such advantage. We estimated its width at above two hundred feet, where it threw its solid bridge of ice over the stream, and not far from three hundred in its greatest length, where it lay along the slope of the gorge. Summer and winter met on this neutral ground. Entering the Arch was joining January and July with a step. Flowers blossomed at the threshold. We caught water, as it dripped ice-cold from the roof, and pledged Old Winter in his own cellarage. The brook foamed at our feet. Looking up, there was a pretty picture of a tiny water-fall pouring in at the upper end and out of the ragged portal of the grotto. But I think we were most charmed with the remarkable sculpture of the roof, which was a groined arch fashioned as featly as was ever done by the human hands. What the stream had begun in secret the warm vapors had chiselled with a boulder hand, but not altered. As it was formed, so it remained—a veritable chapel of the hill, the brook droning its low, monotonous chant, and the dripping roof tinkling its refrain unceasingly. If the interior of the great ravine impressed us as the hidden receptacle of all waste matter, this lustrous heap of snow, so insignificant in its relation to the immensity of the chasm that we scarcely looked at it at first, now chased away the feeling of mingled terror and aversion—of having stolen unawares into the one forbidden chamber—and possessed us with a sense of the beautiful, which remained long after its glittering particles had melted into the stream that flowed beneath. So under a cold exterior is nourished the principle of undying love, which the aged mountain gives that earth may forever renew her fairest youth.

The presence of this miniature glacier is a very simple matter. The fierce winds of winter which sweep over the plateau whirl the snows before them, over its crest, into the ravine, where they are lodged at the foot of the precipice, and accumulate to a great depth. As soon as released by spring, the little streams, falling down this wall, seek their old channels, and, being warmer, succeed in forcing a passage through the ice. By the end of August the ice usually disappears, though it sometimes remains even later.

After picking up some fine specimens of quartz, sparkling with mica, and uttering a parting malediction on the black flies that tormented us, we took our way down and out of the ravine, following the general course of the stream along its steep valley, and, after an uneventful march of two hours, reached the upper waters of the Crystal Cascade.

July 22, 1893

The Glen House Fire

From *The White Mountain Echo and Tourist's Register*

A rival paper of the better known Among the Clouds, *which was printed atop Mount Washington,* The White Mountain Echo and Tourists' Register *was published each summer in Bethlehem beginning on July 13, 1878. The paper was founded by Markinfield Addey, who served as its editor for 20 seasons. After Addey had to give up his editorial duties due to blindness, C. E. Blanchard ran the paper for the next 30 years.* The Echo *was devoted to covering not just its busy home town, but the entire White Mountain tourist community. Its editors were never reluctant to take stands on the major issues of the day, and during the time period when the nearby hills and valleys were being denuded by the great lumber barons of the late 19th and early 20th centuries, the paper often denounced the work of the "wood butchers."*

THE FAMOUS Glen House is no more. That greedy and devouring fiend, fire, has drawn it into its powerful and destructive grasp with such attractive force that all that remains of this, one of the handsomest of White Mountain hotels, is a smouldering mass of ruins, and the tall, weird-like forms of the chimneys, two or three of which have already added their pile of bricks to the debris. The dreaded enemy stopped at nothing, but swept the establishment from the face of the earth as grass falls beneath the sharp blows of the scythe. The ice house was the only one of the attacked buildings that dared to oppose the advent of the fiend, and when I left the scene at two o'clock Monday morning that bade fair to succumb.

While the Sunday evening service was in progress at Wentworth Hall, the telephone rang, and on answering it myself I was informed that the Glen House was on fire, the operator at the Glen, Mrs. Burnell, whose husband is the efficient agent of the Maine Central at Glen Station, having notified her husband immediately the fire broke out. Soon after learning this the operator at the Hall was informed by the operator at Fabyans that the structure had been burned to the ground. In order to keep up the reputation of *The Echo* for being one of the first to get hold of the news, I immediately interviewed *The Echo's* enterprising agent here, Mr. C. H. Hurlin, whose horses I knew had not been out during the day, while the horses at the Hall had each made two trips, and he at once placed his clever little pair of blacks at my disposal. I was fortunate enough to secure the services of "Dick" McInnis, one of the General's trusted drivers, and he drove me over to the Glen and back in good shape.

It was just about half-past nine when we started, the balmy air making the trip most pleasant. Nothing of interest occurred till we were half way up Spruce Hill, when a short distance off loomed up two big high lights and a low one. We immediately decided that it was one of the Glen coaches making for the Hall for the night, and pulling into the bank we awaited its coming. It was a gruesome spectacle. It was nearly eleven, the night was inclined to be dark, we were in the midst of thick woods, with these immense lamps, apparently without any visible support, looking like gigantic fire flys. I don't think either of us will ever forget the impression it made upon him. We hailed them and they halted while I extended to them a cordial welcome to the Hall. Holding the ribbons over the six sturdy grays we could discern the rugged form of the veteran "Jim" McCormick, whose set face was a sure sign that he appreciated the responsibility he bore. Mr. Burnell, who had hastened to the hotel immediately on receipt of his wife's message, led the way with a lantern, his wife occupying a seat on the couch.

Wishing them God-speed we continued on our way till we reached the last turn in the road before the Glen comes into view, and then what a scene met our eyes. Thick volumes of white smoke rose in the air, forming an effective background for the thin, spare forms of the tall chimneys. Where the noble structure had stood the flames rose in most fantastic shapes, dancing in wild glee at the terrible work they had accomplished. The scene closely resembled a field of tall, wavy grass blown about by the wind. Scattered all around were the big tally-hos, trunks, furniture, carriages of all descriptions, mountain wagons, harness, in fact everything that could be carried off before the flames gained too strong a headway. Picking our way carefully through these obstructions, we reached the stables, put up our horses, and then proceeded to make a tour of the place.

On the little lawn in front of the house stood the sprinklers just as they had been performing their duties when the fire broke out, only the flames had destroyed the hose and cut off their water supply. Near them I picked

Glen Ellis Falls.

Crystal Cascade.

C. R. MILLIKEN, Proprietor.

up several smoked knives, forks and spoons, which in the confusion had evidently been hastily thrown out. The picturesque rustic summer houses in front of the hotel had fallen a prey to the fire, as had the lofty flag staff, part of which had fallen while the remainder stood there a charred piece of timber. Some one with more ambition than wisdom had drawn out from the office the fancy scales, which mockingly stood there badly scorched, but yet true to their purpose as they correctly recorded our weights. Stretched out in all directions were the wires that were formerly in use when the house was lighted by electricity. Smoke continued to pour from the furnace smokestack.

Moving round to the back of the establishment, the destruction was more apparent. The engine, which ran the machinery for the laundry, still kept its position, while the machinery it supplied lay scattered in the wreck. Everywhere could be seen the gas and hot water pipes twisted by the heat into all variety of shapes. In another corner, upside down, the printing press was visible. Outside of these objects all that could be distinguished was a gigantic heap of ashes, so thoroughly had the flames done their awful work. They had licked up everything that came within their reach; but though they made several attacks on the stables and employees' quarters, they were repulsed each time.

From the inquiries I made from several of those present when the flames broke out, I gathered that at about half-past six, just as supper was about to be served, smoke was seen issuing from the roof of the house, and an alarm was immediately turned in. When the hose was attached to the hydrants, it was found that owing to the lowness of the streams, or to some other cause which has not yet been ascertained, the water would not reach to the second story. It would not have made much difference, however, for in a very short space the whole structure was completely enveloped in flames, and it being at once apparent that it was doomed; efforts were made to save the rest of the buildings, from which the contents had all been removed to a safe distance.

Most of the personal property of the guests and of those employees who had rooms in the main house, was saved, as was as much of the furniture as could be removed in the short period that intervened in which the blazing building could be entered without danger. The famous Windsor Castle rug was safely removed, as was a large quantity of the silver. But the fire spread so rapidly that very little could be rescued.

The cause of the conflagration is unknown. It is supposed that sparks from the smokestack of the engine room fell on the dry and inflammable roof and speedily ate their way into it before there was any outward indication of danger. This is merely a supposition, however, on the part of those connected with the hotel. As the house is so completely destroyed it is very doubtful if the true origin of the disaster will ever be discovered.

Most of the guests, accompanied by Mr. C. B. Milliken, the proprietor, and his family, and Mr. O. L. Frisbee, the manager, passed the night in Gorham, while the rest, as I have said before, journeyed to Wentworth Hall.

A large number of the employees are thus thrown out of engagement for the season. It is to be hoped, however, that their position will attract attention, and that places will not be wanting for them.

As both Mr. Milliken and Mr. Frisbee had left for Gorham before I arrived at the Glen, I was unable to ascertain what the loss would probably amount to, but was informed by several that it would be fully covered by insurance. Of course I was equally unable to ascertain Mr. Milliken's intentions as to rebuilding or as to the continuance of the stage line. And being pretty well tired I was not sorry about two o'clock to retrace my steps homeward.   J.M.C.

Jackson, N.H., July 17, 1993

Further Particulars

As most of our readers are aware the magnificent hotel that has fallen prey to the flames was an entirely modern structure and the only one of its kind in the mountains that possessed any degree of uniformity. It was not like many others, originally a moderate sized house whose capacity had been enlarged by numerous additions. It is now more than forty years ago that its site was occupied by a country inn, adapted to the wants of the mountain travellers of that period. This in time gave away to a larger structure, destroyed by fire on October 1, 1884, that was also owned by Mr. Milliken. Before that gentleman came into its possession it was the property of Mr. Thompson, whose name has been given to some neighboring falls and who was accidentally drowned during a freshet that occurred in the vicinity of the hotel.

After the destruction of the hotel in 1884, Mr. Milliken set to work to rebuild and by the following season had a considerable portion of the house just destroyed ready for the accommodation of guests; but it was not entirely completed until 1887.

The Glen House was one of the finest of the many handsome houses in the mountains. It was of the English cottage style with the roof line constantly broken by gables, and having octagonal towers at each corner in front. The roof, with its gables, dormers, and towers, presented a picturesque look and a splendid frontage, which extended nearly three hundred feet. The hotel was three stories high above the basement and covered an area of 1700 feet, exclusive of verandas which were 16 feet wide and 450 feet long, and were, without doubt, the best covered promenades in the White Mountains.

It is very fortunate that the stables and the cottage as well as the bowling-alley were saved, although more than once the roof of the cottage was ignited by sparks. The teams of horses and the carriages being thus preserved, the celebrated stage line from the summit of Mount Washington by the Glen to the Glen Station will continue to run as usual throughout the season.

The hotel was, it is stated, insured for $130,000; but Mr. Milliken estimates his loss at $175,000. The help were mostly paid off on Monday, when many of them returned to their homes.

It will not be possible to rebuild the hotel the present season, and it is yet uncertain whether or not it will ever be rebuilt by Mr. Milliken, who, it is reported, will dispose of the real estate. The location is, however, one of such surpassing beauty that the site now disfigured by charred ruins must before long be covered by a new and an elegant structure.

July 18, 1893

Embers from
the Glen Fire

From *Among the Clouds*

THE GROUNDS about the site of the Glen House presented a sad spectacle Monday morning. Every stick of timber and every board had been consumed by the fire which broke out at 6:30 Sunday night. Nothing but the
iron pipes running through the house, and tall chimneys remain to tell
where the magnificent hotel stood only a short time before. The stables and
the cottage and the bowling alley were saved. The middle barn took fire on
the roof, but an employee ascended it with a pail of water and succeeded in
putting it out. At various times during the progress of the flames sparks
started a fire on the cottage roof but it was put out and the building saved.

The origin of the fire is still unknown. Mr. Wilson, the steward, is of the
opinion that it must have originated from a spark out of the boiler chimney,
as there had been no fire in the main part of the house that day except in the
office fireplace. Others state that the first they noticed was smoke pouring
from the attic of the roof of the rear wing over the elevator well, near where
the wing extending eastward joins the main house.

The house was well stocked with provisions, and had been put in complete order for the summer business, which Mr. Milliken states never looked
more promising for a successful season. Many articles, including a large
amount of crockery, had been purchased and had just arrived, all of which
were consumed.

Mr. Milliken puts his loss at $175,000. The insurance is not far from
$130,000. A larger amount had been carried upon the property, some of
which had lapsed only a short time before.

When asked if the house would be rebuilt, Mr. Milliken said he could not yet tell until there was an adjustment. "I am older than I once was," he said, "and can't stand quite as much hard work. It is yet too early to decide what is best." He said that he should keep his stage line running through the season the same as in previous years; but of course will not make an attempt at keeping a hotel this year.

As soon as the fire was discovered, work of saving the furniture was begun. That in the parlors and in the side halls on the first floor was saved, but was considerably damaged in handling. Nothing above the first floor, to speak of, was saved. There were about 40 guests in the house and they had time to escape with most of their personal effects. Some of them in the hurry to get out left small articles in the bureaus, and one party lost a considerable amount of clothing that was in trunks; but all considered, it is fortunate that nothing more serious had happened to them.

The employees were not all of them so fortunate as they might have been. In the excitement some did not stop to put their clothing into trunks but threw them out of the window and much was lost. Several of the girls lost small sums of money, as well as clothing. One threw her pocketbook, containing $11, out the window and at last accounts had seen nothing of it since. Mr. Chas. A. McCormick, the Glen House printer, spent his time trying to save other things than his own clothing, and when he got through found what he had on was about all he had left. He came to the Summit yesterday and found temporary employment in the office of *Among the Clouds*.

The guests were sent Sunday night in coaches to Jackson, and to Gorham, where they found shelter. The employees found quarters in the barns and bowling alley, and a few in the cottage, for the night, but it was a sad time for all, so suddenly deprived of their summer's work and wages. Mr. Milliken made arrangements to immediately pay off his help, and he sent most of them to their homes yesterday. The remainder will stop for a short time and assist in putting what remains in order.

Mr. Frisbee, the manager, and Mr. Wilson, the steward, go to their homes within a short time, — the latter to his farm in North Gray, Me. Few can know what such a catastrophe means to the hundred or more in the employ of the Glen House proprietor. It is too late to get other places this season and the loss of wages is a great misfortune to them. The bell boys were colored young men from the Hampton Institute in Virginia, and they are thus deprived of earning a sufficient amount to carry them through the coming school year. It was indeed a sad time for all, besides that occasioned by the loss of wages, and every one was full of sympathy for those who had suffered most.

The location of the Glen House is unsurpassed. It stands in the very center of a magnificent panorama of mountain peaks. At no place does one get such a clear impression of the heighth of Mount Washington and the neighboring mountains, as from the Glen. It is a grand and impressive sight to look out upon the range of mountains as the clouds drift over them, or the afternoon sun sends it gleams of light over them into the deep valley of Pinkham Notch, or upon the Carter Range in the rear of the famous hotel. It is to be hoped that the site will soon be occupied with another structure, even if Mr. Milliken concludes not to build again. For over forty years the Glen has been famous among the White Mountain hotels, and the name and location are known to about every one who has come to the White Mountains since the first house was built. The destruction of two large houses and the tragic death of the first proprietor by drowning, add not a little to the feeling of sadness coming from incidents that have occurred on the eastern side of Mount Washington.

1904

A Week on
Mount Washington

Bradford Torrey

From *Nature's Invitation*

Weymouth, Massachusetts-born Bradford Torrey (1843–1912) was among the most well-read turn-of-the-century naturalists. Ornithology was his specialty and his frequent White Mountain bird watching ventures were chronicled in books such as Footing it in Franconia, Nature's Invitation, A Rambler's Lease, The Foot-Path Way, *and* Birds in the Bush. *Torrey was also editor of the 14-volume journal of noted 19th-century naturalist Henry David Thoreau.*

I WENT UP Mount Washington in the afternoon of August 22d, and came down again in the afternoon of the 29th. Ten years before I had spent a week there, in early July, and had not visited the place since. In some respects, of course, the summit is badly damaged (I have heard it spoken of as utterly ruined) by the presence of the hotel and other buildings, not to mention the railway trains, with their daily freight of bustling lunch-box tourists. Still the railway and the hotel are indisputable conveniences; I should hardly have stayed there so long without them; and in this imperfect world we must not expect to find all the good things in one basket.

As for the tourists, one need walk but a few steps to be rid of them. As a class they are not enterprising pedestrians. In fifteen minutes you may find yourself where human beings are as far away, practically, as if you were among the highest Andes or on the famous "peak in Darien." There you may sit on a boulder, or recline on a mat of prostrate willow, and imagine yourself the only man in the world; gazing at the prospect, listening to the mountain silence (there is none like it), or eating alpine blueberries, as lonely as any hermit's heart could wish. All this you may do, and then return to the most obliging of hosts, the best of good dinners, and a comfortable bed.

By the time you have been there two days, moreover, you will have begun to enjoy the hotel, not only for its physical comforts, but as an interesting miniature world. The manager and the clerk, the waiters and the bellboys, the editors and the printers, the night watchman and the train conductor, will all have become your friends, almost your blood relations,—such intimate good feeling does a joint seclusion induce,—and at any minute of the day in may come a group of strangers of the most engagingly picturesque sort; having no more the appearance of a sales-ladies or women of fashion, shopkeepers or bankers' clerks, than of college students and professors. They are men and women. They have put off the fine clothes and the smug appearance which society exacts of its members; they look not the least in the world as if they had just come out of a bandbox; their *negligée* costumes bear no resemblance to the dainty, immaculate rig of the tennis court or the golf links. They are "roughing it" in earnest. For at least eight or ten hours, possibly for as many days, they have ceased to be concerned about the cut of their garments or the smoothness of their hair. Of some of them the aspect is fairly disreputable. It is a solemn fact that you may here see gentlemen with rents in their trousers and a week's beard on their faces. And ten to one they will brazen it out without apology.

The dapper clerk and the prosperous merchant and his wife, who have ridden up in the train with their good clothes and their company faces on, may stare if they will. It is nothing to the campers and walkers. They are not on parade, and do not mind being smiled at. A pretty college girl will walk about the office, alpenstock in hand, with her hair tied in a careless knot, her skirts well above the tops of her scratched and dusty boots, her face brown and her sleeves tucked up, and seem quite as much at ease as if she were in full evening dress with the drawing-room lights blazing upon her alabaster shoulders, her laces, and her diamonds. It is heroism (or heroinism) of a kind worth seeing.

You are still enjoying the spectacle when two men enter the door, one with a botanical box slung over his shoulder. It is as if he had given you the Masonic grip, and you hardly wait for him to cross the sill before you make up to him with a question. By which route has he come, and what luck as he met with? Over the Crawford path, he answers, and though the season is pretty late, and Alpine plants are mostly out of bloom, he has found some interesting things.

Two or three of them he cannot name, and he opens the box. His spe-

cial puzzle is a tiny, upright-growing plant, thickly set with roundish, crin-
kled leaves, and bearing a few blossoms so exceedingly small as almost to
defy a common pocket-lens. Do you know what it is? Yes, to your own surprise, you remember, or seem to remember, and you run upstairs to bring
down a Gray's Manual. The plant is *Euphrasia* (eye-bright), an Alpine variety. It was pointed out to you ten years ago, near the same Crawford path,
by the man who knew the Mount Washington flora better than any one else.
You recall the time as if it had been yesterday. Your companion dropped
suddenly upon his knees, eyes to the ground. "What are you looking for?"
you asked; and he answered "Euphrasia." It is good to see it again. You find
it for yourself the next day, it may be, in the Alpine Garden.

And this other plant, stiffly matted and long past flowering? Your new
acquaintance supposes it to be *Diapensia*; and for that you need no book.
And this third one, with its rusty leaves, is the Lapland azalea. You remember the day you saw it first—in middle June—when all by yourself you
were making your first ascent of the mountain, walking alternately over
snowbanks and beds of flowers. So far as the lovely blossoms are concerned,
you have never seen it since.

Next morning your botanist bids you good-by; he is going down by way
of Tuckerman's Ravine; and at noon, after some indolent, happy hours on
the carriage-road and in the Alpine Garden, you are again in the hotel office
when half a dozen campers from the northern peaks make their appearance.
Dusty, travel-stained, disheveled, they bring the freedom of the hills with
them and fill the place with their breeziness. Some of the "transients" clustered about the stove smile at a sight so unconventional, but the manager,
the clerk, and the bellboys are better informed. They have seen the leader
of the party before, and in a minute the word is passed round. This is
Mr. _____, who came up the mountain with his son a year ago on the day
of that dreadful storm, when two later adventurers upon the same path perished by the way, and he himself, old mountaineer that he was, with another
life hanging upon his own, had more than once been all but ready to say, "It
can't be done." Your traveling companion has seen him here before, though
she was not present on that memorable occasion, and presently you are being introduced to him and his friends—a metropolitan clergyman, a university professor, and a younger man, with whose excellent work in your
own line you are already acquainted.

Anon the company breaks up,—the pedestrians are off for an afternoon
excursion,—and you step out onto the platform to look about you. Against
the railing are two men, one of them with what seems to be a "collecting
gun" in his hand. "An ornithologist," you say to yourself, and at the word

you begin edging toward him. A remark or two about the weather and you ask him point-blank if he is collecting birds. No, he answers, his weapon is a rifle, and he shows you the cartridge. He has brought it along to shoot squirrels with. You wonder why any one should think it worth while to carry a gun over the nine miles of the Crawford path for so trifling a use; but that is none of your business, and just then the other man speaks up to say that his companion is a botanist, while he himself is a "bird man." This is interesting (the second ornithologist within an hour), and you set about comparing notes. Did he hear anything of the Bicknell thrushes and the Hudsonian chickadees on his way up? No, he missed them both on this trip, though he has met them elsewhere in the mountains. You drop an innocent remark about the thrushes, and he says, "Are you Mr. So-and-So?" There is no denying it, and when he pronounces his own name it proves to be familiar; and a good talk follows. Then he starts down into the Alpine Garden,—you charging him to be sure to eat some of the delicious cespitose blueberries on the descent,—and ten minutes afterward he turns up again at your elbow. He has left his friend, and has hurried back to tell you of a sharp-shinned hawk that he has just seen. You may put the name into your Mount Washington bird list, if you will.

So the days pass—no day without a new acquaintance. If you and one of the local editors start down the trail to the Lakes of the Clouds after a Sunday-morning breakfast, you find yourselves going along with three Baltimore gentlemen, who have walked up from the Crawford House the day before. ("Well, we arrive!" you remember to have heard the leader exclaim as his foot struck the hotel platform), and are now on their return.

They introduce one another to you and your companion,—Dr. This, Dr. That, and Dr. The Other,—and you pick your way downward over the boulders in Indian file, talking as you go. After a while you and the oldest of the Baltimoreans find yourselves falling a little behind the rest, and the conversation grows more and more friendly. He has come to New Hampshire, as he does every year, for the best of all tonics, a dose of mountain climbing. He has been somewhat overworked of late, especially with a long task of proof-reading. A new edition of his treatise on chemistry is passing through the press, and the moment the last sheets were corrected he broke away northward; and here he is, walking over high places, where he loves to be. "I am an old man," he says; but his strength is not abated. Far be the day! At the lakeside hands are shaken and good-bys said. You will most likely never see each other again, but one of you, at least, keeps a bright memory.

It is a strange place, the Summit House. Twice a day, as on the seashore, the tide rises and falls. But the evening flood is a small affair. The crowd comes at noon. It registers its name, eats it luncheon, writes a postal-card, buys a souvenir, asks a question or two, more or less pertinent ("Can you tell me where the Tip-Over House is?" one women said—for the rarified air plays queer pranks with its victims), possibly looks at the prospect, probably snaps a camera, and then takes the after-dinner train for the base. Evening passengers make a longer stay. They cannot do otherwise. For them the sunset and sunrise are the great events. One would think that such phenomena were never to be witnessed in the low country. They watch the clouds, or more likely the cloud, and go to sleep with one ear open for the sunrise bell.

So much for the larger number of Summit House guests, the respectable majority. A few, two in twenty, perhaps, arrive on foot; and these are the good ones—the salt of the mountain, so to speak. This time I was not one of them, but I had no thought of denying the superiority of their privilege.

July 12, 1900

Victims of the Storm

From *Among the Clouds*

A DAY OF fiercest hurricane and cold. Two stalwart men, each a trained athlete—W. B. Curtis, age 63, and Allen Ormsbee, about 30—both of New York, are pushing bravely up the Crawford bridle path. A night of gloom and fury overtake them, and after a desperate battle with the storm, a temporary refuge is found in a clump of scrub. A final effort is made to reach the Summit, but the older man, chilled and exhausted, falls stunned and helpless to perish in the path two miles from the top. Ormsbee, struggling onward against fearful odds, strives with all his might to reach safety and summon assistance. He wages a heroic yet hopeless fight with the tempest, suffering fall after fall on the icy rocks, until at last, with only a few rods more to shelter, bruised and bleeding and crippled, he too falls to rise no more. Human power has done its utmost,—"For the Angel of Death spread his wings on the blast,"—and the dauntless spirit takes its flight. A struggle such as no other person ever passed through on Mount Washington ends in defeat and death.

Such was the tragedy of Saturday night, June 30. Not for ten years before had a life been lost on Mount Washington, though dozens of untrained and venturesome climbers make the ascent. For two vigorous athletes, accustomed to long and hard walks and mountain climbs, no one would have looked for a disastrous outcome. Except for the storm which was encountered, the severity of which exceeded anything ever known at this time of year by any one now familiar with the mountain, the climb would have been easy and safe.

William B. Curtis, the elder of the two unfortunate men, was for many years one of the finest amateur athletes in this country and was one of the founders of the New York Athletic Club. He was known as the father of athletics in America, and was looked upon as final authority on all athletic questions. Giving up active sports some 18 years ago, he had taken all his exercising in mountain climbing and tramped and climbed extensively. He was perfectly fearless and would climb alone and in all kinds of weather, so confident was he in his strength and skill. He was a man of splendid physique, deep-chested and of the finest type of athlete.

His companion, Allen Ormsbee, was likewise a trained athlete and was a member of the Crescent Athletic Club of Brooklyn.

Messrs. Curtis and Ormsbee with Mr. Fred D. Ilgen of New York came to the White mountains about a week in advance of the Appalachian excursion, which they proposed joining at the Summit House on its arrival. Mr. Curtis alone of the three was a member of the club, in which, however, he had never taken an active part. A fourth friend in the excursion was Prof. H. C. Parker of Columbia University, who came directly to Mount Washington with the club.

The three companions passed several days pleasantly in ascents of Lafayette, Whiteface, Passaconaway, Sandwich Dome and Tecumseh, and on Friday night, June 29, found themselves at Rosebrook Inn, Twin Mountain.

On Saturday they had intended to go to the Crawford House and climb Mount Willard, after which they were to walk up the bridle path to Washington. But Mr. Ilgen had never climbed Twin Mountain, and he finally decided to leave his friends for that purpose, planning to meet the Appalachians that same afternoon and go to Mount Washington with them by rail. So, Saturday morning being fine, Messrs. Curtis and Ormsbee took an early train for Crawford's, while Mr. Ilgen climbed the Twin, joining the club excursion for Mount Washington at night.

Reaching the Summit House, the Appalachians found a furious storm raging, as elsewhere told, and no word of Curtis and Ormsbee. Mr. Ilgen's story at once aroused anxiety, and telephone inquiries were at once made at the Crawford House. The answer was that nothing had been seen or heard of them at the hotel, and that no one was known to have started the path. Messages were sent elsewhere, but nothing could be learned of their whereabouts. The guides with the Appalachian party, Vyron and Thaddeus Lowe, took interns and started for the path, but the wind put out the lights in an instant. To proceed over the icy rocks in darkness and in that fearful gale would have been to go to almost certain death, with scarcely a chance of finding the missing men. Meantime the Club leaders had learned of the arrival of Rev. Mr. Nichols and son over the Montalban Ridge, and of the fact that their guides had started down the Crawford path early in the afternoon. The conclusion was quickly reached that these guides must have met Curtis and Ormsbee and warned them of the terrible weather above, so that they would surely have gone down. Fears were allayed, the guides were recalled from their desperate undertaking, and all were confident that the first fair day would bring Mr. Ilgen's friends.

Sunday passed without news. On Monday morning a large party of the Appalachians went to Tuckerman's Ravine while another went to Madison Hut to pass the night. Mr. Louis F. Cutter of Winchester, however, set out alone down the Crawford path, and about 11:15 the worst fears were realized by his finding the body of Mr. Curtis close to the path, near the Lake of the Clouds.

Mr. Curtis lay in the shelter of a large rock, his head resting on a projected part of the same rock. The left temple rested upon a blunt point of the rock. At the point of contact there was an indentation in the temple.

He had a light crash cap, which had fallen off, and wore a coarse woolen coat, not very thick, a shirt which seemed to be partly cotton, long trousers and heavy, hob nailed boots.

After making the dreadful discovery Mr. Cutter spent some time looking for Mr. Ormsbee. At a point in the lee of Mount Monroe and near the edge of Oakes' Gulf he came upon a camera in the path, and beside it an empty bottle which had contained milk. Close by was an improvised shelter in the scrub, which evidently had been a temporary refuge of the unfortunates.

Mr. Cutter pursued his search as far as the north side of Mount Pleasant. Not finding Mr. Ormsbee and finding a party coming up from the Crawford who had seen no sign of him, he returned to the Summit. Near the junction of the Boott's Spur path he met three Appalachians who were setting out in that direction, Messrs. Coffin, Parker and Weed, and they started at once for the place where Mr. Curtis's body lay. Other Club members who were at the Summit went down upon Mr. Cutter bringing the news. Mr. Davis and Mr. Newhall went down the Tuckerman's Ravine path to intercept the party who would be returning from the ravine about that time, and the men of the party joined the searchers.

Messrs. Coffin, Weed and Parker proceeded to the shelter in the scrub which Mr. Cutter had described and made a thorough examination of it. It was at a point where the ground sloped sharply from the path and was densely overgrown with scrub, just enough space being left to crawl underneath. Once in it, partial shelter was afforded on all sides but the northern, and branches had been hastily broken off and laid over the exposed side. Within,

Lakes of the Clouds Hut and the monument marking the spot
where William B. Curtis met his death in June 1900.

wrapped in paraffined paper, were found two slices of bread and a broken
fragment, and in the dryest corner was Mr. Curtis's camera. The camera in
the path Mr. Parker recognized as that of his friend Mr. Ormsbee.

Having made a careful search and found no trace of Ormsbee, the three
searchers weighed the probabilities of the situation in the light of their discoveries and came to the conclusion that Mr. Curtis had become exhausted
and Mr. Ormsbee had started for help, leaving the older man in the shelter
and placing the camera and bottle in the path to mark the spot. Mr. Curtis,
they thought, had probably survived the night, and on Sunday morning his
companion not returning, he had tried with his diminished strength to
reach the Summit, but had succumbed to exhaustion at the spot where he
was found. From his intimate knowledge of Ormsbee Prof. Parker reasoned
that he would have left the path and gone straight for the top, which would
take him up the more sheltered side of the mountain.

Therefore, after a brief search on the Boott's Spur path, the three left the
Crawford path and set out for the Summit, keeping a little space apart but
following parallel courses. Weed kept farthest to the right, passing Harry
Hunter's monument; Mr. Coffin was next to him, while Prof. Parker kept
to the left, nearest to the Crawford path. Thus they went slowly up the cone,
zigzagging back and forth as a man bewildered by cloud and storm would
have gone, and closely examining the rocks. Finally, about 4:30, when in
sight of the Signal Station and only a few hundred feet below, Prof. Parker

came upon the body of Ormsbee lying upon the rocks where he had fallen. His face and hands bore marks of the terrible struggle he had made with the storm, there being a gash an inch and a quarter long in one hand, besides other cuts, while in the middle of his forehead was a severe bruise.

Some of the lady members of the party happened to be at the signal station when Prof. Parker found the body and he shouted to them to tell of his discovery. The word was speedily passed around and volunteers were quickly found to bear the body to the Summit. It was a comparatively simple matter to bring poor Ormsbee's remains up the little distance he had failed to make in his struggle with the hurricane, but there remained a harder duty, for Mr. Curtis's body was to be borne some two miles up the rock-lined path, which is hard enough to traverse empty-handed.

Materials for making a stretcher were sent down and all the men who were equal to the task set out about 6 o'clock. Others followed after the arrival of the train and relieved the first company near the foot of the cone. There were nearly 20 in all to lend a hand, but progress was slow and it was about 8 o'clock when the Summit was reached. Those who took part in the sad duty, besides several of the Club, were John Camden and John Cam-

Lakes of the Clouds as it appeared to hikers in the early 1970s.

den, Jr., and Etienne Gilbert, employees of the Mount Washington Railway; Nathan Larrabee, driver on the stage line, Patrick Howley, caretaker on the carriage road; George O'Brien, John St. Peter and another, linemen; Howard Langill, bellboy at the Summit House; and Charles H. Carr and G. W. Smith, attaches of *Among the Clouds* office.

Meanwhile, with his accustomed thoughtfulness and promptness, Col. O. G. Barron of the Fabyan House made all necessary arrangements below, summoning Undertakers Charles Bingham and Frank Wells from Littleton and sending them by carriage to the Base, and ordering caskets brought up on one of the evening trains. At the Summit a special train was arranged upon telephone orders from Superintendent John Horne, and left the Summit at 8:20 p.m. bearing the bodies. On the train went Mr. Ilgen, the friend and travelling companion of Messrs. Curtis and Ormsbee, to whom fell the duty of going with the remains to New York. Prof. Parker joined him the following morning.

The remains were taken in charge by the undertakers at the Base, and were removed to Fabyan's on Tuesday morning, where they were viewed by Dr. George S. Gove of Whitefield, who certified the cause of death to be exposure and exhaustion. There were no broken bones. On the left side of Mr. Curtis's forehead was a large bruise about which the blood had settled, producing a condition of ecchymosis, but there was no fracture of the skull. This was at the point which rested on the rock when the body was found. The bruise, Dr. Gove said, could not have been caused by the mere resting on the rock, as had been suggested by observers, but was unquestionably the result of a fall. The blow, he stated, would have been sufficient to produce unconsciousness, and in that condition he would live for awhile and the blood would be effused under the skin. Dr. Gove said it was probable that the older man had become exhausted and his friend had gone forward for help, and while there was nothing in the condition of the bodies to indicate when death occurred, yet he should expect that the younger man would have been the last to die. While it was possible that Mr. Curtis lived until Sunday, yet the chances, he said, were against it, and his opinion was that he died Saturday night. He accordingly certified that both deaths occurred on June 30. The permit for the removal of the bodies was signed by the undertakers and Dr. Gove and they were taken to New York Tuesday night.

What must have been the fierceness of the tempest may well be realized by the fact of its overcoming a man of the almost unequalled strength of Mr. Curtis. His athletic record shows that he was not a man to be baffled by any ordinary storm. "Father Bill" Curtis, as he was affectionately known in athletic circles, was born in Salisbury, Vt., January 17, 1837. In his youth he acquired fame for his skill as an athlete and his wonderful feats of muscular strength. In 1868 he made a lift in harness of 3239 pounds, a record which has never been surpassed with possible exception of J. W. Kennedy's lift of 3242 pounds at Lynn in 1892. In 1868 Mr. Curtis founded the New York Athletic Club and in 1878 the Fresh Air Club. He was an active competitor in athletics until 1882 winning in almost every form of competition. He established records at 60 and 100 yards running, throwing hammer and 56 pounds weight, tug-of-war, rowing in single sculls and double and four oars, lifting heavy weight and putting up dumb bells. He also won 200 yards and quarter mile runs, 100 yard hurdle, mile walk, jumping, swimming, skating and all round gymnastic contests. He was an editorial writer of Spirit of the Times, refereed the N.Y. athletic club games from the foundation of the club, was referee of the games of the Interscholastic Association for 25 years and of the Harvard-Yale games for 15 years. His lowest weight when in training for rowing was 163 pounds, and his heaviest in training for gymnastics 184 pounds. He was so thoroughly inured to cold that even in midwinter he never wore an overcoat. This habit explains the light costume which he wore up the mountain.

One fact which every one concedes is that Ormsbee would have stood by his companion to the last and never would have left him unless to summon help.

Among the Appalachians who have studied the case this week there seem to be three leading theories.

1. That Curtis staid behind exhausted in the shelter while Ormsbee pushed on for help, leaving the camera to mark the place, Curtis afterwards trying to pursue his way and perishing in the attempt.

2. That they both rested in the shelter and set out together, but were forced apart in the furious storm and unable to find one another in the dense cloud.

3. That they were together until Curtis fell, after which Ormsbee started for help.

Those who advocate the first theory are divided as to whether Curtis followed Ormsbee on Saturday night or Sunday morning. Against the Saturday night theory it is urged that he would be more likely to stay over night in comparative shelter than to set out in darkness, which must have come on soon after Ormsbee left. Against the Sunday theory it is argued that he possibly could not have lived through the night, and if he had, why was the bread left uneaten? As to the theory of their both leaving the shelter together, it is asked why did they leave their cameras behind?

There seems no doubt that Ormsbee died Saturday night. His friends

Prof. Parker and Mr. Ilgen agree that with his great strength nothing less than the frightful storm of that night could have overcome him, and that had he survived till Sunday he could easily have reached the top.

An Appalachian who studied the situation carefully says, "They were fast walkers and probably came up through the woods at a high rate. On getting to the ridge and finding the storm they probably hurried and could of course, get no refuge until they had walked four miles along the range and reached the place where they prepared the shelter in the scrub. By this long pull the elder man probably became exhausted. Having been here before, he knew this was all the shelter he would get until the Summit was reached. He therefore remained, and the younger man left, probably about 4:30, when it was still daylight. He would have reached the base of the cone about 5:30, before the lee had formed so far down this mountain; otherwise he could not have climbed so high as he did. He pushed off up the cone, and the higher he went and the later it got the colder it grew. I think he reached the place where he was found between seven and eight, by which time the ice had formed enough to prevent his climbing any higher. The surprise to me is that they did not appreciate the seriousness of this situation sufficiently to have taken a leaf from their notebook and left it in the bottle. I do not believe Ormsbee had any doubt but what he could make the Summit. "Only two miles more and only this rain to hinder—I can do it; what of it?" But as he went higher it became icy, which he could not have foreseen. As we came up the railroad that same night the first snow was seen near Jacob's Ladder, and the ice did not appear till we were near the Summit. So Ormsbee would have been on the cone before he met any snow, and I have no doubt he felt all the confidence that a powerful man would. Once on the cone there was nothing to do but keep going, and he made a gallant fight. It must have been early in the evening, for I do not believe a man of his experience would have left the shelter after dark.

The story was printed Wednesday in a Boston paper that Ormsbee's leg was broken and that when he was found it had been bound up, apparently by himself, with a branch of a tree. Although nothing of the kind was noticed by the persons who examined the bodies at the Summit, Dr. Gove and the undertakers were asked about it. Dr. Gove replied that neither leg was broken, and Wells & Brigham, the undertakers, telegraphed, in reply to a telegram from this office, "It was not bound in any way; was not broken."

On Thursday afternoon the Appalachians who visited Mount Pleasant found in the book in the Club's record cylinder this entry, doubtless the last written message from the two victims of the storm:

June 30, 1900
Wm. B. Curtis, A.M.C.
Allan Ormsbee.
Rain-Clouds And Wind 60 Miles.
Cold.

Unfortunately the writer did not think to write the hour of making the entry.

The time of their arrival on Mount Pleasant is pretty well fixed, however, by two woodsmen in the employ of Mr. Merrill of the Crawford House, who were at work on the bridle path on that day, who say that a little after 2 p.m. they heard men on Mount Pleasant, the wind being in the direction to bring their voices where they were. They called in reply but got nothing which they considered a response.

It has also been learned that the two guides who went up with Rev. Mr. Nichols to the foot of the cone met Curtis and Ormsbee on the path and advised them very strongly not to go up, telling them how bad the weather was.

Thursday morning another link was added to the chain of circumstances by the finding of Mr. Ormsbee's glasses by Mr. T. O. Fuller of the Club.

"I was examining the place where Ormsbee was found," said Mr. Fuller. "Just where his head had pitched forward there was a hole which ran down probably two feet, and just at the point where I was told that his head lay I saw something that looked like gold wire. Reaching down and pulling it out I found it to be a fine pair of gold-bowed glasses. They are double concave glasses, so powerful as to indicate that he was very near-sighted.

"I also made barometrical measurements and found that Ormsbee reached a point within 130 feet in altitude of the platform of the hotel.

"Several of us have been today to the place where Curtis was found," added Mr. Fuller. "We are satisfied from what we saw of the place on our first examination, confirmed by our observation today, that the few stones on which Curtis's head lay had been newly placed there, so that his head might lie in an easier position. The ground where his body lay had been scooped out to make a little hollow. There is no doubt in my mind that they came to the shelter and rested a while and they must have proceeded together from the shelter until they got by the Lakes of the Clouds, where it is extremely windy, and that Curtis stubbed his toe on a rock that would weigh 100 pounds which lay in the path, and fell. I have no doubt Ormsbee laid him where he was found, placing him there as carefully as he could, and then pushing on for help. Although Ormsbee had never been here before he came straight for the top, and the point where he fell was in an exact line between the Lakes of the Clouds and the top of the mountain."

It should be added that Messrs. Weed and Coffin, who examined the body of Mr. Curtis immediately after Mr. Cutter found it, are equally positive that he lay face down where he fell, and never stirred from the spot, the bruise on the forehead resting directly on a point of the rock. They are therefore confident that Ormsbee was not with him when he fell.

It is doubtful if any more light can ever be thrown on the fate of Messrs. Curtis and Ormsbee.

For many years to come the true explanation of the undisclosed facts in the case will be sought with melancholy interest by those familiar with it, and no theory which will be advanced will ever be wholly satisfactory to every one. There remains but the indisputable fact of the brave struggle of two knightly souls, the one, who had in many years of activity done a good work for his fellow man by encouraging their physical development and helping to maintain a high standard of honor and manliness in a friendly rivalry; the other, an equally fine specimen of manhood, to whose sorrowing relatives it must always be a source of comfort to feel that he perished in a heroic effort to save his friend.

June 1905

A Winter Ascent
through the Great Gulf

George N. Whipple

From *Appalachia*

Established in 1876, shortly after the founding of the Boston-based Appalachian Mountain Club, Appalachia *became the official journal of the AMC. Entomologist Samuel H. Scudder, AMC's first vice president and second club president, conceived the idea of publishing the journal. For the most part,* Appalachia *has been published twice a year for the past 123 years. Its early issues are particularly helpful to White Mountain historians as they often contained accounts of early ascents of some of the region's less visited peaks.*

WHILE NOT wishing to exalt unduly the Alpine opportunities of our humble Appalachian system, it is believed that the usual route in the Swiss Alps includes few slopes, where step-cutting is required, of equal height and steepness with that of the Great Gulf on the northerly side of Mt. Washington.

The cone of the Wetterhorn, a snow slope of exceeding steepness, rises from six hundred to seven hundred feet above its base. The Weisshorn, much more strenuous, calls for continuous step-cutting of no greater amount. In his ascent of Les Ecrins in 1864, Whymper encountered a steep slope seven hundred or eight hundred feet high which cost his party six hours' work, and his remarkable descent from the Col Dolent in 1865 occupied seven hours; of it he says: "For the first and only time in my life I looked down a slope more than a thousand feet long, set at an angle of about 50°, which was a sheet of ice from top to bottom." When Leslie Stephen crossed the Eiger Joch in 1859, his party climbed an ice slope about one thousand feet in altitude and with an inclination of from 51° to 52°, which required seven hours of step-cutting,—a feat which Mr. Stephen deemed well worthy of record. The rim of the headwall of the Great Gulf cannot be far from fourteen hundred feet above its base and half a mile or more distant from it, and a party of three spent seven and a half hours in the invigorating exercise of step-cutting up its icy surface on the 27th of January, 1905.

Comparisons aside, it is beyond dispute that this head-wall in winter offers a capital climb to those who find enjoyment in that particular form of "what some people call pleasure," and there surely must be something in a place that costs an hour's time more than is required for the ascent of the Matterhorn, even for a party as slow and inexperienced as we were.

I had had my eye on this particular expedition since the February of 1903, when six of us had made a very sporting ascent of the head-wall of Huntington's Ravine; and therefore it was with peculiar satisfaction that I found myself starting upon it during our stay at the Mt. Madison House in Gorham. This statement needs qualification. I know of nothing more discouraging to complacency, or more likely to sour, for the time being, a naturally sweet nature, than to turn out of a comfortable bed some hours before dawn on a cold winter morning, to indue an exaggerated amount of clothing, to begin a so-called breakfast about the time when the sleigh is announced, to hastily cram a few last necessities into an already over-filled rucksack (wondering at the time how many have been forgotten), to snatch an ice-axe and sally forth upon a quest sure to result in a plethora of toil, and sure of nothing else. Truly, as the psalmist says, we are fearfully and wonderfully made.

The hour was six, the air was cold; a dissipated, gibbous moon was ploughing through a field of watery-looking clouds in the west, and the aspect of Nature did not stimulate hope. What Harlan Perkins and Warren Hart were revolving I know not, for we were morose and uncommunicative; but the third member of the trio marvelled, as he had before on like occasions, at his unaccountable infatuation, and felt capable of sympathizing with a candidate for a first-class asylum for feeble-minded youth. This lasted perhaps an hour, when a magical touch transmuted all. A turn of the road brought us in sight of Madison, then of Adams, and then of Washington, and we all sat up and wondered. The "rose of dawn" flushed their pure snows with radiance ineffable. They soared like mountains of dream in the blue heaven, wondrous in color and in form, and of texture delicate and evanescent. They seemed like clouds that the wind would blow away, as fleeting as thistledown that a breath might scatter. Our spirits revived, our self-respect returned, and we fell to discussing our most sane and delightful trip.

Our plan was to enter the Gulf by way of the West branch of the Peabody; and at 7.45 we slid down the steep bank at the junction of that branch with the main stream, which flows from Huntington's Ravine, and were fairly embarked. This junction is about half a mile north of the Glen cottage.

We found fulfilled the promise of the tickets on which we had traveled to Gorham, — "Good going Jan. 21st to 27th." The going was good. We were able to keep in the bed of the stream, or rather on its counterpane, practically all the way, avoiding all brush and scrub. Hart, possessing a superior knowledge of the route and an ambitious nature, led the procession, and the only incidents which diversified this part of the trip were his occasional partial disappearances. Without the slightest warning he would suddenly subside, sometimes as far as his waist, sometimes as far as his shoulders, carrying down with him a large segment of the roof of the stream. The first time this happened Perkins and I rushed to his assistance in considerable alarm, as it is no joke to get one's feet wet under such circumstances, but were met with such imperturbability and *sang froid* that the subsequent proceedings interested us no more. His feet entirely fast in the mass of debris rapidly being converted into slush, he would survey the landscape in a meditative manner, hazard the prediction that the water must be at least four inches deep, extricate his snowshoes by the aid of a remarkable mountaineering implement in the shape of a long-handled boat-hook which he affected, and clamber out to repeat the process farther on.

Our course upstream led us a little north of west for three or four miles, and then, north of the spur of Washington which starts from above the Halfway House, bent round to the southwest for another three or four miles to Spaulding's Lake. The first part of the way we were opening up views of the Carter and Carter-Moriah range behind us, while later, first ahead and then behind us, Madison and Adams played the drama of "Box and Cox." The grade was very easy for most of the way until we struck the waterfalls a mile or so below Spaulding's Lake, and there were no difficulties whatever on the entire route. We halted for a second breakfast about eleven, and reached Spaulding's Lake at 12.45. The weather had not improved. Light snow began to fall soon after our second breakfast, and as we cowered under a ledge on the shore of the lake to partake of luncheon, a fierce squall swooped down, blotting out all but our immediate surroundings. It seemed very cold, though the glass showed only 14°. We would have parted with the chances of our success for a small sum at that time; but the squall passed, the scenery, such as it was, came back, and we decided to have a try at the thing anyway.

At 1.30 we got under way, and in a few moments found it wise to exchange snowshoes for creepers. Only a few feet of the thick growth above

GUY SHOREY

Winter trampers take a breather outside AMC's Madison Spring Hut
in the Northern Presidentials.

the lake, that is such an obstacle to progress in the summer, projected above
the snow, but the cliffs of Clay and of the head-wall were thinly coated and
looked very forbidding. From the lake the dim disk of the sun had been seen
for a few moments over the neck of Clay, and when we reached the cluster
of boulders, which form in summer such a generous cave, we had a most inspiring burst of sunshine; but it was the last effort on the part of that lumi-
nary, who was forced out of business by his more active rival the snow squall.
A sort of shelf had been formed in the snow by the action of the wind just
at the base of these boulders, and we took this last opportunity to sit down
and gather strength for the fray. The view from this point, raking as it does
the Northern Peaks, extending into the wooded depths of the Gulf, and
bounded by the blue mountains of the horizon, is superb and well repays the
effort required to gain it.

A detailed narrative of the succeeding hours would be monotonous and
unprofitable. Chop, chop, chop. Chop, chop, chop. The bits of ice and crust
went hissing down the slope; the snow squalls descended and enveloped us;
the dark rim of the wall above us certainly seemed no nearer than an hour
ago. How slowly we moved! How slowly the time went by!

It may be said that not so much of it would have gone by had our creeper equipment been equal for all, but unfortunately one of us was poorly provided in that particular, and the speed of the party became the speed of the slowest member, for it was necessary to keep together. On this account practically every step had to be cut. There were stretches where with good creepers and good nerve one might have walked without step-cutting, but the one who, wearying of that exercise, essayed to do it, essayed it but once. For a while he made great progress, an object of wonder and admiration to his fellows, and then like Lucifer he fell. And yet not like Lucifer, for after a slide of what seemed to him like a hundred feet and was actually much less, he was able to bring himself up with the aid of his axe, and held the mountain in a most tight and loving embrace for fifteen minutes before evincing any desire to proceed.

Step-cutting was resumed for all, and we took turns at it. The labor was severe, for the crust had nothing beneath it but crust, and was very hard. From eight to twenty strokes were required to fashion a step, the smaller number on the lower and the larger on the upper part of the wall. The inclination was probably 40° a considerable part of the way. Toward the top, where real ice was encountered, the Architect said 60°. It became too dark to see the steps. We had to feel for them with our axes and drag ourselves up into them with the utmost care. The top of the wall had long ago disappeared. We began to doubt its existence. The higher we got the steeper it grew, and the particles of ice seemed to hiss more loudly as they tobogganed down. Our situation began to resemble that of Leslie Stephen's party on the climb to the Eiger Joch. He says: "The ice was very hard, and it was necessary, as Lauener observed, to cut steps in it as big as soup-tureens, for the result of a slip would in all probability have been that the rest of our lives would have been spent in sliding down a snow slope, and that that employment would not have lasted long enough to become at all monotonous."

As this is not a novel by the ingenious philosopher, Henry James, there will be no description of our thoughts on this occasion. Had we been so fortunate as to be characters of his, we might have reflected on the Evil Spirit that drags men from fairly comfortable homes to climb mountains in winter; we might have tried to reproduce the phraseology of our maternal parents could they have seen us; we might have asked ourselves just what particular business we had in that particular spot; we might have made mental photographs of just what we would not do when we got out if it. Being ourselves and thoroughly delighted with what we were doing, no such thoughts escaped our lips. On the infrequent occasions when we did use our valuable breath for words, the latter were jocular and congratulatory. Our humorous instincts came out strongly. At this distance I fail to recall any of the jokes; but I know that they were received with appreciation, and think that they were probably better than many that are printed.

At last we pulled ourselves over the rim of the wall and struck a match. It was nine p.m. What might have been called in Boston a blizzard—but on Mt. Washington was merely a zephyr—was in progress, and the air was thick with snow. We decided to make for the summit and spend the night as best we might in that abode of luxury, the stage-office. And here a curious thing happened. Hart omitted mention of it in his "Globe" article because he thought it would not be believed. We had located the railroad without difficulty, and started along the line of telegraph posts on its eastern side. We could just make out the post ahead of us as we moved from one to another; but we were actually for some time in doubt as to whether we were going up hill or down. We stopped and experimented and talked it over, and finally decided that we must be going up hill, whether it seemed so or not. The outcome proved that we were, for in fifteen or twenty minutes we reached the top and the shelter of the stage-office. Soon we had a fire going, which quickly raised the temperature from 10° to 30°. We melted some snow and had a delicious drink of hot chocolate, and ate a portion of the small amount of food remaining. We then brought in the old slat bedstead, with its delightfully cool straw mattress, from the adjoining room, placed it with its foot to the stove, and addressed ourselves to undressing for the night. This function was brief, and stopped with the removal of our creepers. Under most circumstances we prefer a bed to ourselves, but for this night only, no one objected to having two bedfellows. We wrapped the drapery of our couch about us (consisting of a charming piece of second-hand carpet which some one had thoughtfully stored in the building), and lay down to pleasant dreams. At least it sounds well to say so. We not only slept but over-slept, for we had planned to start down at three, and we did not wake until four. The fire had been replenished during the night by one of the party whose modesty forbids my naming him (it was not myself) and was still alive, and the thermometer still stood at 30°.

Breakfast was even more sketchy than the preceding meal had been, for the commissary department had gone to pieces. We always begin with fruit; and in spite of our limited menu we were able to maintain this habit. An apple frozen in its passage up the mountain as hard as a stone had been placed on the shelf behind the stove the night before, and was found in a delicious state of pulpiness. A few mouthfuls apiece were quite sufficient. For a second course I think we had half a sandwich, not quite as juicy as the fruit, but very good. At 4.45 we emerged into the cold world, finding the weather much as we had left it. It was dark and it was thick, and for the first half mile of the Carriage Road we had to move slowly and with extreme caution, to avoid losing our way. Once, however, round the bend at the point where the road comes nearest to the Great Gulf, we found ourselves, as Parker would say, "on Easy Street," and trotted merrily down to the Glen, which we reached at 8.15, and refreshed ourselves with hot milk and crackers. It was a good ending to a great trip.

This narrative has but one moral. If you wish to climb Mt. Washington in winter from the Great Gulf, be sure of the commissary department, and do not shrink from an early start.

August 2, 1902

The Mount
Washington Hotel

From *The White Mountain Echo and Tourists' Register*

FOR WEEKS before the opening of the mountain season to the present time when the White Hills are filled with guests from all the corners of the earth, the principal topic under discussion in office and parlor, at table and on the verandas of each and every hotel and cottage has been the opening of the Mount Washington, which the enterprise, love of his native state and the unlimited means of Mr. Joseph Stickney of New York, combined, have made a realization.

A little more than a year's time has passed since work was first begun on the great structure that is to carry off the palm of resort hotels in America, and a curious coincidence connected with its opening on Monday is the fact that on fifty years ago the same day the Summit House on Mount Washington was opened, which was the beginning of a new and prosperous era for the White Mountains of New Hampshire.

From the site of the Mount Washington, on a glacial moraine a third of a mile east of the Mount Pleasant House, is a wonderfully near and compelling view of the Presidential Range, and of the Crawford Notch as well, a combination that gives the Mount Washington precedence over any other hotel in the mountains so far as such a view combination is concerned.

The hotel itself, four stories in height with a frontage of 460 feet and overtopped by great towers, has accommodations that will please the most exacting and be as luxurious as possible in a hotel of this sort.

Very little change was made in the original plans of the architect, with which most people interested are already familiar, and the great work has been successfully and expeditiously carried on by hundreds of workmen under a corps of contractors of wonderful executive ability, as the fact that the hotel is now open so short a time after its commencement testifies.

The coming guest is driven up from the railway station and alights under the great porte cochere and enters the rotunda, which is beautifully decorated, and contains among other interesting features, an enormous fire-place, built entirely from stone selected on the grounds of the hotel. The number of colorings and variety in the stones furnishes an interesting half hour's study for the geologist, while others cannot but stop to admire its beauty.

Passing a number of small parlors and card rooms, one enters the ball room but will pause at the door spell bound for the moment at the beautiful sight of this, the largest ball-room in the country with its cream and crimson color scheme, electric lights half concealed by the cornice, the long galleries, separated by pillars from the main ball-room, thus giving the spectators an opportunity to watch the dance go on without feeling in the way or being subjected to the draught from the large ventilating windows at the top. The stage at the extreme end of the music-room is another feature, and back of it is a great landscape window, which gives opportunity to admire the hills at the same time, with the Crawford Notch in the distance and a bit of pastoral scenery in the foreground.

Behind the office is the great circular sun parlor, from which the finest view of the Presidential Range is obtainable. The wide veranda skirting the house affords a delightful opportunity for a promenade, and a new view greets the eye at every turn.

The large dining-room with its great landscape windows and galleries above, is a beautiful room and not the least pleasant feature in connection with it is the fact that it is quite cut off from the kitchen by a passageway with swinging doors that open and shut automatically, making the entrance and exit of waiters easy and keeping the odors from the kitchen entirely away.

The grand Mount Washington Hotel.

It would take much time and space to enter into every detail of the admirable arrangement of the kitchen, serving and store rooms, but suffice it to say that the facilities for the storage of food and for preparing it as well, are of the most modern character, and that the ventilation could not be improved. There are eleven cold storage closets, a great dish-washing machine, mammoth ranges large enough for a house twice the size of this, and in short, every up-to-date appliance that experience and ingenuity could suggest. The crockery, made to order for the hotel from a special design, is green and white, with a handsome monogram.

A unique feature is the fern garden, which, on the ground floor, is reached from the banquet and dining-halls; also from the ladies' cafe and billiard rooms, as it is situated in an angle between the two wings. An electric fountain will play in the evening, in the midst of a wealth of ferns and green foliage.

The spacious offices and accommodations for transacting the business of the house are worthy of a special mention.

It is in the basement, however, that the most novel features of the house are found, and the swimming pool, 20×65 feet, ranging in depth from four and one-half to seven and one-half feet, tiled in white, and the temperature raised by the introduction of a steam-pipe running about the bottom of the tank and guarded by a brass rail, will be, perhaps, as popular as any.

Then there are spacious play-rooms for the children, bowling alleys with deadened walls, men's cafe and grill-room, barber shop, porters' and baggage-rooms, photographer's room, and rooms for Turkish baths and masseur.

In the sleeping-rooms the exquisite taste that characterizes the furnishing of the hotel is carried out in the furniture, carpets and wallpaper, the latter artistic in design and dainty in coloring, with a large variety in the treatment. Blondes may have their blue, while the brunette will find a charming background in those hung with red, and there are combinations legion in the suites. Best of all are the great closets with plenty of hooks, room for the largest Saratogas and clothes poles for milord's wearing apparel. The baths are beautiful, with porcelain tubs and Tennessee marble bowls and glistening nickel-plated fittings. The furniture is very artistic, and the beds are about equally divided between brass and wood. Nearly every room has a mountain view and some of the suites have views on three sides. The doors are of mahogany and the woodwork of white enamel fireproof finish. Nearly every room has connecting bath, and the suites in the central tower will compare in size and elegance of appointment with those of any hotel in the world.

ROBERT KOZLOW

The Mount Washington Hotel and the Presidential Range
as seen from Bretton Woods.

Between the central and western towers is the roof garden, where a most beautiful promenade may be enjoyed, and a panoramic view of the surrounding country be had from this lofty height.

In short, no feature that could be thought of has been omitted, and the Mount Washington will not only be the pride of the mountains but of all New England as well.

Mr. John Anderson has transferred his quarters to the new hotel, but Mr. Price will continue to reside at the Mount Pleasant, where he will be on hand to welcome the coming and speed the parting guest.

The heads of departments and officials will be as follows: Superintendent, Mr. G. Butler Smith; room clerk, W. S. Kenney; front clerk, James Goodrich; night clerk, C. D. Abbott; cashier, Henry L. E. Smith; secretary to Mr. Anderson, Miss Sawyer; chef, Louis Valet; steward, H. W. Chesley; head waiter, Andrew Fitzgerald; second head waiter, Karl Brackett; head bellman, Harry Annen; general stenographer, Miss Dean.

Much work still remains to be done in the perfecting of the grounds, but under the direction of the efficient landscape architect it is progressing very satisfactorily, and the results already attained are eminently pleasing, while pointing to a splendid effect when finished, as the natural beauty of the place will be preserved by the leaving of the large boulders and the planting of trees upon the hill.

A word should be given to the water supply, which, taken from a point several miles from the house toward the base of Mount Pleasant gives a fire protection unequaled in this section. A recent test was made of the hydrant streams, which were thrown higher than the roof by gravity pressure, without the use of the fire pump. The supply throws fourteen one-and-one-half inch streams to this height. The direct pressure from the reservoir is 135 pounds to the square inch.

On Monday noon, with the boom of artillery and the flaunting of flags, the doors of the Mount Washington Hotel, the youngest and the comliest of the White Mountain hotel family, were swung wide for the waiting guests and the fruition of two years of constant structural labor in the heart of the Bretton Woods was accomplished.

To the credit of the builders and the management the opening occurred exactly as scheduled—on date, July 28.

Among the first to enter the new house were Mr. Joseph Stickney, whose enterprise and capital have made possible the erection of the finest and largest summer resort hotel in the United States; Mr. John Anderson and Mr. J. D. Price, managers for Mr. Stickney of the Mount Washington and the Mount Pleasant hotels. The first to register was Mr. Clarence W. Seamans, of Wyckoff, Seamans & Benedict, of New York, an old patron of the Mount Pleasant House.

Through the afternoon, the porte cochere was the mecca for hundreds of carriages, brakes and coaches, coming from far and near. At dinner, the handsome semi-circular apartment was filled, fully 250 sitting down to the evening meal. On an adjoining banquet hall, the host was Mr. Stickney himself, who spread a feast fit for the gods and called on all his faithful servants in high places to receive his congratulations. These gentlemen, whose energy and fidelity had made possible the opening of the hotel on schedule were the guests:

Charles Ailing Gifford, William Paul Gerhard, Charles E. Knox, William G. Phillips, B. F. Robinson, E. A. Richardson, Anson S. Rice, Mr. Locke, Ray T. Gile of the construction staff; C. H. Merrill, O. G. Barron, Governor Chester B. Jordan, John Anderson, J. D. Price, G. Butler Smith, L. H. Bingham, Dr. J. Blake White, George E. Cummings, James J. Parks, George Lane and William G. Hannah.

In the evening, the magnificent ball room was the fitting setting for 300 of the gorgeously gowned, who came to an informal hop. Preceding the dancing, there was a brief concert, at which Mrs. Jenny-Corea-Bunn sang

A postcard view of the interior of the Mount Washington Hotel.

an appropriate selection composed for the occasion, and Prof. J. Rayner Edmands of Harvard read a dedicatory poem of his own writing. The Virginia reel of sixteen couples, led by Mr. Stickney and Miss Amy Phillips was a merry finale to the day's jubilee.

Mr. Stickney has reared a monument which has not only perpetuated his name for many years to come in the White Mountains, but he has established an enterprise in the hotel line that will be of the greatest benefit to the mountains and to New Hampshire and her citizens as well, and which will go a step farther toward perpetuating the grand old name of the builder of our Nation—"The Father of His Country."

Circa 1915

The Grand Resort

From *A Year-Book of Bretton Woods*

TEN YEARS and more have passed since the far-sighted promoter of Bretton Woods, the lamented Joseph Stickney, of New York, but a native of Concord, N.H., saw that greater things must be done for the traveler in these mountains than had ever been dreamed of, and he built the great hotel, the Mount Washington, that stands as a monument to his enterprise and to his love of his native state. But it was in 1895 that Bretton Woods showed the first reports of progress ever since annually filed and summarized in the creation and perfection of the largest and most modern resort in White Mountain territory. Upon an estate of more than ten thousand acres in the very heart of the mountains, and accessible from all directions by trunk line routes, the Mount Pleasant House was first to meet modern requirements. The Mount Washington was then built to complete a system for the entertainment of a very large and fastidious patronage, and in the Bretton Woods combination every attraction has been supplied, either by Nature or the enterprise of broad-minded men, experienced in the science of resort entertainment.

Fast and luxurious through train service links Bretton Woods direct with New York, Philadelphia, and other great cities to the south; Boston and Portland to the east, and Quebec and Montreal to the north, while prominence upon the "Ideal Tour" route makes the point the Mecca for automobilists in all quarters. Beyond these advantages of location and accessibility, a managing connection with great winter resorts of the far south has ensured an entertaining conduct here invariably at the highest standards and planned to meet the most exacting and critical demands.

The Mount Pleasant is strictly modern, with accommodations for three hundred guests, and is the first to open in the early season and the last to

186

close, ensuring for the resort and its patronage a much longer season than is the rule in mountain locations. The clear, crisp freshness of June, no less than the wondrous color-show periods of October, are in more senses than one Mount Pleasant days, lost to the frequenters of other resort hotels of great size.

The Mount Washington is the newest, largest, and finest hotel in the mountains, with accommodations for five hundred guests, an elevation of nearly seventeen hundred feet above sea level, and a location in superb command of the grandest of New England's mountain scenery. A half-mile distant from its companion house, the privileges of both are interchangeable and identical, and together they provide all that intelligent care can supply of comfort and diversion for a family of eight hundred.

To the majority of visitors mountain interests are of first importance, and the Bretton Woods location is convenient to every point of attraction between the "Old Man" of Franconia Notch, south, to Dixville Notch, north. The ascent of Mount Washington by cog railway and an observation car trip through Crawford Notch are but two of the show points easily reached by rail, and the list of interesting walking and driving trips is legion. Through all the years of Bretton Woods operation the management has had prominent part in whatever might be termed public mountain improvement. By

The Mount Pleasant House (shown above) and the neighboring
Mount Washington Hotel drew thousands of tourists to Bretton Woods
each summer for more than 30 years.

operation with state authority, the Appalachian Club, other enterprising resorts, and public-spirited individuals, much has been done in the building
of new roads and the improvement of old ones, the laying out and repair of
mountain paths, and the encouragement of forest preservation and protection. Wherever within the Bretton Woods preserve a hidden beauty spot of
wood or mountain is discovered, it is developed and its possibilities brought
to common knowledge, and there is each year a never-ending list of path
making, bridge building, and what may be termed nature work for the pleasure of all comers.

Bretton Woods managers took early and prominent place among the
active promoters of automobile touring in White Mountain country, and
co-operated effectively in the spectacular endurance tests up Mount Washington and the earliest long-distance road tests, which on both counts supplied to public interests everywhere proof of unusual auto values, while
drawing to this mountain center patronage which has revolutionized resort
practice. Similarly, the plan and inception of the "Ideal Tour," an approved
route which has mapped and advertised thousands of miles of country for
the same classes of tourists, was a Bretton Woods creation, and it has naturally followed that both houses of the resort have become the official hotels of the most prominent automobile touring clubs, with a finely equipped
garage and established automobile livery equal to all demands.

New ideas as to auto locomotion have, however, made no serious inroads
upon the old and very general preference for the drive and ride. Here was
held the first automobile school for horses, and all stable animals are thoroughly familiarized with machines under the most trying conditions. The
stable service is kept up to the highest mark of safety, efficiency, and correct
style, and the driving department is no more important than the string of
saddlers brought up each season in the exclusive charge of a veteran and experienced riding-master. Records from year to year show that riding and
driving are among the chief pleasures of the season, while walks and paths
leading to favorite mountain springs and hidden bits of sylvan beauty vari-
ously invite others according to their physical strength and desire for quiet
and solitude.

Golf approaches its ideal estate more closely at Bretton Woods than at
any other of the mountain resorts east or west, and the course is equaled by
very few in America. There is full distance and ample variety of fair green
throughout the eighteen holes, and the putting greens are so nearly perfect
that age alone can better them. All the best known golfers of the world who
have played this course have given it their unqualified approval, and while
the sight of a hundred golfers with their caddies scattered over the links is

The flags fly high atop the roof of the Mount Washington Hotel.

no unusual pleasant day picture, the layout of the course is along such liberal lines as to entirely avoid crowding. Circled by the grandest mountain peaks of America, even this royal and ancient game could hardly be more appropriately staged for the pleasure of its devotees. Moreover, it seems to have been left for Bretton Woods management to solve the vexing problem of satisfactory caddie service in a manner which is at once to the advantage of the guests and to a lively lot of city boys. Through co-operation with the South-End House, a social settlement in Boston, about fifty boys, ranging from ten to fourteen years in age, are chosen on the basis of their records in school and settlement club work. They are picked boys, physically fit for the work, who fully appreciate and work hard for their country summer privilege, and who come up from Boston in the care of responsible leaders and caretakers, to be comfortably quartered at The Bretton Woods Inn. They are divided into the Mount Pleasant and Mount Washington camps, and in their own athletic sports—base ball, swimming, boating, track meets, golf, etc.—the rivalry is always keen, and a part of the summer pleasure of many guests. The basis of the arrangement is purely a business one; there is no charity or philanthropy about it. On the one side, the Bretton Woods management pays fare one way and provides a clean and comfortable home place with plenty of good food, and grants to the boys many privileges under the supervision of their own directors. On the other side, the boys buy their own uniforms and equipment, pay a low rate of board, and render caddy service very much better than the average, retaining all their earnings. And for three seasons the plan has worked out perfectly. Many of the guests have found these boys most interesting, and, while golfers have enjoyed perhaps the best caddy service to be found anywhere, the boys have gone back to their city tenement homes, brown and strong after a clean country summer, each with a tidy sum ahead of his expenses. The splendid and sensible discipline under which these boys work and play is, of course, the secret of the plan's success, and as results can hardly be improved on, it will be continued from season to season indefinitely.

Other sports of the green are similarly well staged at Bretton Woods. Base ball is an unfailing attraction always and everywhere, and the beautiful grass diamond located midway between the two hotels is hotly contested ground for teams representing both houses, or visiting teams coming to play in inter-resort matches, where "the honor of the house" is safe to be well defended before large and enthusiastic gatherings. On the Bowling Green, too, that perfect bit of turf which suggests the older world, the quaint old game, lawn bowls of "Merrie England," is well provided for those who love a quieter diversion or whose habit of exercise follows a more deliberate line. Tennis courts, kept up to the highest mark of condition at both houses, are ever in active use, and are training courts for notable tournaments, engaging the best tennis skills, whether in either of the Bretton Woods hotels or in other resorts. And trap shooting, croquet courts, children's playgrounds and swings—each of these minor items of incentive to exercise, sports and pleasure, should be added to the list, since all are sharers in the preferences of a summer's visitors.

Indoors, at both hotels there is recognition of the fact that not all mountain days are sunny days, and that the after-dinner hours are important. The Grand Orchestra of Bretton Woods, divided for the routine musical service of each hotel, comes together alternately at the Mount Pleasant and Mount Washington, and the full instrumentation of twenty-three pieces, augmented by well-trained vocalists, is inspiring to a degree in expression of the world's greatest music. The Swimming Pool at the larger hotel is a point of popular resort, and the daily plunge under the acre of responsible teachers and attendants brings in its train water polo and aquatic sports for the entertainment of larger audiences. Squash courts, bowling alleys, billiards, pool, shuffleboard—all have their adherents; there is a private market wire for those who can't help it; drug store, house physician, store, curio booth, news stand, no detail having been ignored at either house which might make for the convenience or interest of guests.

1904

The Ascent by Rail

Frank H. Burt

From *Mount Washington: A Handbook for Travellers*

Arriving by the early trains from every part of the mountain region, visitors bound for Mount Washington on a single's day trip find themselves at Fabyan's, seven miles from the base of Mount Washington, about 9 a.m. The Union Station of the Boston & Maine and Maine Central Railroads is a general railroad centre for the mountain district, and the early morning finds express trains coming and going in rapid succession. Passengers going up for the night usually plan to reach Fabyan's by one of the express trains arriving in the afternoon from Boston, Montreal, Quebec, or Burlington. The trip between Fabyan's and the Summit occupies one hour and fifty minutes.

The Fabyan House, near which the Fabyan station is situated, is within a few rods of the spot where stood the first White Mountain hotel, opened in 1803; and the site has been occupied by hotels during the greater part of the century that has passed.

The train which runs between Fabyan's and the Base Station is made up of observation cars, and is backed up grade by its powerful locomotive, so that the passengers have uninterrupted views of the great range, yet have no annoyance from cinders or dust. The ascent from Fabyan's to the Base is 1,200 feet, the maximum grade being 316 feet per mile. This, it should be remembered, is an ordinary surface road; but a single engine easily pushes three loaded cars up this unusually heavy incline.

"Train for Mount Washington!" is the announcement to which the waiting passengers at Fabyan's eagerly respond as the observation cars appear in front of the station. The seats are speedily filled, a photographer takes a quick view of the train and passengers, to be ready on their return, and the start is made. There is a stop at Bretton Woods, half a mile east of Fabyan's, to take passengers from the two hotels, the Mount Pleasant and the Mount Washington. Then the train turns to the left, passing Lake Carolyn, and moves toward Mount Washington, which now stands directly before us, supported by its brother peaks at left and right. The track of the Mount Washington Railway may be seen for two-thirds of its length from base to summit.

After a run of a few minutes through the forest the train slows down to give a view (to the left of the track) of the Falls of the Ammonoosuc. For a distance of several hundred feet the swiftly dashing stream has worn a gorge in the solid rock, leaving great basins and fantastic formations, over which the river pours in its headlong rush.

On our left are the high ridge of Mount Dartmouth and the smaller peak of Mitten Mountain, the latter separated from Mount Jefferson by the high pass known as Jefferson Notch.

A long stretch of straight track takes the train directly toward Mount Pleasant, whose graceful dome rises higher and higher as you approach it. A solitary highway crossing is noted on this portion of the route, where the track crosses the Jefferson Notch Road, built in 1901–02 by the State with the co-operation of the hotel proprietors and others interested in the mountain resorts, and extending from the Crawford House to Jefferson Highlands.

At the Base Station the trains of the Mount Washington Railway are awaiting the arrival of the passengers, who quickly change from the observation cars to the small closed cars of the cog railway. The Base is a lonely little settlement lying directly at the foot of Mount Washington, shut in at the north by a spur of Mount Clay and at the south by great parallel ridges coming down from Mounts Monroe, Franklin, and Pleasant.

There is a group of railway buildings, including carhouse, repair shops, boarding-house, etc., and a colony of perhaps fifty people whose presence is necessitated for the operation of the railway. The spot is about 2,700 feet above sea-level.

The trains for the Summit are made up of one car to an engine, the locomotive pushing the car before it and backing down the mountain ahead of it. The cars carry about forty passengers each, and as many trains are run at a trip as travel demands, starting at intervals of three or four minutes. The mountain locomotive is a curious little affair, with boiler tilted down so as to preserve an average level on steep grades. The earliest locomotives had upright boilers, a style which was abandoned after a few years' experience.

A few minutes' ride brings the train to a trestle bridge over the Ammo-

Two Cog Railway trains leave Marshfield Station
bound for the summit of Mount Washington.

noosuc, now diminished to a small mountain stream which dashes down a rocky bed. It was at this point that the building of the first section of the railway began, in 1866. The nearest railroad station was then at Littleton, twenty-five miles away; and every bit of material, including the locomotive and cars, had to be hauled through the woods by ox-teams. Indeed, up to 1876 the passengers for the mountain were brought to the Base by coach. The original railway buildings were clustered about a three-story, unpainted and unclapboarded "depot," with sleeping rooms above for the employees. On the hillside was a boarding-house, the Marshfield House, the place being known as "Marshfield," in honor of Sylvester Marsh, the projector of the road. The name was too pretentious for the spot, however, and the "Base" it always has been called and will doubtless remain.

In 1876 the road was extended down grade a third of a mile to meet the branch built that year from Fabyan's. The old buildings were burned in the spring of 1895.

Crossing the bridge and making a slight turn, we see a slope, nearly a mile long, up which the track ascends at a grade which from this point of view is startling. When near the brow of this pitch—known as Coldspring Hill—we are climbing nearly 1 foot in 3. Far above us the track is seen winding upward above the tree line, and we now begin to discern the varied surface of the upper portion of the range, which looks so smooth from below. Thus far the forest keeps us company, though the railway location is cleared some rods on either side of the track, giving a steadily widening view of rare beauty as we go upward. The spruces and firs of the adjacent forest are intermingled with birch and other hard woods.

Over the brow of Coldspring Hill is the "Waumbek Tank," where the first stop for water is made. A few minutes are allowed us to step out and enjoy the view. We look down into a vast valley, embracing the region of Fabyan's and Bretton Woods, the range which includes Mounts Deception, Dartmouth, and Mitten on the right, and the Rosebrook Range before us. Bethlehem, some twenty miles away, is seen in the west, and far beyond it, with steep sides and flattened top, the noble peak of Camel's Hump in the Green Mountains. Over the Rosebrook Range there rise in succession Mount Hale, the North and South Twins, and Lafayette. The peaks of Monroe, Franklin, and Pleasant are now our near neighbors on the south, and gain in impressiveness as we approach nearer to their level.

Once more in the car and moving upward, we soon see marked evidences of a change of climate. The trees are shorter and shorter, and many are hung with moss, such as is seen in tropical forests. "Half-way up," the conductor tells us, as we pass a trackmen's shelter by the side of the railroad. Now we are above the forest, save only for the scrub spruces; and we look to the left into Burt's Ravine, which lies between us and a spur of Mount Clay. There is a descent of perhaps 1,000 feet to the floor of this ravine, which was named in 1901 by the county commissioners of Coos County in honor of the late Henry M. Burt, the founder of the newspaper, *Among the Clouds*, printed at the summit.

Now the view unfolded toward the north-west embraces the village of Jefferson, prominent in which are the Waumbek Hotel and its surrounding cottages. Over Jefferson rises the long and conspicuous range comprising Mounts Starr King and Pliny, along whose base a straight highway stretches for several miles, guiding the eye from the Waumbek to the village of Jefferson Highlands, only a few miles from the foot of the Presidential Range.

In the broad valley between us and Jefferson glitters Cherry Pond, whose square-cut borders command the notice of every visitor. The valley of Israel's River extends westward to join that of the Connecticut at Lancaster, beyond which we look far into Vermont. Among the nearer mountains in the latter State we note two more sharp peaks of moderate height, but remarkable symmetry, about in line with Cherry Pond, — Mounts Burke and Umpire. Far beyond them is the striking serrated ridge of Jay Peak, near the Canada line. Turning more to the left we see over Mount Dartmouth the massive Cherry Mountain, and many miles beyond, along the horizon, grand old Mount Mansfield, Vermont's highest summit.

But we should leave the distant view and look at our immediate surroundings. The trees have given place to scrub. Now we pass a belt of dead trees, bleached to the semblance of bones by exposure to unnumbered winters. Rough rocks, overgrown with lichens, cover the larger part of the surface, interspersed with coarse grasses and sedges and alpine flowers.

A sudden angle in the track brings us upon Jacob's Ladder, the longest and highest trestle on the road, about 30 feet high, 300 feet long, and rising with a grade of 13½ inches per yard, equal to 1,980 feet per mile, or 37.41 per cent. No higher grade exists on any cog railway in the world save that up Pilatus.

Just at the foot of the Ladder you note the traces of a path, which has been in view for some minutes at our left, running parallel to the railroad, and which here crosses the track to mount a rocky crag at the right. Opened by Ethan Allen Crawford in 1820 or 1821, this was the second path up the mountain; and the name "Jacob's Ladder" was given to the ascent of the steep crag referred to thirty or forty years before the building of the railway. Made passable for horses by Horace Fabyan soon after 1840, it became known as the Fabyan Bridle Path.

Look quickly to the right as you cross the Ladder, and you see the beginning of the Ammonoosuc as it pours its rapid torrent down from the Lake of the Clouds. Monroe, Franklin, and Pleasant are about on a level with us.

For the next half mile the train toils steadily upward, still skirting the edge of Burt's Ravine, until it draws toward the ridge which joins Mount Washington to Mount Clay. All at once a sharp peak rises above this ridge. It is the apex of Mount Adams, the sharpest summit in this region. A moment later the lesser peak, known as Sam Adams, rises at its left; then, nearer, between Sam Adams and Clay, the symmetrical summit of Jefferson. Now, at the right of Adams, there rises a lower but more graceful mountain, Mount Madison, the fourth in height of the Presidential Range. Clay, Jefferson, Sam Adams, Adams, Madison, — this is the order in which

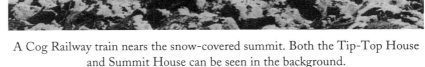

A Cog Railway train nears the snow-covered summit. Both the Tip-Top House
and Summit House can be seen in the background.

they stand as you go from Washington. Swinging to north and north-east,
this magnificent range is easily the grandest feature of the view.

Soon we look into the depths of the Great Gulf, which is hemmed in by
the encircling wall of the Presidential Range, and into which we see the
rocky precipice of Mount Clay descending nearly 2,000 feet. At the right of
Madison flows the Androscoggin through the peaceful Shelburne meadows, while far northward lie the waters of Umbagog and the Rangeley
Lakes, watched over by the mountains of Northern Maine.

A second stop for water is made at the Gulf Tank; and the conductor es-
corts passengers to the edge of the Gulf, giving them their first scramble over
the rocks and their first breath of the stimulating mountain wind. Looking
down into the depths, they see the tiny Spaulding's Lake, named for John
H. Spaulding, an early landlord of the Tip-Top House. In July their eyes
are often refreshed with a glimpse of snow banks on the lower slope of Mount
Clay, and another on the eastern side of Mount Jefferson. With this suggestion of an Arctic climate they are ready to enjoy the nonsensical nickname
of this gorge, which has amused visitors for half a century, — the "Gulf of
Mexico."

Growing profusely among the grasses under your feet is the little white blossom of the Greenland sandwort (*Arenaria Graenlandica*), a veritable Arctic flower, of which Dr. Isaac I. Hayes, the explorer, says that it "only disappears in Greenland at latitude 80°," while it is found as far south as the mountains of North Carolina. It is the most abundant of all flowers found on the mountain.

The Summit House is now in sight, and we will be there in eleven minutes. At the left is seen the carriage road from the Glen House, following the edge of the Gulf. One or two large water tanks are passed, these being reserve supplies to guard against drought, which is sometimes felt in midsummer, even so near the clouds as on this mountain top.

Rounding the last curve before reaching the top, we see on our right the memorial of a tragedy of nearly half a century ago, — the monument of Lizzie Bourne, who perished from cold and exhaustion while climbing the mountain from the Glen House, September 14, 1855.

We have now turned toward the south-west for the last sharp rise. From the left-hand windows we have a hurried look across a vast sweep of mountain and valley, extending across the State of Maine until the eye falls on the Atlantic Ocean. But there is no more time for an outlook; for in a moment the ascent is finished, and the train stops on the platform in front of the Summit House.

Fire on Mount Washington

From *Among the Clouds*

THE INDIANS who once dwelt among the White Mountains, we are told by Thomas Starr King, "had a tradition that Passaconaway, the sachem of Penacook, was once lifted in a car of flaming fire from the summit of the ridge to a council in heaven." Out of the realms of myth Passaconaway's fiery chariot came back to earth on the night of Thursday, June 18, 1908, when in smoke and flame every building on Mount Washington save three fell in ruins. Starting from some unknown cause in the Summit House and fanned by a furious gale, the fire spread with lightning-like swiftness throughout the hotel and thence to the help's cottage, the stage office, the printing office of *Among the Clouds*, the train shed and the United States Signal Station, wholly destroying them all, as well as the broad platform and 247 feet of railway track in front of the hotel, the railway turntable and much of the plank walk leading to the signal station. The Tip-Top House, the oldest house on the mountain, was in a position of safety, the wind driving the flames away from it, and the two stables, a few hundred feet below the Summit, also escaped. In the space of two or three hours the fruit of thirty-five years' development of facilities for summer visitors on Mount Washington was wiped out.

Outbreak and Progress of the Fire.

The last day on which the Summit House was to look down on the world below was a beautiful one. For some days the railway men had been rushing the work of putting things in readiness for summer. Miss Mattie A.

Clarke, manager of the Summit House, was to arrive the following Sunday with the help and the house was to open Monday, the 29th. The section of track along the platform had just been newly built. Preparations to make the house habitable after the long winter of disuse went on through the day under direction of Superintendent John Horne; the telephone was put in and between 4:30 and 5 p.m. the train left to take the employees to the base for the night. Meantime a party of young people from Berlin had come over the range from Madison Hut and prepared to spend the night in the stage office.

The train had reached the base, the men had had supper and were ready for a quiet evening's rest, when there came a sharp ring at the telephone. "The Summit House is on fire" was the startling message from the Fabyan station. So closely is the base station planted under the slope of the mountain that the Summit House could not be seen from it and no sign of the fire had been discovered. Speedily the train was made ready and the whole force of employees except a single train crew set out for the Summit, with Superintendent Horne in charge and Engineer Eugene Armstrong in the cab. Soon the glow of the fire could be seen in the sky, as well as the rising smoke, but not until the Gulf Tank was reached were the flames actually seen. Mounting against the clear, starlit sky they presented a weird appearance which defies description. Drawing nearer to the top it could be seen that the

The charred remains of the old Signal Station in the aftermath
of the June 1908 summit conflagration.

Summit House was already a mass of flames, and that it would be impossible to run the train to the platform. A stop was accordingly made near the drainage chute, a few rods below the water tank, and the men made their way on foot to the scene of the conflagration.

The Summit House roof was already gone and the fire was working its way to the cottage. The stage office had fallen in, and curiously enough the smoke from a fire in the stove was still rising from the chimney in the midst of the ruins. The printing office was ablaze and the long train shed had already been completely destroyed. Fire began to creep up the plank walk toward the old Tip-Top House and Mr. Horne ordered it cut, but the precaution proved unnecessary, as the high wind kept the flames from traveling further. Soon the Signal Station caught from the fire in the train shed's ruins and an unbroken line of flame surmounted the crest of the peak.

Nothing could be done to stay the whirlwind of destruction and the train crew could only look on, and watch the progress of the flames, while thinking of the changed conditions and increased hardships which were to attend their summer's work.

What the Carriage Road People Saw.

On the east side the news of the fire traveled as rapidly as on the west. It was seen at the Glen House by the housekeeper, who at once telephoned to the E. Libby & Sons Company at Gorham and to the Half-Way House. Superintendent George C. Baird of the Carriage Road, with his employees, at once hitched up a team to start for the Summit. While they were busy with the horses four boys came down the road. They were a part of the Berlin party who were at the top when the fire broke out and had hurried down to give the alarm. Near the five-mile post Mr. Baird met the rest of the party, one of whom, a young lady teacher from Berlin, said that the flames had first been seen breaking from a window in the corner of the hotel toward the printing office. Some of the party had entered the house in hopes of putting out the fire, but found it too much for them. They tried to raise somebody on the telephone, but were unaware that it had been cut out when the workmen left in the afternoon.

Mr. Baird and his party reached the top in time to see the fire at its height. The wind which spread the fire so swiftly from house to house was the means, Mr. Baird says, of saving the stables. Again and again were blazing fragments of shingles and clapboards hurled on the roof of the upper stable, only to be lifted in an instant by the next gust and sent flying toward Tuckerman Ravine, so that the roof was hardly scorched. Before midnight the fire had

AMONG THE CLOUDS

The Tip-Top House (far right) stands as the lone survivor
of the great 1908 summit fire.

burned itself out, and the spectators left the Summit, so sadly changed in
appearance, to keep a lonely watch over its own ruins.

The Fire as seen from Below.

At the Fabyan House the discovery of the fire was made probably within a
few minutes after its breaking out. The sun had already set in the valleys but
on the peaks the light still lingered, for this was almost the longest day of
the year. Mr. Trafton, the bookkeeper, had come out from supper with two
friends and caught sight of a glow on the Summit House. Thinking, as did
others who saw it, that it was the reflection of the setting sun on the windows, he called to the friends who were following him, "Come out here
quick if you want to see a pretty sight." At the same instant Mr. Harry B.
Warden, the clerk, detected a flickering of the light, which revealed the true
situation. Colonel Barron, who was at the cottage, was hurriedly called by
telephone and came out and looked at the mountain. The flame had died
down and Mr. Barron said, "Why, that's what I've seen a thousand times—
just the sun shining on the windows." But another outburst of flame confirmed the alarm, and in less time than it takes to tell it the telephone had
carried word to the Base. Gen. W. A. Barron was summoned from the

Crawford House and the group of sorrowfully interested spectators kept watch as long as the flames lighted up the slowly darkening sky.

Mrs. O. G. Barron and Miss Maude Barron were much impressed with the resemblance of the scene to an eruption of Mount Etna, which they had witnessed, differing only in the absence of the streams of lava which flowed down the sides of Sicily's famous volcano.

Mr. John Anderson, who watched the fire from the Mount Pleasant House, studied its progress with the aid of glasses, seeing one building after another take fire. "At one time," he said, "the fire seemed to die down and the printing office, Tip-Top House and Signal Station could be seen standing out against the blaze. Then it seemed to start up again, taking first the printing office and later the Signal Station."

Mr. St. John of the Bretton Woods printing office says that at the first appearance of the fire those who saw it took it for the rising moon.

Mrs. C. H. Morey, who lives at the old Bemis place in the Notch, saw the fire when returning homeward from a drive a few miles up the Notch and thought at first the workmen were burning rubbish. The truth soon became evident and she hastened home to bring her husband back to a point from which the fire could be seen.

Among the first to notice the fire in the vicinity of Gorham were Mr. Charles E. Philbrook, who telephoned the news to town from his home, Grove Cottage, and Mr. B. B. Bickford, the well-known guide.

The Buildings Destroyed.

Of the buildings destroyed, the Summit House, cottage, train shed and printing office were owned by the Mount Washington Railway Company, the stage office by the Mount Washington Summit Road Company (controlled by the E. Libby & Sons Company of Gorham), and the Signal Station by the United States government. The hotel was fully furnished. The Signal Station had been abandoned for many years, and merely contained old furniture. The printing plant of *Among the Clouds* included a Hoe cylinder press, which was put in by the founder of the paper, the late Henry M. Burt of Springfield, when the paper was printed in the old Tip-Top House; an Alamo 7-horse gasoline engine, nearly new, and a comparatively new outfit of type. A nearly complete file of the paper was destroyed, but the editor fortunately had a duplicate file at home. Files of the paper from the beginning are kept in the state libraries of New Hampshire and Massachusetts, the library of the Appalachian Mountain Club in Boston, the Bretton Woods library and the Gorham public library, the town of Gorham having secured a set a year ago through the forethought of Judge Alfred R. Evans.

Plans for Rebuilding.

The flames had not died down when the telephone wires were put in use to make arrangements for rebuilding the hotel and affording shelter for visitors during the season just opening. The Messrs. Barron were speedily in conference with the railroad officials and it was at first hoped that by almost superhuman efforts a new hotel might be ready for use by the first of August. Further study of the situation showed the impracticability of so doing, in view of the uncertainty of weather and the difficulty and danger of working in the exposed situation on the mountain top, where storms were liable to interrupt the work for days together. It was remembered that it took two years to build the hotel and 250 train loads to carry up the material. The wisest course was evidently to go slowly. Meanwhile, for temporary shelter, the obvious thing to do was to restore the Tip-Top House, that ancient landmark of pioneer enterprise, to the original purpose of a place of entertainment and shelter.

Working under Difficulties.

The work of clearing away the debris and restoring the destroyed track began at once. Along the whole length of the platform the railway ties and supporting timbers had been burned and the rails twisted into a hopeless mass. "We must have that track and a platform ready by the 29th," was Mr. Horne's word to the veteran roadmaster, Patrick Camden. And ready it was, though on the last day the wind was so furious that while a carpenter was using the auger another man had to hold him down to keep him from blowing over. So the first regular passenger train made its trip on Monday, June 29, according to schedule.

The repairs of the Tip-Top House were hustled along and surprising indeed was the sight that it presented the first of July. The old partitions, floors and sheathing had been ripped out and new material put in, and with the windows once more open to daylight the house was as cheerful and cosy as when newly built. The old hewn timbers, drawn up by horses more than half a century ago, seemed as sound as when put in, and the smooth inside face of the rugged stone walls showed the skill and thoroughness of the original mason work.

For the use of the workmen the observatory room at the back of the house was fitted up with a bench around the sides and a little stove, and here the editor shared with the railroad men their excellent lunch on his first visit after the fire. This room is to serve as kitchen for the restored house.

The Restored Tip-Top House.

To the Tip-Top House are transferred the energies of the manager of the Summit House, Miss Mattie A. Clarke, and the clerk, Mr. A. Frank Curtis, with as many of the help as can be accommodated. Mr. James H. Powers again takes charge of the postoffice. Here, under the roof which sheltered visitors as long ago as the days of the Civil War, visitors find food and hospitality. It is a return to the "simple life" such as visitors of late years have never dreamed of, and is a picture from the past which it is worth a long journey to see. The modest walls of the Tip-Top offer a hospitable greeting as in days of old, with the good cheer and comfort that an earlier generation enjoyed.

Many are the travelers of recent years who have said, "My father slept in the old Tip-Top House forty years ago," or have told of some other family association with the old place. Only a year or two ago a lady visitor recognized the room she occupied there on her wedding tour. To such visitors, whether from their personal recollection or from stories their parents have told them, the reopening of the Tip-Top House will bring a pleasure that they never dreamed of realizing. Those visiting Mount Washington in 1908 will have a unique experience which will stand out in their recollections above any other mountain trip of their lives.

May 16, 1912

Grand Plans
for the Summit

From *The White Mountain Republic-Journal*

One of several weekly newspapers published in Littleton, N.H., at the time, The White Mountain Republic-Journal *gave in depth coverage to an ambitious new plan to develop the top of Mount Washington in the aftermath of the 1908 conflagration. The proposal outlined in the following* Republic-Journal *story never came to fruition as hard economic times and several other factors derailed the hotel/electric railway plans by the end of 1912.*

ACCORDING to plans prepared by the Boston & Maine railroad, the summit of Mount Washington, the highest point of land east of the Rocky mountains, is to be crowned with a massive hotel structure that will have about it several features to make it unique among the hostelries of the world. The building will be located upon the very top, in fact, the tiptop point of the mountain will protrude itself through the lower floor, and will be absolutely fireproof. In shape it will be that of a great circle, with two ells projecting almost radically and forming a huge V with the apex at the circle.

The approach to this modern masterpiece of hotel construction will be one of unrivalled splendor. For almost twenty miles the new electric railway will swing through the mountain region, climbing heavenward 4750 feet and reaching many of the most noted scenic points in the mountain district. It will traverse the slopes of Mount Jefferson and Mount Clay and encircle the summit of Mount Washington twice.

A prospect almost boundless will unfold itself to the passengers as the car swings along, bringing into view the southern peaks, Monroe, Franklin,

Webster and Pleasant, and the country beyond those. Only a short distance below is the Lake of the Clouds and here the road takes a turn abruptly to the left giving a wonderful view down into Tuckerman's ravine. Climbing still higher it runs above the Alpine garden, so-called, and unfolds to view the southern and eastern parts of New Hampshire and the western part of Maine. Swinging back toward the left, the road doubles on itself and crosses the carriage road, looking down into the Great gulf, with Spaulding lake 1200 feet below. Crossing the old cog road for the second time, the electric line completes a circle of the summit, makes another turn, and the car will come to a stop in front of the new hotel. Views have been given from every point of the compass at different altitudes, and no one who has ever been at the summit of Mount Washington need be told that this railroad will surpass anything at present extant in scenic display and engineering skill. A short time ago this paper in an exclusive story printed a detailed account of the plan whereby the railroad and hotel were to be erected and financed, printed a topographical map indicating the path to be traversed by the car and the various points of interest where the line touched.

The building of the old cog railway was a simple proposition when compared with the difficulties that beset the engineers charged by the Boston & Maine with carrying out this comprehensive plan for developing Mount Washington. The railway now in use presented no greater troubles than the selection of a straight pathway to the top, the cutting down of trees, leveling up by stonework and trestles the roadbed and the laying of the rails. The new project made it necessary to take into account the defacements of the landscape, the attainment of easy grades, the reaching of points from which desirable views were to be obtained, and the guarding against landslides and avalanches in winter. Not only these but the form of power to be made use of was unheard of in the days of Sylvester Marsh.

The hotel will be constructed solidly of steel, stone and glass. Every room in it will be an outside room, and in spite of its high location it will be provided with every modern convenience of the modern hostelry. Distributed throughout its three stories will be 180 sleeping rooms, many of which will be provided with private baths. One of the most remarkable features of the structure will be the fact that it has been especially designed so that it "will not get in its own way."

The development of the plans called for an immense amount of time by the officials in charge and the working out of the details was left to Architect R. C. Reamer of the engineering department of the New York, New Haven and Hartford railroad, whose wide experience in connection with the world famous hotels at the Yellowstone National park particularly fitted

him for the task of crowning the highest peak east of the Rockies. It was realized that the season would be short, and that many of those who visited
the mountain top would go merely to spend a few hours, while others, disappointed perhaps by disagreeable weather would desire to remain over night
on the summit. With this idea in mind, provision has been made for a dining room to accommodate three hundred to four hundred people in the day.

The especially remarkable feature about the building will be the circular
observatory, one hundred and fifty feet in diameter. The ells jutting from
the side will be so positioned that only forty-eight out of a total of three hundred and sixty degree of the circular view from the observatory will be cut
off. This observatory will run up through three stories, and will be side-
walled by many and heavy glass windows. On the roof, surmounting the
building proper, will be a circular walk, and a glass skylight ninety feet in diameter and circular in form. Above all will be placed a searchlight of several
hundred thousand candle power, which will be seen at Portland, Me., and
other points favorably situated and at a similar distance.

The depot or station where passengers will enter the building from the
cars, will be situated on the south side of the hotel and it has been so arranged that the freight and passenger traffic will be separated. One passageway from the depot will run directly into the hotel building and it is through
this that passengers will proceed to the main structure, while another, leading to the service and store rooms, will be used for handling the freight. In
the basement the plan shows the main kitchen, boiler and engine rooms,
wine room, barber shop, billiard room, laboratories and servants' quarters.
From the passageway which goes into the side of the mountain, one goes up
a flight of stairs or via an elevator nearby into the lobby, which is, by the way,
entirely apart from the circular rotunda. Here will be the service rooms,
some sleeping rooms, the great dining rooms, and the news and souvenir
stands. Above this are two stories, similarly arranged, in which the rooms
run around the observatory well and are in both of the wings.

As verandas and porches are little use on the summit of this mountain,
the "verandas," as they might be called, are inside the observatory part itself.
However, there will be arranged around the outside of the first floor a wide
terrace and the glass sides of the rotunda will open so that the visitors may
step from there directly out-of-doors on to the terrace. The part known as
the observatory will be centered on the highest point of the mountain and a
picturesque point will be the fact that the top of the mountain will project
itself through the floor. One may stand on the summit and gain an unobstructed view of the horizon for 312 degrees out of the entire circle. Inside
the rotunda a row of pillars will support the upper stories but on account of

the fact that these will have a common centre the view will be obstructed and between the pillars and the walls of the observatory there will be a clear space of about twenty-five feet.

On the second story surrounded by the sleeping rooms will be a circular gallery looking down into the rotunda. Around the circular skylight on the roof will be a space thirty-five feet wide.

The building will be handsomely furnished throughout and the interior finish will be rich and expensive. In the method and system of interior lighting some novel effects have been planned but all the details have not as yet been fully worked out.

The new project of an electric traction road up Mount Washington and the building of such a large hotel on the summit is really an out-growth of the old plan upon which the present cog railroad was built.

The cog road was not, it is said, a paying proposition, even with the present high rates of fare. The cost of repairs at the beginning of each season, the expense of maintenance in operation were too great for a road which was trying to effect economies and increase revenues.

After several makeshift plans had been arranged and discussed the whole cog road system was dropped and the engineers took up the idea of building a traction road. Chief Engineer A. B. Corthell of the Boston and Maine railroad was placed in charge of working out the problems. Under his direction Engineer F. S. Darling made reconnaissance's, studied grades and mapped out several routes. Finally a grade of six per cent was decided upon, and on this basis routes were studied. One ran around the Lake of the Clouds, between Mount Washington and Mount Monroe. Another was planned to run along the Great Gulf side of Mount Clay, but the sheer precipise on this side caused that plan to be abandoned.

All the time the engineers had to keep the idea in mind of making the route scenically beautiful as well as economically as possible. At length a route was decided upon which would afford the finest view to the north and west, reaching the picturesque heights known as the Ridge of the Caps and the Castellated Ridge, and then going along the northern range to near the summit of Mount Washington, where it would make a complete circuit, affording views in every direction. One advantage of this plan was the fact that it would make it possible at little comparative cost to run a spur back to Mount Adams, and at one point the track route runs within a mile of Madison.

Engineer Darling celebrated the Fourth of July, 1911, by beginning the actual work of surveying the route. His work done, the engineers collaborated and the result was the evolution of the hotel design. In a few days, it is understood, application will be made to the public service commission of the state of New Hampshire for a charter for the electric road. The total costs of the improvements will be in the neighborhood of $1,500,000, and this represents an effort by the Boston and Maine railroad to carry out its promise of improvements for the benefit of New Hampshire.

The cost of construction will be defrayed by an issue of stock of the Concord and Montreal railroad. This road finances the proposition because of the fact that it owns the present road from Fabyans to the Base station, with valuable rights at the base and summit, and also owns the stock of the Mount Washington railway. The public service commission of New Hampshire has the necessary authority to grant permission for the extension of the Concord and Montreal line and the construction of the power station which will generate the electrical energy to keep this vast establishment in operation. The power plant will be located on the Ammonoosuc river.

All the preliminaries have been complied with. In view of the fact that such a large sum of money is to be expended there is little doubt that permission will be given soon. The rates of fare on the new road will be very much less — probably one-half those that prevailed on the older road. When completed the railway and hotel together will form one of the most noteworthy of New Hampshire's many attractions, and will be a fitting ornament for New Hampshire's mountain region, and particularly its "peak of peaks" — Mount Washington.

August 1960

The Last Climb
of Old Peppersass

Winston Pote

From *New Hampshire Profiles*

When it comes to photographing Mount Washington, few who have ever aimed a camera at the mountain can match the work of this well-known professional. Winston Pote's (1899–1989) magnificent pictures, taken at a time when Mount Washington was gaining notoriety for its spring skiing in Tuckerman Ravine and its weather extremes, aptly captured the era between 1925 and 1945.

The Massachusetts native, who lived in New Hampshire for the last 52 years of his life, produced many stunning aerial shots of the Presidential Range at a time when few such shots were being taken. He was a frequent contributor, both as a writer and photographer, to the popular Granite State publications New Hampshire Troubadour *and* New Hampshire Profiles.

ONE HUNDRED years ago, when the first climb of Old Peppersass was only an ambitious dream, Sylvester Marsh, a native of Campton, applied to the state of New Hampshire for a charter to build the Mount Washington Cog Railway. He got it in 1858, after much ridicule. One legislator suggested he be given the right to build his railway to the moon if he wanted. The public was equally amused, and no one but Marsh himself took the project seriously.

The rack rail and the cog locomotive were his own inventions, and for the next twelve years he devoted his own capital and a great deal of energy to carry them from patents to actuality. The first mountain-going locomotive was built by Campbell & Whittier of Boston, shipped to Littleton, the nearest rail point, then hauled 25 miles to Mt. Washington piecemeal by ox teams.

When it was assembled, it was quickly nicknamed "Peppersass" for its resemblance to an old-fashioned peppersauce bottle. The "bottle," or boiler, with its flared smokestack, was mounted on trunnions to keep it vertical regardless of grade. The locomotive had no cab and only a single pair of cylinders. A wood-burner, it was designed with the cog-wheel at the front to pull itself up the steep incline.

Finally, in August 1866, a test run over the first quarter mile of track proved entirely successful. Railroad men and the public were equally impressed by Marsh's invention and his enthusiasm. From that point on, work progressed rapidly. A company was organized to build the road, and on August 14, 1868, the track was completed to Jacob's Ladder and the railroad formally opened.

Those early trips with passengers were so popular that the completion of the road was rushed with all possible speed. It was finished on July 3, 1869 when the first passenger rode to the summit on a load of lumber. The beginning of paid passenger service was the next day.

It was a great vindication of "Crazy Marsh" and an equally great accomplishment in terms of back-breaking man-hours. The track climbs an average grade of 25 percent, or over 1100 feet per mile. It is three and a quarter miles long, laid partly over a trestle of varying height. Aside from the timber in the trestle itself, all the material—rails, cars, locomotives—were hauled in from Littleton as Peppersass had been, by oxen and horses.

So, here on Mt. Washington's 6284 feet above sea level was the first mountain-top railroad terminal. Subsequently Marsh's inventions served as the pattern for similar railroads in Switzerland and on Pike's Peak, Colorado. All proved equally safe.

Sixty years later, long after Old Peppersass had become a museum relic, the same old locomotive was returned to Mt. Washington for one last trip over the cog road—with disastrous results. During the descent over the long trestle just above Jacob's Ladder, the cog mechanism snapped, Peppersass careened down over 2000 feet, and jumped the track from a reverse curve. One man was killed, and four others jumped for their lives. The writer was one of those four.

It was a tragic trip—one that never should have been made. Yet strangely enough, this is a story that has never been properly told. July 20, 1929, and the newspaper accounts of the day ran such headlines as "Old Peppersass Explodes!"

This first engine had an active lifetime of only twelve years and was discarded as worn out before 1877. During its early years, when it was used to push building materials up the completed portion of the track on a flat car, it had no tender. Apparently wood for fuel was picked up along the way.

During its early years of passenger service, Peppersass was accompanied by three other vertical-boiler locomotives of an improved type, with an enclosed cab and a much larger cog wheel working in the rear, which gave more speed. Peppersass would travel only two miles an hour. Then in 1878 the road adopted a fleet of much improved horizontal boiler engines, and the original locomotive was retired.

In 1893 it was exhibited at the Columbian Exposition in Chicago, and for eleven more years it remained in that city in the Field Museum. In 1904 it was displayed in St. Louis and then went on to the Baltimore and Ohio Railroad and was lost in obscurity for 23 years.

It was the late Rev. Guy Roberts of Whitefield—who in 1916 had come to the rescue of the crumbling Old Man of the Mountain at Franconia—who took the initiative in the twenties in finding Old Peppersass and returning her to her rightful home.

Over a period of two years, following 1927, the locomotive was shipped to New Hampshire and put into the Concord, N.H., repair shops of the Boston & Maine Railroad, who owned the Cog Railway at that time. Here she was thoroughly overhauled and redecorated in gay colors, under the eye of E. C. "Jack" Frost, who was to be her engineer on the trip up Mt. Washington.

According to Frost, some trouble was experienced in getting up steam during tests. The water foamed! The repair crew bored a hole in her wrought iron boiler in an attempt to find the cause of this strange phenomenon. They discovered the boiler half filled with nuts and cherry stones, stored there by squirrels, some fifty years before when the locomotive had been on display at Bretton Woods.

The repair crew also found it necessary to weld part of the frame which held the forward wheels and the drive shaft—worthy of note in view of what later happened. It should also be emphasized that the cog wheel of this earliest engine was much smaller than more recent models and could more easily jump the rack rail.

During this period of repair, elaborate plans were made for the return of Old Peppersass after her 36 years of wandering. A temporary grandstand and speakers' platform were constructed at the Base Station. Everything was gay with flags and bunting. The gala day was set for Saturday, July 20, 1929, with 500 guests officially invited, including the governors from six other states. The original intent was to run Peppersass a few hundred yards up and

Guests from the nearby Crawford House depart via horse-drawn wagon for the Cog Railway base station to witness the last run of Peppersass.

down the track, but engineer Jack Frost had his heart set on taking her for one last trip to the summit.

The day was perfect—clear, warm, and without wind. Thousands of spectators turned out. Regular trains were cancelled, and six were decorated and waiting to carry the invited guests to the summit, which could be seen clearly above us. The Whitefield band was there, and photographers and correspondents from every important newspaper. At least four newsreel companies had cameramen on hand, so arrangements were made to have them shoot pictures of Peppersass from a flat trailer car in the rear of the last train.

The exercises took place at two o'clock, with Col. Barron of the Crawford House presiding as toastmaster. He had obtained a bottle of water from the Lakes of the Clouds to christen the engine.

At the proper moment Old Peppersass came chugging up the track, blowing her whistle in answer to the cheering thousands. Engineer Jack Frost and fireman William Newsham were dressed in bright red shirts and tall beaver hats.

Governor Charles W. Tobey officially received the locomotive for the state of New Hampshire, and she was christened by President George Hannauer of the B & M. Soon after, the six cog trains were loaded to capacity with guests and there was a scramble for space on the small trailer car for photographers. I managed to squeeze in behind the newsreel cameras and altogether too many folding camp chairs.

I had arrived on the scene a bit late with a friend and no certain plans for going up the mountain. With me I carried a Graflex camera, a doctor's leather bag full of extra lenses and film, and a Filmo movie camera.

It was not until I found myself on the flatcar that I realized that the lunch was still locked up in the car and that my keys were in my pocket. In my haste to get pictures of the ceremonies I had not taken time to eat, and now there would be no food available for several hours. The fact of my increasing hunger was to be a fateful one in the decisions I made that afternoon.

The cog train we rode climbed as slowly as possible in an effort to keep the slow moving Peppersass within camera range. All of us were trying to get pictures at once, some hopping off and on our train and even hitching rides on the old locomotive for an effective close-up. For it was hard to hold a camera steady, what with the jolting of the cog wheel.

Our train made frequent stops, since no one knew how far Peppersass would attempt to climb. At the first water tank an official appeared to signal for her return, but Frost continued on upward with her to the Halfway House, a small building near the track. There she stopped for more wood, which was quickly loaded onto the queer tender. And again she continued upward instead of starting back down as we half-expected she would. After she had climbed a few feet, we distinctly heard a loud bang.

"That doesn't sound so hot!" said a newsreel camera man. There was no further comment about it, but I was to hear a very similar sound on our descent.

Another quarter of a mile, perhaps, and we crossed Jacob's Ladder with Peppersass following slowly in the distance. Engineer and fireman were busy waving those tall hats and blowing the whistle which made little white puffs in the almost calm air. A perfect day for the festivities!

Above the trestle we stopped again, and Rev. Guy Roberts climbed off accompanied by at least one photographer. I decided to do the same and try for a different picture, but my Graflex had slid under all those chairs and feet, and I couldn't get to it because of the angle of ascent.

Even so, I had half a mind to hop off and recover the camera later, as the train started. But the thought of possible difficulty in boarding a crowded train or walking down on an empty stomach caused me to stay aboard.

That decision cost me what might have been the most dramatic movie sequence of my career, for shortly after Peppersass flew by this spot completely out of control. It also almost cost me my life. And — ironically — the

WINSTON POTE

A large throng gathers at the Cog Railway base station to watch Peppersass
head up the mountain one last time.

only thing that went to the bitter end with the old locomotive was my
Graflex!

The procession continued upward over "Long Trestle" to the Gulf Tank,
where Peppersass stopped to take on water. I remember that they filled it
so full it ran over. More pictures were taken of the process, and I climbed
out with all my gear. When my train moved off toward the summit, only
a short distance, now, I did not rejoin it but stayed watching the old locomotive.

Frost had evidently received orders to take her back down, but still he
waited, looking longingly upward as though his goal were fading away.

By now it was five o'clock, and the absence of that lunch was becoming
serious. The thought of a hike to the summit with all that gear became less
inviting by the moment. If I rode back on Peppersass, I might get a few more
interesting shots, and at least there would be lunch in the car. All the movie
film had been exposed, but I could re-load on the way down.

As I watched, Peppersass took on two more passengers—the engineer's
son Caleb, a boy of sixteen, and Daniel P. Rossiter, who was official photographer for the railroad.

Still I made no move to join them, even as the old engine started steam-
ing slowly down the moderate grade of the area. Then, annoyed at my own

indecision, I grabbed up my equipment, and, with both hands filled, tried to run over the rocks—a strange chase after a strange engine.

It was only moving at two miles an hour, so I was sure I could catch up. Yet twice I stopped, as though to give up. It was as though there were some restraining force holding me back. I chalked it up to an empty stomach and ran on, catching it at last. Frost stopped, reached down with a helping hand. Then, with a clank and a roar of steam, we were off down the mountain.

My first need was to load the movie camera. I had done it on a moving dog sled and on a speed boat, but this jolting conveyance was the worse yet. Young Caleb Frost lent a hand, and together we struggled with the camera on the pile of firewood, which was taking up most of the room. We got it finished just as the engine reached the steeper grade.

Watching Peppersass from above, I hadn't realized how noisy and rough she was, once in motion. Conversation was limited to brief shouts. Engineer Frost stood by with a huge oil can and used it when his aim was good. Newsham, the fireman, tossed a chunk of wood into the flaming firebox.

Here were two fine closeup shots, and I shouted into Frost's ear that I would like such pictures if he could stop. It was impossible to hold the camera steady otherwise.

"You can get that at the base"—I could just make out the words. At that point we reached the top of Long Trestle, and I could hear the engineer's words as he yelled to Newsham: "How do you like the looks of that!" I was not alone in feeling apprehensive about this ride.

We passed two climbers who waved. . . . Down we dropped—a different kind of jolt, now. . . . Rossiter sat holding his camera, near the doorway. My equipment was scattered on the woodpile. . . . What a fine, clear day, I thought—and how hungry can you get. . . .

There was a loud sledge hammer crack. We seemed to bounce a bit and lurch to one side. As we picked up speed, there was an ominous grinding sound. Frost grabbed the old hand brake wheel, which spun loosely and seemed to have little effect. I could see his mouth opening, shouting *Jump, Jump!* I'm sure I didn't hear the words, so terrifying was the clatter.

Struggling to the woodpile, I grabbed the bag of film and lens equipment, carefully threw it out the doorway, and watched it roll over on a grassy place. I should have gone with it. Caleb was the only one with presence of mind to jump this soon and got away with only a torn short from the bushes that cushioned his fall.

The brake must have been holding partially; we were not going more than fifteen miles an hour—but it was unpleasant. The engine rocked violently, and pieces of flaming wood and embers flew from the firebox. Af-

Peppersass embarks on its fateful July 20, 1929 run up the mountain.

terward I found burnt holes in my clothing. Rossiter still sat with his camera.

I lurched back to the woodpile and reached for the Graflex. It was in a far corner, and as I went after it I found myself looking at a breathtaking view of Jacob's Ladder. Still thinking of pictures, I forgot the Graflex and grabbed the Filmo, tightening the wrist strap.

But we were going too fast now. Then something else gave way, and we started to roll freely, a sudden drop, like a high speed elevator. Any braking action was gone.

(I believe an axle had broken at this point, the ends of it dragging on the ties which were splintered for a long distance. Later I saw a trainman with one wheel and part of the axle wrapped in newspaper, showing an old progressive break.)

I was sure the old engine would tip over. And the sensation—an all gone feeling, as trees and rocks whizzed by. Engineer and fireman hung on in the doorways, on opposite sides, looking for a soft spot.

Down we rushed—first a deep hole in the mountain, then rocks all blurred, near the track. As I jumped from the woodpile, I caught one toe on the Peppersass sign. So it was head first, a dive instead of a jump, with no sensation of falling, only of speed.

Sky—rocks—sky—then a huge rock looming up for a landing. I tried to throw my head back to protect my face.

Stars I saw plenty, but I remember better seeing the engine like a comet with a long tail of steam. I seemed to be on my feet, but there was no camera. An eye witness said I immediately jumped up and pulled a handkerchief from my pocket.

I knew I had a broken jaw, because I could hear the bones rattle! I tried to find the camera, but something was wrong with one knee. I was very close to Jacob's Ladder, and some time later remember seeing the engine's smokestack under it. It was here that Rossiter had dropped off, or was thrown, after hanging on the tender with his camera.

He was killed instantly. The engineer and fireman suffered broken bones but recovered, in time. Frost had made a miraculous 30-foot jump on the high ravine side.

Old Peppersass had shot off the track on a reverse curve just below Jacob's Ladder, the wrought iron boiler bouncing over the rocks and into the scrub trees, with only a few dents to show for it. The ash pan remained on the tracks and slid over 900 feet, almost to the Halfway House.

The events that followed are a blur of excitement and confusion. I remember a hiker hurrying down with my black bag. . . . Hunting for my lost movie camera, a painful process. The next day, I found I had a fractured knee cap. The jaw fracture was compound. I walked around holding it together with my hand because it felt heavy. And somehow I hiked far enough up the mountain to get a lengthy ride back down again when the excursion trains descended.

No one on these trains had realized what had happened, of course, until they came to the Peppersass fireman and engineer sitting beside the track. They pulled me up the high step, but I refused to sit inside if they were going on down and stayed on the back platform trying to answer questions for a newspaperman.

Before long they descended to the damaged section of the track where further descent was impossible. So it would be essential to go back up the mountain and down the auto road. But there was no water here and not enough steam for some of the trains. We waited for hours, the area swarming with people, some walking down, many waiting for an eventual return to the summit.

There was a good sunset. A trainman arrived with my movie camera, not badly damaged.

Much later the upper two trains made it back to the summit. The hotel was packed with guests—all staring at me. I was told later that my head had swollen up like a balloon. I couldn't swallow milk. If only I had eaten that lunch!

Newspaper men fought over the use of the telephone, and one of them pulled out the wires. Frantic news—the engine was not to be seen, so it must have exploded!

I continued to hold my jaw together manually until I arrived at a hospital at 1:00 the next morning.

They say the following day the mountain was like an ant hill, with souvenir hunters carrying away anything that was light. Fortunately, most of the engine pieces were heavy. The steam gauge went across the Presidential Range, while the whistle found its way into Pinkham Notch. The only thing that remained on the old engine was my Graflex—and pieces of that eventually turned up at the University of New Hampshire. I never did find the lens.

Before the summer was over, the parts of Old Peppersass were assembled in the Concord repair shops, and eventually it was placed on display at the Base Station, where it may be seen today. It should never have gone up the mountain that day, nor was the trip planned officially. It was a relic of the past, far different from the modern trains with their perfect safety record.

Many photographers went up Mt. Washington July 20, 1929, looking for special pictures. All of us missed the big one. However, I had the fastest ride on the slowest locomotive ever built, and lived to remember the last climb of Old Peppersass.

January 1933

Robert S. Monahan

From *Mount Washington Reoccupied*

When he first climbed Mount Washington at the age of 12 years, Robert "Bob" Monahan (1908–1994) probably wouldn't have guessed that someday not too far in the future, his name would be linked forever to New Hampshire's grandest summit. The 1929 Dartmouth College graduate, who also attended the Yale University School of Forestry, was among the "reoccupants" of Mount Washington during the winter of 1932–33, when weather observers returned to the summit for year-round occupation. The following piece features excerpts from Monahan's daily mountaintop log entries for January 1933. After his stint atop the mountain, Monahan went on to work for the U.S. Forest Service for 15 years. For several years, he supervised Civilian Conservation Corps (CCC) crews in the White Mountains. Later he became manager of Dartmouth College-owned timberlands throughout the state and region. He was also a member of the New Hampshire legislature in the late 1950s and early 1960s.

January 1

I turned out at three this morning to refuel the fires and make sure that the wind had not caused any damage, and especially to ink the barograph pen which was pumping so vigorously in the gusty wind that the ink supply was fast exhausted.

Today was open house on Mount Washington for no less than thirty-nine names were registered in the log, of whom fifteen are remaining overnight either in Camden or the Observatory. This has been a very busy day welcoming friends, preparing for this evening's illumination, making the usual observations and occasionally enjoying the fine view, especially to the south where Monadnock seemed to rear higher than ever before.

We have had many distinguished guests today including three climbers from Cambridge, Massachusetts, all of whom have acquired enviable mountaineering records: Miss Jessie Whitehead, who returned to Pinkham via Boott Spur; Henry Hall, who made an hour's visit before returning to the Glen House; and Brad Washburn, who is spending the night. Also we are entertaining Al Sise and Josh Crosby, who packed up three ponderous volumes produced by the United States Polar Year Expeditions of fifty years ago to Lady Franklin Bay and Point Barrow. The books were loaned by the Baker Library at Dartmouth upon request written on the summit December 29. Some service!

Fortunately both temperature and wind velocity have moderated considerably today, enabling the holiday visitors to enjoy a regular field day on the heights.

For supper we had the first fresh meat we've enjoyed for some time, also a dessert of vanilla ice cream with chocolate sauce. In the evening we could readily detect the Portland lights and were very much pleased with the fine visibility conditions. At nine p.m. we lit six magnesium flares, which were carried to various high points on the summit, and flashed the 400-watt lamp from the roof. Meanwhile, Brad was recording the holiday display with the standard movie camera which he has loaned us for the winter. While the torches were still glowing we had a phone call from the Mountain View House at Whitefield informing us that the lights were seen from that point and shortly thereafter we received a similar message from South Lunenburg, Vermont.

At ten p.m. we repeated the lamp for five minutes and also lit two more flares. By eleven p.m. the others had turned in but Sise and I used the lamp again and at midnight burned two more flares. An answering light in the direction of Bridgton, Maine, indicated that our flashes had been seen from three states. The wind was blowing hard again at midnight and a flying spark burned the gauntlets Sise was wearing and another spark burned my bare hand slightly.

We enjoyed the novelty of lighting off the fireworks and will wait in suspense for replies from those who may have seen the light. It is unfortunate that the same conditions did not prevail last night as tonight for we suppose many more people were looking in this direction at that time.

January 2

Only one group climbed the mountain today but it was not until midafternoon that the last (Sise) of our overnight company had left for the lowlands.

At eleven a.m. the clouds rolled in again bringing to a close the brief period of clear weather. In the afternoon Mac put in a lengthy sked with Mr. Shaw at Exeter. We were quite surprised that he was able to carry on at all after Sise's alterations to his equipment!

Today we shared a quart of fresh milk, the first such article that has ever graced the dining table of the Observatory. Evaporated milk for cooking and our eighty-five pound drum of parlac for cereals have substituted satisfactorily.

At the 7:15 p.m. sked with Pinkham we were quite surprised to hear Sise's voice at the other end and even more surprised and horrified to learn that an accident had occurred that afternoon in Huntington's Ravine involving Jessie Whitehead and her climbing partner, Walter Sturges. Progress reports were dispatched on frequent schedules to keep us posted on developments until almost three a.m. when Joe and Wen returned from the North Conway Hospital with the news that Jessie was alive, but still delirious and obviously in very serious condition.

January 4

Today was an historical day for a distinguished company of visitors called on us for two hours in the afternoon: Joe Dodge (his first day on the summit since December 3), Elliot Libby (his first winter climb up the auto road and the first time he has been within his Stage Office during the winter), Wen Lees and Itchy Mills. Landlord Libby presented no rent bill and seemed well pleased with the transformation we have wrought at the summit terminal of the auto road.

The quartet had driven 100 yards beyond Five Mile Turn in the "Hearse," a Pierce Arrow mountain-geared sedan possessing a lengthy and proud record of difficult travel. We had hoped they would remain overnight but they had made plans to return late in the afternoon. Fortunately, both temperature and wind were mild, and the summit cloud cap was thin.

They brought up a batch of mail, including Sal's Massachusetts Income Tax Return blanks. Inasmuch as he has volunteered his services for several months, we suspect the forms will help start the next fire.

Confirmation of our lights represented the bulk of the mail. The most distant reply received indicated that the nine p.m. display was seen as far as Boothbay Harbor, Maine, approximately 95 miles airline from Mount Washington. Ralph B. Jenkins of that town reported seeing the light "with the naked eye very clearly." William W. Graves and Marshall H. Metcalf climbed the fire lookout tower on Mount Ararat, near Topsham, Maine, about 80

Chief observer Sal Pagliuca takes a reading off the sling psychrometer
during the winter of 1932–33.

miles distant, from which they could distinguish the mountain light "without difficulty." The lights were also reported from Lisbon Falls, Maine, and Farmington, N.H., both 64 miles from the mountain. Additional replies were received from many distant points including Lakeport, N.H., Otisfield and Lovell Village, Maine. Probably the most unique setting in which the light appeared was the quiet water of Lake Winnepesaukee, for Clifton F. Shaw of Concord reported seeing not only the stars but the summit light reflected for a few minutes upon the surface of the water.

January 5

In clouds all day. However, the telephone conversations between the Base Station and the thrice daily radio phone skeds with Pinkham Notch relieve any monotony that might have developed. At present, we are so busy with our regular observations and calculations that the hours fly by, yet many of our friends below cannot understand what we do to "kill time."

In the afternoon we burned the Christmas tree. It served its purpose nobly but the coal gas in the atmosphere of the room is more telling on the tree than on us. So that much appreciated symbol of the Christmas spirit had to be junked.

Today we heard the sad news that Calvin Coolidge has died. A living ex-president seems about as short-lived as a stretch of clear mountain weather.

At six p.m. we were very much surprised to hear someone open the door. He proved to be the forerunner of a group of four boys and advised us that one of the party was in a bad way, so Sal and I picked up the emergency kits and set out down the mountain. However, we met the rest of the party a few hundred feet from the Observatory—a false alarm, for which we are thankful. The youths had no intention of climbing to the summit when they set out but they could not resist the temptation, so, despite their inadequate equipment, they managed to push through to the summit. They knocked in vain on the garage door thinking it the Observatory and next they mistook the snow gage in the center of the parking area for the stove pipe of our snow-blanketed quarters. Our four "stowaways" have been supplied with blankets and food, including some of the several cases of baked beans which Friends Brothers supplied us for just such emergencies.

January 8

During last night the temperature fell rapidly from 20° at eight p.m. to −14° at eight a.m. this morning, accompanied by a considerable increase in the wind velocity.

During the day we were visited by two groups of three each from Littleton and Whitefield, who climbed via the railroad. At noon the sky was clear for the first time since January 1. The maximum temperature was only 2° but the climbing conditions were ideal and the visibility excellent.

Mac worked Mr. Shaw again in the late afternoon. At 5:30 p.m. we flashed the 400 watt lamp for which he looked in vain from the summit of Stratham Hill near Exeter, N.H.

Our period of clear sky was short-lived, for at 6:30 p.m. Cumulus clouds sneaked in from the west and enveloped the summit, thus denying us a moonlight view of the snow covered peaks, and outlook of which we shall never tire.

While waiting for the 7:15 sked which would advise us whether Burho had started up the mountain, we were quite surprised to see him stagger through the threshold and slump into the nearest chair. The round trip, burdened on the upgrade with the 45 pounds of mail and special supplies, had proven almost too much. We have now adopted a standard treatment for such cases of exhaustion and promptly restored Ralph to his usual genial self.

Later in the evening Sal and I brought up his load from the Cow Pasture lower turn, 1¾ miles below the summit, where the pack had been cached.

The summit party during the reoccupation of Mount Washington 1932–33 included, l–r, Alex McKenzie, Sal Pagliuca, and Bob Monahan.

This is the second successive time that our mail has been abandoned in the vicinity of the Cow Pasture. The long pull above the Stone Crusher has proven exceedingly disheartening and now Sal refers to the Cow Pasture as "le pont de l'ane" (the donkey's bridge or the packer's critical point).

January 10

A terrific wind blew all night and at seven a.m. was sweeping across the summit at a ninety-mile velocity. During the night the pressure dropped rapidly, reaching a record low for the Observatory of 22.881 at four a.m. The snowstorm which raged all yesterday finally let up some time during the night. The gages caught about 5½ inches but the wind and −4° temperature formed a windpacked crust over the peak.

The cat returned this morning triumphant from his conquest of Camden Cottage in which he reduced the summit population by three.

In the afternoon the clouds opened up at 2:45, the temperature increased appreciably and the wind diminished slightly. Sal and I took advantage of these conditions to refuel the gas tank and haul by toboggan several bags of coal from the garage. An attempt was made to photograph a striking scene to the northeast in which the upper edge of the almost full moon was peeking over a formidable lenticular cloud riding quietly over the shadow of Mount Washington.

At eight p.m. Sal and I started the hourly watch of the weather changes for the eleventh and twelfth of this month are International First Order Days when all Polar Year stations are urged to make detailed observations. Sal stood the first watch so I am turning in early.

January 11

Either Sal or I made the rounds of the instruments all night. At 5:30 p.m. the sky suddenly cleared overhead heralding a glorious sunrise thoroughly enjoyed and welcomed by the observer on watch. All night the wind continued very gusty and reached an hourly average velocity of from 55–60 m.p.h. The sky clouded over again at 7:30 a.m. and remained overcast all day with dense haze forming a 360° horizon.

The wind was so gusty that pilot balloon and nephoscopic observations were impracticable but we watched the cloud formations closely until 3:45 p.m. when we went under again. At 5:30 p.m. snow began to fall which, together with the rime already forming, should whiten our summit aspect considerably.

In the evening Mac carried on his usual sked with WIFGA, Mr. Henry Shaw's Exeter station, in the customary mutually encouraging manner. Since Mr. Shaw's company, General Radio, loaned us the 56-mc. equipment, we are especially pleased that Mr. Shaw can share with us the thrill in developing this unique form of communication.

A raging blizzard swept over the mountain all evening. The wind-driven snow reduced visibility to a minimum and added considerable difficulty to the task of making the hourly outside observations.

Between readings I am studying Hobbs' "North Pole of the Winds," an altogether appropriate book to read while we ride out this raging snowstorm.

January 14

A bank of low clouds which appear to the lowlander as Stratocumulus but which are classified by us as "advection fog" rolled in from the coast all morning. At noon the Sandwich Range went under and soon thereafter Mount Pequawket and Doublehead were enveloped as the mass swept around Moosilauke and invaded the lower summits of the Franconia Range. By one p.m. the dense blanket had concealed the southern half of Pinkham Notch. The very crest of Wildcat and Carter Dome remained clear, for the upper limit of the fog is about 4300 feet. The few peaks over that altitude emerge above the inland sea as so many scattered islands on a vast ocean. Because of the barrier nature of the Presidential Range the cloud bank's advance is halted in our immediate vicinity and the region to the north of us remains clear.

We are enjoying the first calm weather experienced since December 27 and no time was lost in taking advantage of these fine conditions. The Kohler tank was refueled, soft coal and kindling wood hauled by toboggan from the garage and the water supply replenished. Mac was enabled to accomplish some outside soldering for the first time in many weeks. Reports from the lowlands indicate distinctly disagreeable weather but we are basking in continuous sunshine and moonlight.

The wind was from the southeast but gradually veered westward during the late afternoon. The anemograph installed on the railroad platform has been overhauled and we are all set for the next storm.

A party of six Dartmouth students climbed from the Base in the afternoon, remaining overnight in Camden Cottage. It is unfortunate that prospective climbers in the valley do not realize the remarkable conditions prevailing on the upper slopes, for we are sure they would flock to the mountain to share with us the unusual view.

The almost full moon this evening reveals the various currents and eddies of our inland sea. Especially fascinating are the clouds which sweep over Wildcat and through Carter Notch, for they pour down the north-facing slopes in a great cascade. Snow flurries occurred in the valleys but we have had no precipitation of any kind. The frost is rapidly evaporating under these conditions and I was obliged to turn "road monkey" in order to improve the snow surface on our "skid road" from the garage to the winter quarters.

One of the Dartmouth students tested our telephone hook-up by calling his home in New Jersey. He reported perfect transmission on probably the longest phone call to date.

January 15

Only a thin layer of Cirrostratus above the eastern horizon obscured the sky. All else is blue. During the night the blanket of fog covering the lowlands broke up to some extent allowing sunshine to filter through at times, but up here we are blessed with constant sunlight. At 11:30 a.m. a few masses of Cumulus floated by causing a decided jump in the pyrheliometer recorder. The reflected sunlight caused by these clouds increased the millivolts registered by about 50%.

The morning's weather report indicated snow falling in Boston but we are still favored with clear skies. However, the wind is increasing from yesterday's calm, our first quiet weather since December 27, to a velocity averaging forty m.p.h.

In the afternoon Joe and John Eddy in the latter's Ford roadster drove up the unplowed summit road as far as the Halfway House without undue difficulty reaching that point at three p.m. where they were met by Sal and Mac. They were obliged to shovel only twice: at Adams Lookout and just below Jenny Lind Bridge. The fact that a car could be driven halfway up the mountain on this date is concrete evidence of the mild winter thus far in the valleys. But past experience indicates that more wintry conditions may be expected in March and even during April than this month.

The mail was exchanged at the Halfway House and Sal and Mac returned to the summit with a considerable amount of mail, fudge, radio equipment and cold weather clothing. And so our weekly mail service has continued!

A beautiful red moon provided an unusual setting as it rose behind Cirrostratus. We tried to reproduce part of the effect photographically but even our array of filters and special lenses will fall far short in duplicating the scenes as we observe them.

January 18

This morning brought bright sunshine and absolutely clear skies, a very welcome change from yesterday's disagreeable combination of wind-driven snow and fog. The temperature is lower today, ranging from $18°$ to $1.5°$ between eight a.m. and eight p.m. Dense Altocumulus clouds were noted in the western valleys moving this way. At sundown the shadow of the mountain was cast upon the haze over the northeast horizon, a common portent of unfavorable weather.

The anemoscope recently installed at the end of the trestle had to be demounted for additional repairs. The canvas cover does not seem to be the best device possible to protect the clockwork and record rolls from the fine snow which is driven into the smallest cracks.

We had hoped to conduct at least one balloon run today but the extreme gustiness of the northwest wind prevented. At seven a.m. the velocity was 78 m.p.h.

January 19

Inasmuch as every indication of immediate bad weather has been noticed, I left for Pinkham Notch soon after breakfast with an 87-pound load including the sixty-pound pryheliometer recorder which will have to be repaired in the valley. We have been able to make all other instrument repairs on the summit but this requires special attention. At present there is very little loose snow on the road so we are anxious to complete all the back packing necessary while the traveling conditions are still good.

The hygrograph showed an almost vertical rise between seven and eight a.m. accompanying the sudden approach of clouds and snow. The wind slowly veered from SW to W during the day and increased steadily in velocity from 24 m.p.h. at seven a.m. to 85 m.p.h. at eight p.m.

Pushed downhill by the heavy load and the increasing wind, I made good time down the road covering seven miles in exactly two hours to the One Mile, where Joe and Itchy had just hauled the latter's car out of a ditch with the aid of Elliot Libby and his "hearse."

The wind blew hard all day, even in the valley. A sign near the Glen House, which had withstood numerous severe blows, was knocked down. During the evening sked between the summit and Mr. Shaw the recorder continued to increase its tempo so the clicks were sent over the radio at a time when the wind was clocked at 96 m.p.h. To accomplish this transmission the relay connected to the anemometer was placed in the keying circuit of the 56-mc. transmitter which was operated on ICW (interrupted continuous wave).

January 20

The wind velocity let up appreciably early this morning, reaching 44 m.p.h. at four a.m. but it soon increased rapidly and blew at hurricane velocity (No. 12 Beaufort Scale) all day. Outdoor activities were rendered extremely difficult because of the wind gustiness and flying ice. The rapidly forming frost has made it impossible to obtain accurate readings even when the full charge of heat is passed through the present anemometer. We constantly look forward to the day when the new improved anemometer will be in operation and we can hope to obtain a continuous record of the air passage under all conditions.

An attempt was made to use the Tycos portable anemometer but the frost rapidly formed in the air gap making a reading impossible. The velocity must have exceeded 125 m.p.h. and this storm will doubtless go down in history as the most violent in January, 1933.

At 12:30 p.m. the barograph recorded 22.610, which is much lower than the previous existing minimum of 22.961 indicated by the mercurial barometer at 2 p.m., December 31. Today's reading resulted from an instan-

This postcard view from the 1930s, taken by Mount Washington
Observatory staffers, shows the summit encased in rime ice.

taneous dip in the ragged curve, for the barograph pumped vigorously
all day.

Perhaps it is just as well that we are above tree line, for Mrs. Mary
L. Roberts, of Grasmere, N.H., succumbed to a heart attack when today's
high wind felled a large maple tree in front of the house where she was
staying.

On account of the severe weather I remained in the valley, for we follow
a policy of not attempting the ascent unless weather conditions are wholly
favorable. It is hard enough to pack up a load when the going is excellent.

When Sergeant O.S.M. Cone was relieved because of sickness 55 years
ago today, it is reported that he loaded all his belongings on an improvised
sled and started down the track. The crude safety brake failed when about
halfway down and the Sergeant with his assistant, Private D. C. Murphy,
were thrown from the trestle and Cone's belongings were strewn over the
mountainside. Both observers narrowly escaped fatal injuries.

January 21

At seven a.m. the driving snowstorm which had been raging for almost 48
hours finally stopped leaving an average catch in the six gages of 6.2 inches
unmelted and 1.2 inches melted. Today's weather has been much like that
of the 18th, a flash in the pan, for the disagreeable weather of the past two

days has given way to relatively calm, warm and clear weather. At nine a.m. the sky cleared completely revealing banks of Cumulus moving from the west 1500 meters above sea level. At two p.m. the wind was recording 28 miles, a marked difference from that of the past two days. I returned in the early evening accompanied by John Eddy of the U.S. Forest Service.

January 23

The snow let up at one p.m. but the fog and frost persisted all day. The wind reached 72 m.p.h. at two p.m., but the temperature remains moderate. The two instrument technicians of the Eppley Laboratory, Newport, R.I., reached Pinkham Notch this morning to repair the Engelhard recorder of the pyrheliometer which they have furnished us. The trouble is caused by a broken suspension spring weighing a fraction of an ounce but to make a satisfactory repair it was necessary to pack the sixty-pound instrument down the mountain.

Rough frost formed early in the day but as the wind shifted more northerly the usual rime took its place. A diffuse aurora was observed from the Base Station in the evening but the mountain cloud blanket prevented any summit observations by eye, camera or La Cour star box.

This is the 62nd anniversary of one of the most violent storms experienced by the Hitchcock-Huntington Expedition and offers ample proof that mild temperatures in early January are no criterion of continued moderate weather through the month. On January 10, 1871, a temperature of 37° was noted, which is higher than any of our readings since December 1, 1932. But the extreme weather occurring later that month is best described in the Journal of that expedition:

"January 22. Having a gale today, and not only a high wind, but a temperature below anything I have ever experienced before, now at nine p.m −34° inside the door. The wind is 80 miles, blowing steadily. At two p.m. wind 72, Professor H. measured the velocity. He had to sit with a line around him, myself at the other end indoors, as an anchor; even then it was almost impossible for him to keep his position. Temperature −31°. I put up a pendulum this morning in our room, it is four feet long, and the rod passes through a sheet of cardboard, on which are marked the points of the compass. The oscillations when the wind blew in gusts were in every direction, changing suddenly, and sometimes had a rotary motion. When the wind was steady the oscillations were northwest and southeast. With two fires the room is cold tonight. Had a long talk with Littleton and Concord, all anxious to know how cold it is here."

"January 23. The wind raged all night. The house rocked fearfully, but as we had no fear of a wreck, it did not disturb us much. Sometimes it would seem as if things were going by the board, but an inspection showed everything all right. It is a sublime affair, such a gale—only we do not care to have it repeated too often. Nobody was hurt or scared, though there was not much sleep for our party, with such an uproar of the elements. Evidently the spirits of the mountain are angry at this invasion of their domain. Toward morning the wind ceased, and all day it has been nearly calm. The temperature outside −43°. Professor H. and myself sat up all night to keep fires going. The pendulum gave oscillation of an inch and a half at times during the night. Temperature tonight ten p.m. −40°; a changeable climate this."

January 24

Today the wind blew steadily from the west and northwest at 55–64 m.p.h., discouraging me from returning to the summit. So I improved my time in the lowlands by packing up two loads to the Halfway House, including the original recorder and a spare instrument should the former one give us further trouble.

The summit temperature ranged during the day from 3° to 8° and the sky cleared at four p.m. with every indication of improved weather conditions. Very low humidity readings were observed today. At eight p.m. the minimum reading was recorded: 15% resulting from a 5° depression at a temperature of 11°. This is far below any humidity we have calculated before.

January 27

Washburn and Hawkins left this morning for the Glen with Observatory mail. We certainly can't complain about our mail service to date. During the night the summit went under and we awoke to find the station engulfed in fog, snow and wind, our usual combination. Judging from the hygrograph record the first clouds struck the summit at one a.m.

The wind has blown steadily all day from the ENE and NE, an unusual quarter. As might be expected with the wind blowing from that direction, the frost deposit is a very heavy accumulation with considerable water content, termed "rough frost." This thick frost, which lacks the delicate structure of the usual rime formed by the west wind, built out at the rate of one inch per hour from noon to ten p.m. on a stick used for measuring snow depth. A plentiful harvest of water is promised when the present storm abates.

We understand that this storm has caused appreciable damage along the New England coast and that violent weather is expected today. The tem-

The Tip-Top House and other summit buildings are captured
by Observatory photographers cloaked in winter white.

perature has remained surprisingly constant during the last few days for it
has varied little from 15°. The Nantucket Lightship was dragged 30 miles
from her permanent position by the high seas and gale, according to reports.
Sure hope our anchor chains hold better!

In the early evening the frost accumulation proved too much for the
heated anemometer for it rapidly came to a standstill, despite the 600 watts
being sent through the heating unit. The apparatus now under construction,
we hope, will continue to operate despite such unfavorable conditions as
prevail tonight.

January 29

Today was a real mild Sabbath and judging from lowland reports our weather,
though cloudy with light winds, is much more pleasant than the windy raw
weather of the valley. We remained in clouds throughout the day. This has
certainly been a cloudy month and the last few days are no exception. At
four p.m. the snow of the past two days ceased, leaving about six inches in
the gages. This snowstorm has been a welcome addition to the scanty snow
cover in the lowlands. Now there is a fine foundation for the winter's snow
cover which we hope will provide the best of skiing for many weeks to come.

Sal and I went down to the Halfway House in the forenoon to meet Dr.
H. C. Willett, acting head of the meteorological department at Massachu-

setts Institute of Technology, who will be our guest at the Observatory for a few days. A Salem party packed up eight heavy duty insulators and some other gear forwarded from Pinkham. The insulators were sent us by the Corning Glass Works when we made known the severe requirements our antennas must withstand. These are tested for a 4500-pound load and we surely hope they will solve the antenna problem.

A large group of skiers were met at the House including a contingent from Berlin under the guidance of our old friend, Henry Barbin (for whom we have named the drift where we turned back to the summit during the storm of December 12). Skiing was excellent on the lower four miles and above the Halfway House the road was skiable its entire length for about the first time this winter, if one were equipped with "rubber-tipped" skis.

Ray Lavender and Ray Pressey, both of whom had visited the Observatory earlier, accompanied Sal and me on the climb, had a late dinner and returned to the valley in the afternoon with Salem, Mass., as their ultimate destination.

This is the fourth Sunday we have worked Sise on the 56-mc. band from Mt. Wachusett. He was unable to drive more than halfway up the mountain road but nevertheless exchanged words with Mac for several minutes.

Dr. Willett, who is a specialist on fog and cloud formations, certainly has ample opportunity to study not only the dense fog which cloaks the mountain so often but the frost accumulation which it leaves.

The extensive low-pressure area has remained stationary over Nova Scotia causing heavy snowfall in its rear. The storm of the past three days has left extensive alterations along the coastline and storm damages approaching two million dollars have been estimated. The combination of spring tides and gigantic storm waves appear to have caused great losses along the waterfront.

January 30

Today is one of those fine invigorating days which we wish were only more common. At seven a.m. the fog became thinner, revealing clear sky with dense Cumulus in the eastern valleys. A two p.m. balloon run indicated prevailing northwest surface as well as upper winds.

I shot 100 feet of 16 mm. film for these is no telling when we shall have bright sun again immediately following a long frost storm. Both near-by and distant views are very striking today and we hope that some of these vistas were recorded photographically. But one must actually be here to appreciate the grandeur of the cloud and frost formations prevailing today.

Several outdoor chores were attended to, such as refueling the Kohler tank and hauling coal from the garage. The skidding surface is the best we have experienced this year so Sal and I hauled up several loads of hard and soft coal.

On several occasions during the afternoon a double fog bow was observed. This formation showed some color, especially in the primary bow and was caused by refraction and internal reflection of sunlight in the liquid droplets in the air. At sunset the quite common shadow of the mountain was cast on the dense valley clouds to the northeast and on top of this shadow we noticed a corona of striking color.

A trio of M.I.T. students arrived in the afternoon, having waded through the deep snow up the Tuckerman Right Gully with blankets and supplies for several days on the summit.

January 31

A fog bow and solar corona were observed at sunrise. The former is quite common when the cloud cover over the mountain is very thin. The trees are reported heavily frosted down to about 2300 feet on both sides of us. The completely white Franconias and Moosilauke are especially impressive.

In the morning Dr. Willett cleared up several difficulties we have encountered in decoding the Arlington weather dispatch and preparing a synoptic weather map. He also indicated several points that will help in analyzing these charts. Some 200 stations report prevailing eight a.m. and eight p.m. weather conditions, in this way enabling us to learn much about the prevailing general weather conditions and when the more pronounced disturbances may strike us.

In the afternoon Dr. Willett helped us plot balloon runs so that now we can confidently proceed to use the records already obtained for studying the nature of the upper air currents.

This evening we all talked over the 91-mile circuit to Mr. Shaw in Exeter. His voice came through exceptionally fine and he was able to understand perfectly all our comments. It certainly is a great boon to discuss our problems and triumphs with this constant friend and supporter of the expedition. We feel the same thrill as that experienced by the 1870–71 group when they enjoyed thrice weekly telegraphic schedules with their director, Professor Hitchcock in his Hanover office. The telegraph company allowed the observers to use their line directly through to Hanover whenever the company business had been completed, and all the latest news was forwarded to the staff over this hook-up.

This has certainly been a mild month for our mean temperature, calculated according to Weather Bureau practice of averaging the daily maxima and minima, is only 12.6°, which is a warmer January average than any recorded up here from 1870–1887, except the one year of January, 1880.

Only seven clear days were enjoyed. The lowest temperature was recorded when the thermometer registered −19° January 1 and the second coldest day on January 12–13 with −16°. The only above freezing temperature was registered on the 23rd when 33° was recorded.

The January mean temperature in Boston was 10° above normal with only two days having a mean temperature below normal. The mean temperature in New York was 9.5° above normal. Portland, Oregon, also had cloudy weather this month with 27 cloudy days on 26 of which it snowed or rained!

This month brought deficient snowfall in the East but the opposite condition prevailed in the West where unusually heavy snowfalls have been reported.

The Polar Year observer at Point Barrow must have put in a chilly month, for he reported twenty days with a temperature of −30° or lower; fifteen with temperature −40° or lower; three days with temperature −50° or lower, and one day with temperature −60°!

Fortunately his is not a windy location for the maximum velocity of the month was 17 m.p.h. We shiver when we think of his 34-minute pilot balloon observation with the temperature at −41°!

1979

"We Recorded
the Greatest Wind
Ever Measured on Earth"

Wendell Stephenson

Though he worked atop the mountain for just a year and a half, Wendell Frank Stephenson (1908–1990) happened to be at the summit in April 1934 when the greatest wind ever measured blew across the mountain. The Aurora, Illinois native and 1930 University of Chicago graduate worked for the newly organized Mount Washington Observatory during a portion of the winter of 1932–33. He was a full-time weather observer the following winter, then went on to work for the Appalachian Mountain Club, and eventually became a teacher. Stephenson's wife, 87-year-old Eleanor Ballard Stephenson, met her husband-to-be on top of Mount Washington in the fall of 1933, during a hiking trip to the summit with her dad. The couple were married the following summer, just four months after the record wind. Mrs. Stephenson still lives in Bethlehem in the home she and her husband built more than 30 years.

ON APRIL 12, 1934, the greatest wind ever measured on the face of the earth—231 miles per hour—was recorded by three weather observers atop Mt. Washington, New Hampshire. The previous high of 152 mph had been recorded only a year earlier. No wind higher than the 1934 howler has ever been recorded, not even during a hurricane.

Salvatore Pagliuca was the chief observer on the weather team in the hut on the mountain top. Cook, forecaster, and repairman Wendell Stephenson, and radio operator Alex "Mac" McKenzie, were the other team mem-

Witnesses to the record wind of April 12, 1934 were, l–r, Sal Pagliuca, Alex McKenzie, and Wendell Stephenson.

bers. Two hikers were windbound with them that day. This is Wendell Stephenson's account of the record-making occasion.

Nothing on the radio or the weather maps on April 11, 1934, gave any clue to the extraordinary events that were about to happen. The temperature was warm for the mountains—low 20s—and a heavy, almost clear ice rime was rapidly covering everything. When we came back in the house from our routine inspection of gauges and recorders, the melting ice from our storm clothes left puddles everywhere.

Mac and I took a break from normal procedures in the late afternoon. This was tea and doughnut time, as we all were fairly free from duties before supper. Sal commented that if the wind kept increasing, we'd keep a 24-hour watch. He'd take the early shift, Mac would go from 1 to 4 a.m., and I, low man on the pole, would get the shift from 4 to 7 a.m. Well, it kept getting wilder and wilder, with gusts around 100 mph, so the all-night plan, a rather common occurrence in those days, went into action.

We were all young, in good shape, happy with our munificent salary— and why not? The first year it had been $5 a month and now it was $5 a week! We had no trouble sleeping in our unheated bedroom, so Mac had to thump me awake, and in that half-awake state I stood by the stove to dress and tune myself to what was going on outside. I had the tingly feeling that it was blowing about as hard as I'd ever heard it. The house shuddered in a steady throb. You see, up there the wind blows steadily, not in gusts, so it has a tone for any given velocity. We had learned to guess quite accurately how fast the wind was going by, and I decided to check my guess of more than 100 mph.

Our anemometer sent electric impulses to a recorder in Mac's radio shack. At the passing of a mile of wind, a pen kicked up and made a short, straight line, perpendicular to the line on the clock-driven recording sheet. A fast count of the straight lines over a five-minute span could easily be figured to miles per hour. I counted several blocks but couldn't get much over 90 to 100 mph. I knew that was inaccurate, which meant only one thing —so much ice had built up on the mast carrying the anemometer rotor that it was shielding the rotor from the full force of the wind. This happened whenever rime was forming rapidly, and one of us would go up the ladder to the roof, bash and beat the ice away, and scurry down to take a few fast stopwatch readings and make a note on the chart to explain the sudden increase in velocity.

I could wax dramatic from this distance, but then and there it was my job—so into the storm gear and out the door I went. I began to be suspicious of the situation when I could hardly get the door open against the vacuum of the wind screaming by. I was further convinced when I got knocked down as soon as I stepped out. I had leaned, as usual, into the northwest wind when I stepped out, but the blast was from the southeast and dead against the ladder. It took two tries to get started, with me carrying a club to break the ice and trying to keep my parka from blowing up over my head and arms. I wasn't afraid or apprehensive, just annoyed that I had to go so slow. I hooked a leg around the ladder, hung on madly, and beat away the huge ice shield that had indeed formed. I finally threw the club down, crawled back under the ladder, and ducked around the corner of the house and in the still stubborn door.

Before I even took off the parka, I grabbed the stopwatch and began counting. Once I tried—but couldn't believe the answer. Twice—but it still seemed too fast. Three times—"Ye gods," I whispered, "186 miles an hour!"

And so it was. Had I known, I might never have gone out. But there was more. When Sal and Mac came down, I was almost out of control, and, if anything, the wind was even wilder. We sent the 186 figure on our morning weather report, and did we get reactions! The most important and fortunate break came when Dr. C. Brooks of the Blue Hill Observatory called to check and Mac plugged the anemometer into the radio and let Dr. Brooks time the gusts for a while. Our new high was the famous 231 mph at 1:21 p.m., which Dr. Brooks also timed to lend support to our claim. Sal held the stop-watch as the gust velocity climbed first to 229 and finally to 231.

The wind blew ferociously into the afternoon of the 12th, but by the 13th we were back to normal—which for Mt. Washington is about 80 miles an hour. The house hadn't blown over, collapsed, or otherwise suffered, thanks to the 20 or more inches of heavy ice rime.

People are still always asking me if I was frightened up there that day. Well, I was just a young man not too long out of the University of Chicago. McKenzie hadn't been long out of Dartmouth either. We were all in our twenties and full of life. Do you know what we did when that wind hit a record high? We cheered! We were in on a record setter, and we were part of it. We recorded the greatest wind ever measured on earth.

June 1934

The Great Wind
of April 11–12, 1934

Salvatore Pagliuca

From *Monthly Weather Review*

For the first two years of its existence, Sal Pagliuca (1899–1944) served as chief observer for the Mount Washington Observatory. Pagliuca, who hailed from a small town outside Naples, Italy, was an electrical and mechanical engineer. After leaving the Observatory following the winter of 1934, he took up postgraduate work in meteorology at the Massachusetts Institute of Technology (MIT) in Cambridge, and for a few years was the chief observer of the nearby Blue Hill Observatory. During World War II, while serving in the U.S. Army Air Force, Pagliuca was tragically killed in a jeep accident while testing weather equipment on Mount Mitchell in North Carolina.

THE LOW pressure which caused the greatest 24-hour wind movement ever recorded on Mount Washington, N.H., and the highest wind velocity ever officially recorded anywhere in the world by accurately-tested instruments, was preceded there by a period of 48 hours of fair weather with normal pressure, temperature, and other meteorological elements. On the afternoon of April 10 a singular period of near calm was experienced. But the pressure fell slowly from the afternoon of April 11 until 6 a.m., April 12, and then more rapidly, under the influence of the low-pressure area centering over the eastern part of the Great Lakes region.

On the morning of April 11, there was an emissary sky with Cirrostraus, Cirrus densus, Cirrus filosus, and some Altocumulus lenticularis, moving from the west. At 8 a.m. low Stratocumulus was seen rapidly advancing over an extended front from the east. At 11 a.m., while the upper sky was covered with eight-tenths Cirrostratus, Cirrus filosus, and Cirrus densus, the low Stratocumulus from the east began arching over the summit of the mountain. The southeast wind had reached a velocity of 80 miles per hour, and was steadily increasing. The temperature held about 22° F. without any appreciable change. Rough frost began forming soon after the summit became enveloped by clouds.

The afternoon of April 11 was characterized by a heavy southeast wind of moderate gustiness, reaching a maximum of 136 miles per hour. During the following night the hourly wind movement was never less than 107 miles and rough frost formed rapidly.

The morning of April 12 was characterized by a rapidly increasing southeast wind of appreciable gustiness, steadily falling pressure, slightly rising temperature from a minimum of 15° F., reached at 2 a.m., and a light fall of granular snow. Rough frost accumulated heavily throughout the day, with a fairly well defined feathery appearance, icy structure, high water content, and producing a characteristic deep-blue light reflection.

At noon, April 12, the hourly wind movement had risen to 155 miles with gusts reaching a velocity well above 200 mi./hr. From noon to 1 p.m., while other conditions were comparatively unchanged, the wind attained its extreme force. Between 12:25 p.m. and 12:30 p.m., a 5 minute average wind velocity of 188 mi./hr. was recorded on the Weather Bureau type multiple register. Gusts were frequently timed by two observers, with stop-watch and Nardin chronometer, and the values obtained corrected by means of the extrapolated calibration curve of the United States Bureau of Standards.

While frequent values of 225 mi./hr., including two-thirds mile at this speed, were obtained, several gusts of 229 mi./hr. were timed, and at 1:21 p.m. the extreme value of 231 mi./hr. for a succession of 3 one-tenth mile contacts was timed twice. This is the highest natural wind velocity ever officially recorded by means of an anemometer on Mount Washington or anywhere else.

The hourly movement between noon and 1 p.m. reached a peak of 173 miles.

The barograph, 6,284 feet above sea level, showed vigorous oscillations of two-tenths inch maximum amplitude. The lowest pressure of 22.82 inches was recorded at 12:45 p.m.

In the afternoon the force of the wind decreased rapidly, while the snowfall increased in intensity. The pressure rose rapidly between 4 p.m. and 6 p.m. and more gradually thereafter. At 8 p.m. the total snowfall for the previous 24 hours was 10 inches and had a water equivalent of 3.87 inches. The

COURTESY ELEANOR STEPHENSON

Wendell Stephenson (on phone), Alex McKenzie and Sal Pagliuca
sit down for a meal in the summit observatory.

huge accumulation of rough frost had reached a maximum thickness of 3 feet on the most exposed objects.

The maximum 24-hour wind movement was obtained between 4 p.m. April 11, and 4 p.m. April 12, with a total of 3,095 miles and an average of 129 mi./hr.

Although the anemometer was well exposed to the southeast wind, the rapid accumulation of rough frost around the lower portion of the 10-foot staff seemed to have had the tendency to break somewhat the force of the wind, since the wind-movement curve shows decided increases of velocity following each cleaning of the anemometer post immediately below the instrument. The figures obtained, therefore, should be considered as somewhat conservative.

Every mile of wind was recorded by the special electrically heated anemometer.

No serious difficulty was experienced by the observers in attending to their outdoor duties necessary under the extreme conditions. The much discussed question whether a man can stand up under the heavy pressure of such a strong wind remains still a matter of speculation. Experienced men seem to react to the impact of the wind with various adjustments such as bending themselves toward the wind, lowering the body by spreading the

Observatory crew members Wendell Stephenson, Salvatore "Sal" Pagliuca, Robert Monahan, and Alex McKenzie pose for a group shot atop the summit.

legs, and exposing the side of the body to the wind. The various counteractions, difficult to evaluate in terms of force, and variable with different individuals, together with the fact that the wind pressure is less by one-fifth part or more at the summit than at sea level makes it possible for persons to withstand the force of extremely strong winds with tolerable difficulties. Besides the velocity is much less near a rough rocky surface than in the free air where the anemometer is exposed.

Only slight damage occurred, chiefly to the exposed instruments. A structure supporting a special wind vane, situated at the end of the trestle, partly collapsed and badly smashed a snow gauge. Another wind vane on the trestle was slightly damaged, and the wind vane on the summit tank developed trouble. The observatory building shook considerably under the severe impact, but obviously the heavy covering of rough frost on the exposed east side, and on the roof, must have increased greatly the rigidity of the structure. The delicate pyrheliometer bulb did not suffer the slightest damage, and was found to be covered by a singularly small amount of frost. The telephone line from the summit to the base station was also undamaged.

From 12:35 to 1 p.m. April 12, the one-thirtieth mile contact clicks from the anemometer were broadcast from the observatory's ultra-short (5m) wave transmitter and were received at the Blue Hill Observatory in Milton,

Mass., 142 miles south, by Director C. F. Brooks, who timed the contacts by intervals of 5 seconds. Five samplings of one or two minutes each from 12:37 to 12:55 p.m. showed "true" velocities by 5-second intervals ranging from 108 to 216 mi./.hr. The fastest 40 contacts, representing a true mile, came in only 17 seconds, or at a rate of 3½ miles a minute (210 mi./hr.). The mean velocities by whole minutes ranged from 148 to 192 mi./hr., and for the 5½ minutes as a unit, a random sampling of this windy hour, 172 mi./hr.

1956

The Long Trail

Arthur E. Bent (1897–1976)

From *Winter on Mount Washington*
Published by Mount Washington Observatory

The measure of some trails is in miles or days, others in years, or even a lifetime.

I. The Blizzard, 1920–1941

The door of the Observatory was a good safe place from which to look at the blizzard. I took hold of the handle of the door carefully and turned it tentatively. A door behaves strangely in a hurricane—sometimes it feels as if someone was holding it from the other side and sometimes it strikes against you as it blows open, depending on the direction of the wind. All action in the hurricane should be careful and tentative, as a matter of fact, because the margin of safety is so small that the consequences of everything must be weighed and considered.

Standing just outside the door, I listened to the storm. The roar of the wind was like the sound of a passing express train. Now and then a gust reached into my protected place as if trying to snatch me out into the roaring wind. The snow was so thick in the air that the light of morning was subdued—as in late afternoon. Driven by the gusty wind, the snow streaked by in horizontal lines, now blotting out everything and not giving a glimpse beyond. The visibility was poor, as the Summit House could not be seen. Very faintly the instrument tower appeared 50 feet away. The temperature was 10, not very cold, but, because of the hurricane, the cooling power was great, comparable to a much lower temperature at low air velocity. When the wind is over 75 miles an hour it is a hurricane.

The question was: to go down or not. There was no particular need to go that day. Several days had passed, however, without much better weather and in January on Mount Washington you cannot expect a calm day. Such a decision must be on a very personal basis, no one else can really advise at all. Looking out again, I thought of the usual things. Would I be too cold? Could I find my way across the bare Home Stretch Flat? Could I find the turns in the road? Could I stand the battering of the storm long enough to get down to where it was not so severe? These are the thoughts that go flashing through the mind and there is no definite answer. One thing is certain: the more experienced you are, the more clearly you see all the difficulties. Down through the years, how many men must have looked out on the Mount Washington blizzard and wondered.

Once the decision is made, there is a satisfying activity to take the mind off anticipated troubles. There is always the pack to arrange. Why is it that, going up or down, there is always something to carry? Windproof clothing is put on and crampons adjusted on the feet. That is one of the advantages of going down—you can prepare yourself in the security of the building and go forth fresh and ready to face the storm. While the men were writing last-minute letters for me to carry, I arranged the hood of my parka about my face. The idea is to cover up as much as possible and still leave a little opening to see out of and breathe through. The hood should be big enough to leave room for wrapping a woolly scarf around your neck so as to leave a little open space near your mouth. If anything touches your mouth it is likely to freeze to you because of the condensation of the breath. These things are not only a matter of knowledge and experience, but also of having proper equipment. Little details are important, like having a flap to cover every pocket so it will not blow full of snow.

Going down the steps of the Observatory is rather awkward because the long spikes of the crampons give one a feeling of being on stilts. I held on to the railing so that a gust of wind would not push me over. Down on the snow and ice the crampons bit into the surface and I felt at least secure from slipping. After a brief wave at my friends in the door, I started off, and almost at once the building faded from sight.

My first feeling was of relief; it is not as bad as I thought it was going to be. Objects on the summit of the mountain are close together so that by steering a course from one to the next it is possible to have quite a good idea of location and direction. Down the slope near the Stage Office I went, keeping the railing of the summer stairway in sight. In a moment the stone wall marking the outer edge of the road appeared beside me and I turned to follow near it, a small and lonely figure in the storm.

* * *

When a man thinks of telling of the blizzard there are many reasons why he hesitates. Looking back through the years, thinking one by one of the men who have lived on Mount Washington, of mountaineers and explorers everywhere, who is there who will assume that it is fitting he should tell the story? Where are the words to confine on narrow lines the impression of the impact of the hurricane upon man?

Beyond this is the more fundamental query which leaves one wondering where the objective reality of the storms is. We can measure the blizzard in certain scientific terms; miles per hour, pounds per square inch, but even then it is elusive. Suppose we say the wind is blowing a hundred miles an hour. Our first thought is of the even progress of an airplane, an express train; but this is not the blizzard. There is a certain satisfaction in the numerical value, but it signifies little. Our scientific instruments integrate the velocity of the wind over relatively long periods. Close study shows an infinite variability in speed from almost nothing to the full force of the storm in a few seconds, so we fall back on saying the average velocity is so much and the gusts are hitting so much. As soon as we qualify our measure, we begin to lose our grip on reality of definition, and probably it is well that this is so. There is nothing original in the thought that if we are to learn the real significance of the impact of situations upon men we must look within the personality and not seek an answer in the measure of physical qualities. The blizzard may be likened to a chemical reaction: the reaction of the measurable external forces upon the individual.

This is why it is so very difficult to describe the blizzard and why one is so hesitant to try. As a human experience the blizzard may be the final defeat in which the individual goes to destruction, or it may be a glorious adventure, and it may be both these things at the same time to different people. To a few on Mount Washington it has been the former, fortunately to many more it has been the latter.

Reduced to simple terms, the blizzard is wind, snow, cold and cloud, coming at you over ice, and the severity is measured by the relative combinations of these factors. One of the first descriptions of a real storm is found in Mawson's *The Home of the Blizzard*, where hurricane snowstorms in the Antarctic of over a hundred miles an hour are told of. Many other brief references are found in the literature of mountaineering and exploration. It is a strange thing that of all the places where scientific measurements have been made, the winds of Mount Washington are apparently equal to the worst. Dr. Charles F. Brooks, in a recent article, *The Worst Weather in the World*, concludes that the severity of Mount Washington is about equal to those found in other notoriously stormy spots. Of course, it is well known that the highest natural wind ever officially recorded by an instrument was observed at Mount Washington in April, 1934, when the maximum reached 231 miles per hour.

The first encounter with the blizzard is apt to come as something of a surprise because anything like it is so far removed from the experience of most of us. A long time ago, at Christmas-time in 1920, I was wandering around alone on the summit. We were camped for a few days in the Stage Office enjoying a winter trip on the mountain. I came to the corner of the old Tip Top House and, creeping around, was met by a solid wall of wind and snow. I was startled and bewildered, and, after struggling a few feet, retreated. That was something to think about. A fellow could get lost in that pretty easily, with his face being plastered with snow.

The next sample was more convincing. Several years later there were three of us on the summit, camped in Camden Cottage, and we wanted to get down. The wind was roaring over the top of the mountain and again it was snowing. We tried an experiment by opening the door and throwing out a board—it simply disappeared horizontally. Probably it was nothing unusual as a storm, but it seemed so to us. Fortunately, we had proper equipment. Putting on our windproof clothing, "Submarine Suits" salvaged after the last war, we roped together and started down. Sheltered from the northwest wind by the summit rock we followed the road to the edge of the flat area just below the top. Nowadays the men call it Home Stretch Flat. I was ahead and I put my head down against the wind. Very soon though, my eyes were covered by the freezing snow. I was afraid that I might not be able to wipe it away many times. We huddled together and decided to go back. The next day it was not so bad.

Leaving the immediate summit area, the way leads along the sheltered east side of the mountain. A false feeling of security is likely to develop here, but those who are very familiar with the mountain know that the worst place of all is just beyond. Plunging down a short slope and turning a little more toward the wind, the road leads across the large flat area. There is no shelter from the northwest wind and no obstructions impede its full velocity. In recent years a line of cairns has been built across this area close to one side of the road. The individual piles of rocks are about as high as a man and are spaced about 50 feet apart. In summer they seem ridiculously close together.

And so, about the time you are thinking it is really not so bad, the full blast of the wind strikes you. The hurricane wind is not something you can lean against; it is gusty and treacherous, and you have to struggle against it with every ounce of your strength. That is why the time element is important: you can only stand the battering of the wind for just so long without getting rather worn out. Curiously enough, too, this struggle against the wind brings another problem. The exertion is so severe that the traveler becomes quite hot, and the driven snow melts on his face. Occupied with the struggle against the storm and having hands cased in cumbersome mittens it is difficult to do anything about it, but it may be necessary to stop from time to time to break the icicles from the eyelids. It is easy to see that all this is rather wearing and when you reflect that through it all it is only possible to see three or four feet, one can appreciate that the Mount Washington blizzard is a fearsome experience.

Raising my left hand to get what shelter I could for my face, I peered down near my feet with my right eye. There is no use looking ahead. Near you there may be a raised bit of old footprint or the straight line of a snow-drift to give a clue as to the direction. From time to time a cairn would loom up ahead to show that I was on my way, but mostly I just plunged along in the center of my little circle of visibility of a yard or so.

There isn't much time for philosophy, for reflection on misdeeds, or future plans; all the attention is required for the problems of the moment. Very fleeting ideas come darting in and out, vague impressions connected with immediate events. In a sense, though, there is a philosophy of the blizzard, which I suspect varies a great deal with individuals. In my own case one idea which helps is to try not to visualize the whole journey, the thought of the long hours against the storm can be very discouraging. Concentrate on some immediate objective and when that is attained pick out another. While the physical progress may be more or less continuous, the effect mentally is of a series of short dashes, a little easier to summon courage for. Another thing is not to fight the storm harder than you have to. When you feel the surge of a great gust of wind, don't push ahead just then, but wait a second or so to make your effort at a time a bit later when the strength of the wind is less. All the time, too, you should be weighing the chances. There are certain parts of the mountain where the climber is rather caught, where retreat is almost as difficult as advance.

An impression which was quite strong at the time of the climb I am describing was that of the pitiful insignificance of the individual contrasted with the mighty power of the storm. The human frame, protected by an inadequate layer of clothing, seemed too puny to wage such a contest with the elements. Mere existence was extremely tenuous, drawn out to a very fine thread. In more senses than one the lonely figure was walking near a precipice.

Why do this alone? Well, there are a number of reasons. For one thing, there is not very much that men can do for each other at such a time. Even speech is practically impossible. When visibility is low, it is difficult for two to keep in sight of each other. Adjusting your pace to the changes of gait of another person imposes an additional burden which can be irritating. Possibly there may be some mental support derived from the presence of another person, something reassuring. If this is so, it may be another reason for being alone. To experience the blizzard to the ultimate you must be alone.

I had been thinking that it was going to be easier when I turned the corner, and I remember the brief sinking feeling when it wasn't different. Then came the moment when things didn't look right any more. I saw a hump of snow beside me, so I sat on it, braced against the wind. Turning the corner had been confusing—the direction of the wind was different and things looked different. There was no particular sensation of being lost because I knew fairly closely where I was, but I did not want to go wandering off on the mountain if I could find the road again. In a very short time the density of the drifting snow decreased for a moment and I could see eight or ten feet. I was sitting on the outer wall of the road and the Great Gulf was just beyond. A glance was enough to give bearings again, and on I went.

Below was another flat area known as the Cow Pasture. Here again there was little to define the way, and at the beginning and end were difficult turns, where it is easy to go astray. Confidence was increasing, however, as every step was taking me lower down the mountain out of the fierce wind, and occasional breaks in the swirling snow gave glimpses ahead. While the storm was still rough, I was getting into the region where nothing more was likely to happen, and soon it was just a matter of the long trudge down the road to skis at the Half Way House.

In the shelter of the forest it was hard to believe that the storm was raging above.

May 1913

Ice Trail of the Presidential Range

James Walter Goldthwait

From *Appalachia*

A preeminent geologist and professor at Dartmouth College, James W. Goldthwait (1890–1947) is best known for his pioneering studies of the glacial cirques and terminal moraines of the Presidential Range. His findings, contending that the last great ice sheet covered the Presidential Range peaks after previous glacial activity had formed such notable geological landmarks as Tuckerman Ravine, was first reported in The Geology of New Hampshire, *published in 1925 by the New Hampshire Academy of Science. At Dartmouth, Goldthwait was actively involved in the 1909 formation of the Dartmouth Outing Club and was well-known among DOC circles for his snowshoeing exploits. Coincidentally, he was president of the New Hampshire Academy of Science (NHAS) in 1932 when Joe Dodge made a pitch to the organization for start-up funding of the planned Mount Washington Observatory. Dodge came away from the May 1932 meeting with a promise of $400—an amount which basically emptied the NHAS treasury, save for a few dollars earmarked for the next planned membership mailing.*

THE Presidential Range before the Ice Age was probably a good deal like the range to-day. Thousands upon thousands of years had elapsed since the wrinkling up of the rocks, allowing time for the weather to loosen and for rivers to remove the rock waste from the mountain sides until the very roots of the original mountain structure—contorted gneisses and schists—were exposed at the surface. These crumpled or foliated rocks, glittering with mica flakes and peppered with crystals of secondary minerals, can be seen all over the range both in the loose rock and in the ledges. During the crumpling, hot masses of granite invaded the structure from below and shot through it irregular veins wherever tension permitted. Probably the form of the range at no time corresponded directly with the forms of the folds, as the crumpling process occupied vast lengths of time and the surface was being degraded by weather and streams then as now. It is a serious mistake to think of the White Mountains as having formed simply or chiefly by this upwrinkling of strata. There is no agreement between the present form of the range and the underground folds in the rock. The presence of broad summits and ridges with gentle side slopes where rock structure would lead one to look for towering peaks of alpine form and size is accounted for by the extensive degradation which this region has suffered in the long interval that has elapsed since the crumpling of the mountain structure was completed. The decay of the mountain sides and the removal of the waste or weathered material by rain and running water reduced the range to a semblance of its present form during the several geologic periods which preceded the Ice Age.

This degradation, however, did not consist in a steadily progressing reduction of the mountains to their present proportions. At one time during the long period the general form of the range appears to have been even more subdued than now. On all the sides of the dome-like summits long graded slopes of moderate declivity stretched down to the lowlands, where now lie the deep intermount valleys. Scraps of this old mountain topography still remain. The summits of Washington, Jefferson, Adams, and Madison retain much of this primitive symmetry in spite of ravages by the ice sheet. The flat "lawns" which border them and stretch forward to the brinks of the great semicircular ravines are fragments of the undulating side slopes of the ancient range. Here and there one may see long narrow remnants of the ancient surface extending down a smooth crested spur. Chandler Ridge, especially, when viewed from a distance and from a point slightly above its own altitude, shows very strikingly the gentle gradient of this old surface. Here and in many other places one may see how the side slopes of the range flatten into insignificant relief where now the altitude is 4,000 feet above the sea. To restore this surface fully one would have to fill up the great ravines and torrent valleys evenly to the level of the lawns and smooth-topped spurs. The "gulfs" which to-day so deeply indent the sides of the range and give it its height had not then been carved out, because the region then stood nearer to the level of the sea.

This subdued topography which appears on the broad summits, lawns, and the larger spurs is probably part of the great stream-leveled surface of Cretaceous time which Professor Davis has called "the peneplain of Southern New England." While the maritime portion of New England was worn down to a low undulating plain, the more remote interior, particularly the White Mountains district, drained as it was by headwaters of several river systems, remained comparatively mountainous, although this, the greatest of the ranges, rose but a thousand feet or two above the neighboring intermount lowlands.

When, at length, this worn-down surface of New England was elevated to approximately its present position, the rivers which had coursed sluggishly along the lowlands between the subdued ranges, the ancestors of the Connecticut, Merrimac, Saco, and Androscoggin, were turned into mighty agents of erosion. As they entrenched themselves in the lowland floors, new mountain torrents developed all around them on the graded mountain sides, and thus a new topography, consisting of deeper, steeper-sided valleys was carved out beneath the smoothly graded surface of the old range. From that time to the present the deepening and widening of the valleys both by rivers and glaciers, at the expense of the old upland area, has tended to restore to a slight degree the grandeur of those ancient mountains whose roots we see in cross section in the contorted rocks. At the beginning of the Ice Age the Presidential Range had become deeply carved by these rejuvenated streams, whose rather crooked valleys, with V-shaped cross section, reached back from every side toward the still unconsumed upland along its axis. Some of these torrent-worn valleys still remain, hardly changed by glacier or ice sheet; more of them suffered considerable alteration while occupied by moving ice; and a number of them have been quite made over, at least in their higher stretches, by the mountain glaciers which are later to be described. Here, indeed, is a range of New England where typical river-made valleys are less numerous than glacial-carved valleys. One of the best examples of stream-carved ravines is the valley of Snyder Brook, near the north end of the range. Starting as a little V-shaped valley below Madison Hut, this grows rapidly to the proportion of a full-sized valley as it makes it steep descent to Randolph. A view down the Valley Way Trail brings out two significant features; the V-shaped cross section of the valley, and the alternately overlapping spurs which result from the bending of the stream from side to side. The significance of this is appreciated only when one contrasts such valleys with those which mountain glaciers have occupied, as will presently be seen.

Signs of the Former Existence of Local Glaciers

We come now to a chapter in the glacial history of the White Mountains which has curiously been neglected—namely, that of local glaciation. It is no new idea—this idea of systems of river-like glaciers extending down the valleys from snow fields on Mount Washington and neighboring summits. Agassiz conceived it; Guyot, Hitchcock, and their contemporaries accepted it and sought to demonstrate it, although without permanent success. Much of the evidence which these men offered of local valley glaciers is now recognized as the record of the great ice sheet; some of it has been forgotten or set aside in a spirit of skepticism, which it must be admitted has not always been undeserved. It is unfortunately true that just where the valley glaciers should have left their most distinct records, that is, at their heads amid the mountain tops, the pioneer glacialist found no evidence of them. If others searching more recently in the White Mountains have come across such records, they have not published descriptions of them so far as I know.

The most characteristic feature produced by mountain glaciers, according to modern physiographers, is the cirque, or corrie. This is a bowl-shaped glen or amphitheatre, carved by the glacier, far up on the mountain side where the stream of ice tears loose from the thinner snow field and starts down the valley. They are enclosed by great crescentic cliffs or head walls several hundred feet high. From a distance they look like great hollows cut out of the mountain side by a gigantic sugar scoop. The semi-circular line of cliffs marks the place where the glacier headed at a semicircular crevasse called the "bergschrund," a place where the moving ice, torn away by its own weight from the thinner snow fields of the surrounding slopes, carried with it a plentiful supply of the blocks which excessive frost action at the foot of the crevasse is continually loosening. Over-steepened by this quarrying process, the head walls are trimmed farther and farther back on the snow-covered mountain, until at length they may overlap, giving to the surface of upland the appearance of a sheet of dough from which a lot of round biscuits have been cut.

Around the Presidential Range well developed cirque forms may be seen in the Great Gulf and its two largest branches, Jefferson and Madison Ravines, in King, Huntington, and Tuckerman Ravine, and in the ravine of the Castles. The bowl-shaped Bumpus Basin and the Gulf of Slides are doubtless of the same origin, although less well developed and less well preserved. Oakes Gulf and a number of broad ravines alongside the southern peaks appear to be cirques also. It is a pity that so many of these White Mountain cirques have been so long named "ravines"; for they differ so completely in form and origin from ordinary stream-worn ravines. The words "gulf" and "basin" used in a few cases on Mount Washington, are much more discriminative.

It is the gulfs that give the Presidential Range its peculiar charm. Their towering walls and steep crags furnish the mountaineer with much exhila-

Shadows creep across glacially carved Tuckerman Ravine
on the southeast slope of Mount Washington.

rating sport and occasional opportunities for a dangerous climb. In their deep recesses the mountain torrents, fed from belated snow banks and ice-cold springs, rush and toss with loud roar, which in the stillness of the night may rise momentarily with startling crescendo, rousing the sleeping camper in the fear that an avalanche is descending the mountain side. Nowhere in the mountains do the lightning strokes seem so brilliant nor the thunder claps so ear-splitting and persistently reverberating as from under an over-hanging ledge or a protecting boulder at the foot of one of these mighty head walls. The dwarfs who bowled at nine pins in the cirque-like glen of the Cat-skills could have had no more noisy playground then King Ravine.

The only topographic map yet published which does justice to these glaciated ravines is the one made for the Club by Mr. Cutter. This map was my chief inspiration last summer in studying the ancient glaciers, and it will long continue to express in a graphic way the care which this Club is taking to guide summer travelers over the Great Range. In the map the cirque form of several gulfs of the northern peaks is plainly seen in the form and spacing of the contours. The representation of King Ravine particularly is true to nature. One may see how the great head wall a thousand feet high was eaten far back into the gentle slope on the north side of Mount Adams, and the right and left walls were similarly eaten away with the widening of the gla-cier bed until Durand Spur was more than half consumed, forming the "Knife Edge." It would be hard to find two valleys more unlike than the deep, glaciated trough of King Ravine and the narrow stream-carved valley of Snyder Brook which lies close beside it; and Mr. Cutter's map shows keen perception of that difference.

In valleys which have recently been abandoned by mountain glaciers one might hope to find certain other marks of the ice, notably scoured and scratched surfaces on the rocky floor and rock debris derived from the walls and banked up near the lower limit of glaciation in concentric lobes or ter-minal moraines. These marks are missing in the White Mountain ravines, at least in those already mentioned. No great concentric moraine lies at the lower level of King Ravine. Neither are there any well-defined transverse ridges of local drift back within the cirques where they might be expected to mark spasmodic readvances of a dying valley glacier. Instead, the lower two thirds of the ravine floor is occupied by ground moraine deposited by the continental ice sheet, similar to that of the neighboring Randolph low-land. The upper-half-mile above Mossy Fall is occupied, to be sure, by a gi-gantic pile of blocks which has a convex forward margin; but, inasmuch as this deposit lacks the definite linear expression of a true frontal moraine, it is apparently not of glacial origin. The scooping out of so vast an amount of rock from the enclosing spurs and the mountain side as a comparison of King Ravine and Snyder Brook Valley proves to have taken place, must have been accompanied by the depositing somewhere of moraine of equal proportions. There can only be one explanation for the absence of the local moraines and the presence in their place of regional ground moraine; these valleys were ice carved *before* and *not after* the great ice sheet swept across New England, and only those records of local alpine glaciers remain which the ice sheet did not obliterate.

Inasmuch as the evidences of burial of the Presidential Range by the continental ice sheet are clear and convincing, while the record of local glaciers, as already marked, is fragmentary and incomplete, one might ask whether the cirque-like valleys were not perhaps shaped by the ice sheet when it buried the range. Detailed studies of valleys elsewhere has shown that the ice sheet frequently widened those valleys which lay nearly parallel to its course — especially in regions of high relief, where the flow of ice was much faster through the hollows and cols than on the upland and summits; and that where the ice advanced in a direction oblique or transverse to the valleys these were steepened by a plucking process on the iceward side and made gentler by a scrubbing process on the other. It is significant that the well-formed cirques of the Presidential Range trend in all directions. This is brought out by Mr. Cutter's map. The movement of the ice sheet while the range was buried beneath it was from northwest to southeast. The deflection around obstructing slopes was often considerable, however, and it is altogether probable that in pushing against the northwest side of the range the basal portion of the ice would turn and tend strongly to follow any well-defined valley whose axis lay in the northwest and southeast quadrants of the circle. Most of the ravines already named lie thus in positions where they might be expected to suffer severely from the southeastward glaciation. The Ravine of the Castles trends northwestward, King Ravine and Bumpus Basin nearly northwest, Madison, Jefferson, Huntington, and Tuckerman Ravines eastward; but the greatest of all, the Great Gulf, trends northeastward, lying directly transverse to the movement of the continental ice. It is significant that although the head wall and the left or northwest wall of the Great Gulf retain the steepness characteristic of cirque walls, the slope to the right or southeast side has plainly been reduced by regional glaciation and covered with blocks, which locally constitute the bulk of the ground moraine where crags furnished the ice sheet with a plentiful supply of coarse debris. The asymmetry is strong, but not excessive. Moreover, were the gulfs developed by the southeastward movement of the ice sheet, we would expect two different types of forms at the heads of the valleys on opposite sides of the range. While an ice sheet which moved southeastward might widen valleys which trended either northwest or southeast, it would hardly produce steep head walls in them on both sides of the divide. The valleys on the northwest side up which the ice pushed, as, for example, King Ravine, would have their heads roughened and oversteepened by plucking. The fact is, however, that the wide ravines which open toward the northwest are similar in form to those which open to the southeast. It appears to have mattered little whether they faced toward or away from the center of regional glaciation. On the other hand, in support of the view that the cirque form was developed before the ice sheet came across the range, it is notable that the head walls of the valleys which open towards the northwest are somewhat less precipitous and less ragged than those which descend towards the southeast. A more convincing disproof of wholesale ice-sheet erosion as the cause of cirques is the presence of such normal stream-carved valleys beside them as the valley of Snyder Brook. This valley, which lies between the two cirques, King Ravine and Bumpus Basin, and which trends parallel to them, shows no sign that its lower portion was widened and straightened or that its head was enlarged and steepened by the ice sheet. If the continental ice sheet in its southeastward advances across the range had hollowed out the two gulf-like ravines on either side, it would have carved out a similar gulf along the line of Snyder Brook. The existence of this normal torrent valley between the broad ravines or gulfs is natural enough, however, if they are true cirques, for not every valley on the mountain range is so favorably situated as to gather a full supply of snow and to support an alpine glacier. Some, like Snyder Brook valley, might pass through an epoch of local glaciation unchanged, while neighboring ravines might be profoundly altered.

The full extent of these ancient alpine glaciers is as yet unknown. That they filled the broad, gulf-like ravines down as far as the side walls are steep is clear enough. The King Ravine glacier, for instance, was not less than one and a quarter miles long. Those in the Ravine of the Castles and Tuckerman Ravine seem to have been approximately the same size. The Great Gulf glacier was several times as large and seems to have hollowed out its valley at least as far as the blunt end of Chandler Ridge and the mouth of Madison Ravine. It would not be safe to say positively that these glaciers lay thus wholly within the shadow of the peaks, simply because their characteristic topography disappears before one reaches the neighboring lowland. Subsequent erosion by the great ice sheet, which was more intense in the lower ground and broader depressions, and heavy and extensive deposits of glacial drift have combined to obscure whatever records may have existed there. The U-shaped cross section of the Crawford Notch, Carter Notch, and

WINSTON POTE

The Great Gulf separates Mount Washington from the
northern peaks of the Presidential Range.

other deep passages through the mountains makes one wonder whether
possibly the alpine glaciers were long enough to reach out through them;
but the situation of these notches high up on the main divide leads rather to
the opinion that investigation will show them to be pre-glacial notches
which were widened and rounded in cross section by the accelerated flow of
ice in the great ice sheet. More light will be shed on this question of the extent of local glaciers when other high ranges among the White and Green
Mountains are examined to discover how far their ravines are cirques. On
the northwest side of the Carter-Moriah Range several broad hollows seen
from the Gorham road look like possible cirques; but a distant view from
one or two points is not sufficient examination. In a general way the exhibition of cirque forms on this range seems to be poor, and hardly lends hope
that study will show that extensive distribution of cirques which is de-
manded by the long-cherished view that the White Mountain glaciers
stretched far down the Androscoggin, Connecticut, and other valleys.

If the discovery that these local glaciers were confined to the flanks of the
range comes somewhat unexpectedly, the discovery that the glaciers operated before rather than after development of the last great ice sheet is a genuine surprise. It is not yet possible to assign the local glaciation to any
specific part of the glacial period. Perhaps it all took place during one of the

early epochs of that period, long before the last ice sheet made its appearance. If, however, the rock piles in the heads of the cirques prove on further study to be rudely constructed moraines of recent valley glaciers, it will appear probable that there were local snow fields and glaciers both before and after the development of the ice sheet in the last glacial epoch, as well as more effective cirque-carving glaciers in corresponding early and late stages of the preceding epochs.

1960

Skiing and the Mountain

F. Allen Burt

From *The Story of Mount Washington*

OF ALL PLACES in New England where skiers get together, there is none where snow lingers longer, or where everybody from novice to hardened expert may have more fun and thrills, than in Tuckerman Ravine on the eastern flank of Mount Washington. On a sunny Sunday in spring, when snow still lies deep in the ravine and up the headwall, and when the snow field is colorful with scores of happy, lusty skiers, it is hard to realize that skiing as a sport on Mount Washington dates back only fifty years. This first descent by a skier took place on Thursday, 16 February 1905, when Norman Libby of Bridgton, Maine, made the ascent from the Base Station, accompanied by the winter caretaker of the railroad's property, and slid down the mountain on skis.

Mr. Libby, who was assistant editor of *Among the Clouds* for two summers, was not content with being the first man to "slide down Mount Washington," but returned in February 1907, with a friend, intending to climb to the Halfway House for the ski ride down the carriage road.

But at the Glen House the proprietor promptly offered to secure creepers that would make it possible to reach the summit. So, while waiting for the creepers to be sent from Gorham, the two men made the trip to the Halfway House, wearing skis bound with rope. The road was piled with from three to four feet of snow, and along some parts of it Mr. Libby reported that "the drifts were small mountains." After eating dinner by candlelight in the boarded-up Halfway House, the two men fastened on their skis for the run of four miles to the Glen House, which they made in a running time of twenty minutes.

Next morning they made Halfway without incident. Just above the house, at Cape Horn, where the road makes a sharp U-turn, Mr. Libby reported the snow as making "an unbroken slope from the top of the spur down hundreds of feet to the threatening gulf below. Not even a twig offered a clutch in event of mishap, and, our creepers not yet put on, it was a thrilling moment as we passed this declivity." On their return, just after they crossed this same spot, a large area of their path slipped from the ice beneath the hard snow and shot into the valley, a thousand or more feet below! Around the Horn they found a deer, frozen and blown dead against the rocks.

Their creepers were moccasins split and laced at the toe, with two ankle straps for adjustment outside overshoes. On the sole and heel were pieces of steel, the edges of which were turned down like a cooky-cutter. These gave security on crusted snow, but were of little help on ice.

From a point four and a half miles up, to the fifth milepost, there is another snow slope that is dreaded by winter climbers. It is like the one at Cape Horn, only more frightful. Here, for nearly a half hour, the two men picked their way, step by step, "daring to look neither to the right nor left, for fear of dizziness."

Between the fifth and sixth mileposts was their longest test of endurance. It was a snow-packed road again, on which the creepers made not the slightest dent. Somehow they made their way across, and from there to the summit the mountain was blown free of snow.

It was even before these ascents — back in the 1890s — that there had appeared at Dartmouth College the first crude homemade skis, awkward contraptions that garnered more laughs than followers. A new era began in 1909–10 when Fred H. Harris of Brattleboro, Vermont, the first Dartmouth man who was a really proficient ski runner and jumper, proposed the formation of an outdoor club. Early in January 1910 the Dartmouth Outing Club (or D.O.C.) was organized, with fifty or sixty members. Fred Harris '11 was its first president. On Saturdays a group of snowshoers, led by a few speedy skiers, would hike out over the snowy fields and hills, their odd clothing and clumsy gait provoking more derision than enthusiasm among the undergraduates. But the seed was sown and sprouted swiftly, and, as one Dartmouth man said, "The college has never fallen so quickly for any other new sport as it did in 1910 for controlled ski running."

As the D.O.C. grew and prospered, the slopes and hills around Hanover became a bit tame. The long finger of Mount Washington was felt, if not seen, beckoning across the snowy heights, and in March 1913 Fred Harris, Joseph Y. Cheney, and Carl E. Shumway, all members of the Club, were skiing at the very top of New England. That the D.O.C. was the first college club to make that ascent by skis was altogether fitting, for now their alma mater owns that summit.

Early ascents by the Dartmouth Outing Club (prior to winter opening of the Pinkham Notch Camps in 1926–27) were made by snowshoe from the Glen House up the Carriage Road, across on the Raymond Path, and into the floor of Tuckerman Ravine. Then began the laborious job of cutting steps in the hard-packed snow to the rim. If conditions on the cone were good, the hike with crampons above timber line was the easiest part of the trip. One of the dangers pointed out by Robert Scott Monahan, leader of these ascents and later one of the leading spirits in the founding of the Mount Washington Observatory, was the fact that by the time the groups were ready to start down the headwall, the slopes were usually frozen. As Bob Monahan explained: "When the afternoon shadow hits the main wall of the ravine, the snow, if it is at all soft, will 'tighten up' suddenly, and make for tricky descents. One stunt was to 'glissade' down the lower slope, but not always with the same technique used by the alpinists!"

In 1923 Charles A. Proctor, professor of Physics at Dartmouth, widely known as the "Granddaddy of American College Skiing," was the moving spirit in the establishment of the Eastern Intercollegiate Ski Union, formed by Dartmouth, New Hampshire University, and McGill University. From this, and from the famous Dartmouth Winter Carnival, which had its beginning in 1911, sprang the still-growing enthusiasm for this great winter sport at most northern colleges.

Two of the most notable of the Dartmouth skiers to visit Mount Washington were John P. Carleton, who commenced skiing on the mountain in 1916, and Charles N. Proctor, son of the professor. Both held numerous championships, and both had competed in the Olympics. With two such skiers as these making frequent visits to the summit of Washington, it could be only a matter of time before the greatest thrill offered by the rugged old mountain would be attempted—the descent of the Tuckerman headwall, that sheer drop of 1000 feet into the bowl below. Of that event Carleton writes: "So far as I know the rumor is correct that Charles Proctor and I were the first to run the headwall. That was on April 11, 1931."

In the 1924 Olympics, John Carleton, then a Rhodes Scholar at Oxford University, competed as captain of the Oxford-Cambridge Ski Team. Later a practicing attorney in Manchester, New Hampshire, Carleton was the first American ski-internationalist.

In 1928, at St. Moritz, Charley Proctor was the only native-born American on the United States Olympic Ski Team. He had already been Intercollegiate Champion in ski jumping and downhill and slalom racing, and in

Early ski instructor Sig Buchmayr executes a jump turn on the
Tuckerman Ravine headwall in the spring of 1932.

1927 he had been All-Round Ski Champion of Canada. During the 1930s he became Winter Recreation Director and purchasing agent for all tourist facilities in Yosemite National Park, California.

That was the time when skiing was becoming a full-time winter interest for White Mountain landlords and winter sports fans. As more and more people learned how to ski, and as snow trains commenced drawing thousands of beginners and advanced skiers to winter playgrounds, overnight facilities were strained to the utmost on week ends. But Sunday nights the camps and hotels were deserted.

Although the first descent of Mount Washington by skis took place in 1905, five years before the founding of the Dartmouth Outing Club, and although that club has always been a leader among ski enthusiasts, yet it remained for a little group of Harvard students from Boston to start the first club in America devoted solely to downhill skiing. Robert Livermore, Jr., of Boston and Topsfield, of the United States Olympic Ski Team of 1936, Robert S. Balch of Jamaica Plain, and W. Bradford Trafford of Boston, all members of the Harvard class of 1932, were its originators in 1928–29.

About this time a Swiss watchmaker working at the Waltham Watch factory asked permission to join an outing of the Appalachian Mountain Club. It turned out that Otto Eugen Schniebs was an accomplished skier. The three Harvard boys decided that he was just the man they needed to complete the perfect foursome. And thereupon the Stem-Like-Hell Club was formed.

Bob Livermore and his friends like to recall that they "discovered" Otto Schniebs, who soon quit watchmaking for the more exciting job of coaching Dartmouth skiers. Later he became coach of the St. Lawrence University ski team at Canton, New York.

The Stem-Like-Hell Club members were pioneers in more ways than discovering talent. In February 1930 Bob Livermore became the first Harvard man to enter the Dartmouth Winter Carnival. To the surprise of his Dartmouth hosts he won the slalom race and placed second in the downhill race. In 1931 the club members spent three or four days in the Camden Cottage, and were the first party of skiers to go down from the summit over the headwall of Tuckerman. This was a week after Charley Proctor made his "first" run over the headwall from the lip, with John Carleton following.

It was during that winter of 1931 that Balch, Livermore, and Trafford secured permission to represent Harvard in ski events held under the auspices of the Intercollegiate Winter Sports Union. Although not officially recognized, a ski team was active at Harvard beginning with the winter of 1933. Skiing was officially recognized as a minor sport by vote of the Harvard Athletic Association on 5 February 1940.

WINSTON POTE

A trio of skiers take on the snowfields of Mount Jefferson, just north
of Mount Washington along the Presidential Range.

On 2 January 1932 a heavy snowfall made possible the first thorough testing by skiers of the recently improved Forest Service Trail from Pinkham
Notch to Tuckerman Ravine. Its moderate grade and negotiable turns proved
its attraction to both expert and novice skiers, and have been of invaluable
assistance in getting injured skiers out to Pinkham Notch when emergencies have arisen.

After those exciting days in April 1931, ideas about ski racing in Tuckerman Ravine began to bud in the minds of America's top-ranking skiers. The
Nansen Ski Club of Berlin, New Hampshire, the Hochgebirge Ski Club of
Boston, and the Deutsche Ski Club of New York, to say nothing of all the
college ski clubs and the ski enthusiasts of the Appalachian Mountain Club,
turned speculative eyes toward the Tuckerman headwall.

Just under a year later, on Sunday, 20 March 1932, those budding ideas
bloomed into the "Mt. Washington Spring Snow Fest," featuring, under the
auspices of the Nansen Ski Club, the Glen House, and Joe Dodge, a series
of races and jumping events for girls, boys, and senior skiers. The climax of
the day's events was the eight-mile race down the Carriage Road, the first
ever attempted. Sanctioned by the Eastern Amateur Ski Association, this
race attracted Olympic, college, and individual stars from far distances.

In advance publicity describing the race the four miles at the top were spoken of as "the four hardest miles of skiing on the continent. Wind-blown crust, ice, huge drifts as large as ocean waves impede the progress of skiers. The last four miles, from the Halfway House down, are comparatively easy, and afford some of the best skiing in the country. This [lower] four-mile slope is wide and averages a little over a ten percent grade." It had been covered by a member of a Dartmouth ski team in 8 minutes, 16 seconds. Up to that time no one had been known to run from the summit against time, but it was expected that nearly forty minutes of terrific strain would be necessary for the eight miles.

The Nansen Ski Club, under whose supervision the race was held, was the pioneer ski club of the northeastern United States. The race was promoted by Alf Halversen, a coach of the Olympic Ski Team, and a committee headed by Olaf Nelson, president of the club. Assisting the Nansen Club were Joe Dodge and Bob Monahan from the A.M.C. Huts in Pinkham Notch. The Glen House was represented by Elliott C. Libby, the manager, and C. M. (Charlie) Dudley, ski instructor, and former recreational ski instructor at Dartmouth College.

Of course the eight-mile grind from the summit to the Glen was the feature of the meet. But Mount Washington was in no mood to cooperate with flying skiers. Conditions of snow and weather, including a seventy-mile gale, caused officials to give up hope of staging this event. But the five experts who had entered this hazardous race were not to be turned back by a mere hurricane. Facing death at every turn while traveling at blinding speed in the face of the gale, they completed the first race from the summit to the Glen House in a little over twelve minutes.

Over 6000 persons were waiting at the end of the road to cheer the racers as they whizzed like human bullets down the mountainside, ending the race so closely that the winner, Edward J. Blood of the University of New Hampshire, was only twenty-five seconds ahead of the last man to cross the line.

Although they wore special goggles and helmets to protect them from slashing ice particles whipped up by the wind and their own hurtling speed, their noses and mouths were frostbitten, and tiny particles of ice were imbedded in exposed portions of their faces.

Three members of the 1932 United States Olympic Ski Team took top honors in the Carriage Road race, in this order: E. J. Blood, 12 minutes, 20 seconds; Nils Bachstrom, Swedish Ski Club of New York, 12 minutes, 30 seconds; and Bob Reid, Nansen Ski Club, 12 minutes, 35 seconds.

Asked what it was like to rocket down the mountain at a speed sometimes in excess of eighty miles an hour with certain death always jogging his elbow, Ed Blood said:

It was like watching a ribbon of white uncoiling beneath me. I could hear a roar in my ear and see a blur of black as I came below the timber line. I could hear a peculiar singing sound as the skis rasped over the snow crystals, and I got the impression of the world flying up to meet me, as if I was falling from an airplane . . . but that's about all, except that we had some mighty close shaves. I never had seen a race so evenly matched. We swung around the turns just as if we were actuated by a single mind, every man in his own place, neither gaining or losing a yard.

To apprise the spectators and timers below of the start of the race, a gigantic rocket specially prepared for the occasion was discharged at the summit. The simultaneous start in a ski race is rarely possible in this country, but inasmuch as the first half of the race was above tree line, and the road quite open, the competitors had plenty of room to spread out. Mr. Blood's statement indicated that they early found their respective places in the group and held them to the end.

On Easter Sunday, 16 April 1933, the dream of a ski race from the summit of Mount Washington down over the Tuckerman headwall came to reality in the first "American Inferno." So hazardous was the event considered that it was quickly dubbed a "suicide race."

Sponsored by the Ski Club Hochgebirge, whose motto is "Dash and Abandon," with Joe Dodge as chief official, every precaution was taken against accident. Expected times were three minutes from summit to rim of headwall, where runners were to zigzag almost to a dead stop between slalom flags; one minute down the thousand-foot drop of the headwall; then through the tortuous path past Hermit Lake and down the Forest Service Trail, which had been done in three minutes fifty-five seconds.

Of this first Inferno Race, in which fourteen skiers entered, Winston Pote, color photographer, wrote: "The best time was around 17 minutes, by Hollis Phillips, though that was down the 'right' or north gully. It was in a driving rain and very heavy snow and he was the only skier who came down there on his feet."

Records on Mount Washington depend upon many factors which may never be repeated. While the bowl of Tuckerman usually is 200 feet deep in snow in April, in 1933 there was enough more to form the required angle at the upper rim for an expert skier to make a perfect run of the headwall.

This snow always continues skiable into June. But in 1933 Tuckerman Ravine set up a new record by furnishing skiing on the Fourth of July. Easter week end, however, is likely to be the most popular time of all in Tuckerman. Each year finds a growing host of skiers trekking up the muddy trail from the Pinkham Notch Camp to revel in a sun-blistering paradise of snowy slopes mounting up, up, up, to the pinnacle of all skiers' dreams—the lip of the Tuckerman headwall. Gwendoline Keene gave this picture of Easter week-end skiing, "when Tuckerman's bowl is best":

> Caught between winter's isolation and the summer "goofer" season it is a little world of its own, a pocket warmed by the sun and cooled by the cold that rises from its floor of marble snow, a pendant world where midget skiers come to climb and slide, to climb and slide again, to rest on the warm exposed summits of its few great rocks, to laugh and chatter and hum and hear far-off sounds . . .
>
> That day's big event may be some one running the headwall. Perhaps it's Charley Proctor, and you watch carefully to see the little speck that appears on the rim and is he. The speck starts, swoops, doubles back, swoops again, zigzagging at ever-widening angles until it dashes breathlessly straight down and stops at the bottom in one last side-slip of a Christie.

But spring in Tuckerman is not all sun-bathing. Sometimes a blinding blizzard will fill the bowl. Snowslides may add to the excitement, and at times people have been carried along, buried waist deep, and may even have to be dug out of the snow.

Illustrating what terrific and swift changes in the weather are to be encountered on Mount Washington: On a beautifully warm and sunny 17 June 1933, at one o'clock in the afternoon, a sudden cold wind blew an immense black cloud over the headwall of Tuckerman. It spread out on the sides of the ravine and shut down like a curtain at the rim of the bowl, leaving the bowl enclosed like a tremendous tent and lighted by a queer twilight. After a few claps of thunder and ten minutes of severe hail, there followed a driving snowstorm which lasted an hour and deposited about an inch and a half of snow in the ravine before clearing again to bright sunshine. Next day young Simon Joseph of Brookline, Massachusetts, perished on the plateau land near the Lakes of the Clouds in a similar storm.

From 1933 to 1939, weather and snow conditions permitting, an Inferno Race was run on skis from the summit of Washington down the cone, over the headwall, and out the Forest Service Trail to Pinkham. In the Inferno of 1934 the Stem-Like-Hell Club again made history. All the contestants went to the summit. During the time they were climbing up there was an avalanche on the face of the headwall, but none of the skiers knew about it. Bob Livermore was one of the first over the lip, going over far to the left of the summer trail, and turning sharply to the right under the overhanging crag. As he did so, he discovered that there had been an avalanche, and realized that he was running directly into the path it had left, which meant disaster. Turning abruptly to the left he attempted to schuss straight for the foot of the headwall. But near the bottom he ran head-on into the debris left by the avalanche. His skis were snagged, and he was thrown into the air with terrific force.

In those days skis were fastened securely with straps. There were no safety bindings to free the feet in case of accident. Where the skis went the skier went also. And in this case Bob went into the air; turned a perfect triple somersault—somebody caught a movie of the dramatic event—and landed with unbroken skis to go on and finish the race, then to find that in his landing he had sprained both ankles!

Perhaps the most remarkable performance of all was the schussing of Tuckerman headwall by Toni Matt, who afterward served as head instructor of the Sun Valley Ski School, and later conducted his own ski school at Whitefish, Montana—one of the most brilliant skiers of all time. Born at St. Anton-am-Arlberg, birthplace of the renowned Hannes Schneider and his famous ski school, Toni strapped on his first barrel staves so early in life that at six he won his first race. At fourteen he was a full-fledged instructor in Schneider's school. For five years he taught as St. Anton, also taking part in most of the big Continental events.

Chosen by Schneider, in 1938, to assist the "Skimeister" in operating his school at North Conway, New Hampshire, and knowing almost no English, Toni Matt began teaching there through the medium of sign language. In the late winter of 1939, while only nineteen, he began to blaze a trail of ski victories that carried him through to practically every major downhill and slalom title in the United States. In the first season of American competition, he won the Eastern Combined at Stowe, Vermont, the Harriman Downhill at Sun Valley, the National Open Downhill at Mount Hood, and the Gibson Trophy at North Conway. This he won five times, retiring one cup and possessing two legs on another. But of all Toni's victories, the most remarkable was the April 1939 Inferno, when along the race course a shout went up that was echoed throughout the entire skiing world: "Toni Matt schussed the headwall!"

Even in a race, the headwall is generally handled in a series of turns. But Toni was not in a conservative mood that spring day, and his line was as straight as a die. "Uncorking one of the greatest schusses in all of skiing history, he took the Headwall in one long dive that left the 4000 spectators literally gasping for breath. Shooting across the outrun at sixty miles an hour, he roared over the Little Headwall and down the Sherburn Trail at full throttle to record a stunning 6:29.4 mark . . . a full minute better than that of second place winner Dick Durrance."

Winston Pote adds a word to one of the most spectacular records ever made on Mount Washington: "There is no doubt that Toni Matt made the first real 'Schuss' down the headwall, from practically the top, and I dare say the last! Just like the airplane landings, the elements were kind and snow was favorable. He came over the top very near where I was standing, and made only one turn, some 75 feet below, then straight down! He said afterwards, 'I intended to make two checks, but the snow felt so good I pointed them down!' He had run the cone almost straight, and that was wind-blown. So this unusually deep powder on the headwall must have seemed good."

How swiftly skiers can run into difficulties in Tuckerman Ravine is illustrated by what happened on 19 April 1947, when more than 350 ski racers and spectators were gathered high up in the Ravine for the annual Harvard-Dartmouth slalom race. Suddenly, a ski patrolman, investigating snow conditions above the race course, touched off an avalanche which plunged 450 yards down the steep racing stretch known as "Hillman's Highway" just after the race had started.

Brooks Dodge, son of Joe Dodge and then the seventeen-year-old Eastern Downhill champion, was halfway down the course when the slide started. He immediately let his skis run straight for the bottom, and outran the avalanche.

But avalanches cannot stem the enthusiasm of Mount Washington skiers. The sport is a part of them—is in their very blood—and must be served. So year after year they come back to the rugged old mountain to its most popular ski slope—Tuckerman Ravine.

September 21, 1967

Crash of the Cog Railway

From *The Littleton Courier*

First published in 1889, The Littleton [N.H.] Courier *(now know simply as* The Courier*) has been covering news of the western White Mountains and northern New Hampshire for well over a century. Over the years the weekly newspaper has covered nearly every major event to occur on Mount Washington, including its devastating summit fires, the fatal 1967 Cog Railway accident, and numerous search and rescue incidents.*

A TRAGEDY of staggering proportions took place on Mt. Washington late Sunday afternoon when a Cog Railway passenger train left the rails on the next to the last southbound trip of the day and toppled at the Skyline Switch of the scenic mountain ride, about three-quarters of a mile from the summit.

Before night was over it had been learned eight passengers had died and 72 people including members of the train crew were sent to Littleton hospital for treatment of injuries that varied widely in extent of their seriousness. Two more came in for checkups later in the day, and two were sent direct to St. Louis hospital in Berlin.

All of the fatalities occurred at the scene of the crash, with no one succumbing to injuries after they had been rescued.

The unique steam engine and a newer-type aluminum and steel passenger car left the Summit about 5 p.m. Sunday for the return trip to the Base Station while the last train up for the day was enroute to the top.

The southbound train was moving over a switch to the spur to the main line when the center switch which had been tampered with threw the engine and coach from the center cog, causing the engine to leave the track and crash about six feet to the rocks.

It was reported that the passenger car then picked up speed and travelled an estimated 400 feet before it left the rails, dropping 6–8 feet onto the ground with its human cargo including people who had gone to the top by railroad and hikers who were returning from the mountaintop.

The car landed on its side and was later returned to its wheels by those less seriously injured to permit full rescue operations.

The train crew included Gordon Chase of Lincoln, engineer, Charles Kenison, Jefferson, fireman, Guillean "Rusty" Aertsen, a brakeman who was firing, Nate Carter, South Woodstock, brakeman on the passenger car, and Peter Carter, a brakeman who was riding on the downhill side of the cab during the trip.

As darkness settled in, the plight of the victims became more serious. The railroad management worked heroically to effect the rescues, using equipment including a flat car with emergency supplies for transportation of litter patients, 11 at a time. Dr. Francis Appleton of Gorham directed the handling of the injured at the scene.

All injured people had been removed to ambulances at the Base Station by 9:15 p.m.

The priority was agonizing as rescue workers with flashlights attempted to determine the more seriously hurt in the darkness. While warmer than usual weather conditions prevailed, nevertheless it was cool, adding to the discomfort of many of the victims. Relative calm prevailed, with many acts of mercy.

The site of the crash determined that rescue operations could best be carried out only by the Cog Railway and its Base Station more than 2½ miles below.

The rescue was effected by the upbound train being joined in rescue operations by another train and its crew, and volunteers. The latter crew included Griffin Harris, formerly of Littleton, and his brother, David of Littleton, and another member who had just completed the last trip down for the day. They added a flatcar to the passenger train and worked through the long hours to bring down the injured. "Grif" has been an engineer for 12 years and was doing weekend duty, being a teacher in the Lin-Wood Elementary School in Lincoln. David Harris is employed by New England Power Co. The third member of this crew was Robert Kent of Essex Junction, Vt.

One of the hospital patients, Bertrand Croteau, 31, of Thornton, who was accompanied by his wife, Elmae, 30, his son, Bertrand, Jr., 6, and daughter, Deborah, 11 (the son was also hospitalized) is a teacher of French and social studies at Lin-Wood High school in Lincoln. He was thrown through a window in the crash and was buried under the bodies of other passengers.

He told of the nerve-wracking conditions that existed as passengers endeavored to free themselves and to get attention for their injuries.

The bodies of the eight victims were brought to the Pillsbury Funeral Home in Littleton where all-night operations were carried out including identification. When the information had been compiled funeral directors in the home areas of the victims were notified and the fatalities listed as follows: Eric J. Davies, 7, Hampton; Kent Woodward, 8, New London; Monica Gross, 2, Brookline, Mass.; Mary Frank, 38, Warren, Mich.; Shirley Zorzy, 22, Lynn, Mass.; Charles Usher, 54, Dover; Beverly Ann Richmond, 15, Putnam, Ct.; Mrs. Esther Usher, 56, Dover.

The bodies were viewed by Dr. Leandre P. Beaudoin of Berlin, Coos county medical examiner. It was determined that all had died on the mountain.

An estimated 30 ambulances were pressed into emergency service to transport the victims from the Cog Railway to the Littleton hospital. The vehicles came from Littleton (Pillsbury Funeral Home, Ross Funeral Home, and the Fire Department), Bethlehem Fire Department, Lincoln, Whitefield, Lancaster, Groveton, Berlin and North Conway. Each vehicle was capable of carrying two litter patients.

The Littleton hospital was so geared to meeting the emergency under its Disaster Plan that the entire group of victims was brought to this institution. Hospitals at Lancaster and North Conway had been alerted but their services in treating the victims were not immediately required.

Dr. Harry C. McDade, chief of surgeons at Littleton hospital, said the Disaster Plan which had been prepared for any emergency eventuality was put into action about 6:30 p.m. Sunday. The first ambulance delivery was made about 8:15 and the last admittance to the emergency quarters of the hospital was made about 3 a.m. Monday.

The Littleton hospital has a bed capacity of 61 patients and it was fortunate at the time of the tragedy the patient count was at a lower level, about 30.

The entire medical staff, the nursing staff, administration staff personnel headed by Assistant Administrator Robert McLean, and dietary personnel, totaling about 40, were pressed into service and the Disaster Plan was carried out with remarkable efficiency to meet the heavy responsibility placed on the Littleton hospital by one of the worst tragedies in the state's history.

The victims were wheeled into the emergency area or walked in, and dispatched to whatever treatment area was required. Those who were fortunate to require only first aid were released as their conditions permitted, some being sent to private homes for the balance of the night. Three of the

Trains congregate at Skyline Switch, scene of the fatal September 1967
Cog Railway accident that claimed eight lives.

victims with serious head wounds were sped to Mary Hitchcock Memorial hospital in Hanover, three sent to Brightlook hospital in St. Johnsbury, Vt., and two to Weeks Memorial hospital in Lancaster for care.

On hand at the hospital as the patients were received for the all-night emergency action were volunteer litter bearers who handled the stretchers with care and dispatch. These stretcher bearers included members of the Littleton Fire Dept., U.S. Forest Service and innumerable volunteers from the Base Station.

The victims of the mountain tragedy were treated for a variety of hurts including head injuries, broken bones and serious lacerations and bruises. There were many particularly pathetic cases such as one mother who consoled her young daughter suffering from facial injuries while aware that a second daughter had been killed in the accident. There were many instances of families endeavoring to be re-united following their harrowing experience. The exclamation, "We're all alive!", was heard more than once during the heart-rending scenes of the nighttime drama.

On hand to render their services wherever possible were the ministers and priests of churches in Littleton, Whitefield, Lisbon and Lincoln. Rev. Raymond Desjardins of Lisbon, Rev. Gerard Supper of Littleton and Rev. Michael Griffin of Whitefield were present at the Base Station during the rescue operations and later came to Littleton hospital.

The victims ranged in age from very young to elderly couples from throughout New England and several other states. One youngster, James B. Dixon of Portland, Me., will long remember his 12th birthday which occurred Sunday.

Of concern to everyone was the inability during the night to identify one child who was among the three dispatched to Hanover hospital for treatment of head injuries. No family member had come forward to assist authorities with the identification.

As the night wore on the well-organized hospital personnel carried out their professional duties with compassion and sympathetic understanding, bearing up under the heavy strain with remarkable stamina.

During the night the hospital was besieged by news media of all kinds for latest information concerning victims, and as the casualty list climbed it became more evident that it was miraculous that more fatalities had not occurred.

As of Monday 11 patients were at the Littleton hospital for continued treatment, the balance of the 72 admittances having been transferred elsewhere or approved for release to pick up the agonizing details of reunion with plans to retrieve their autos at the Base Station and return to their homes.

The major emergency was controlled to provide little or no anxiety for the regular patients at the hospital. Special emergency supplies arranged for under the Disaster Plan were put to immediate use, and anticipated requirements for blood resulted in one shipment of whole blood plasma and blood derivatives being sent from Brightlook hospital and other supplies made available from other sources but not needed.

State Police of Troop F at Twin Mountain under Capt. Kenneth Hayes and Lt. Henry Genest were pressed into full emergency service at the Base Station and at the hospital, controlling traffic situations, compiling accident data and generally expediting the night rescue operation, carried out by personnel of the Cog Railway and others. Nine State Police were at the Base and three at hospitals.

Mrs. John Morgan of Greenfield, sister of Mrs. Arthur S. Teague, president of the Mt. Washington Cog Railway Corp., assisted at the scene as did Thomas Baker of Littleton, fiance of Miss Margaret Teague; Miss Marjorie Bargar, Cog Railway nurse; Cass White and Paul Philbrook of the Cog Railway staff.

For the most part, regular hospital staff members had little or no sleep before reporting for regular duties Monday morning, and continued follow-up work in the emergency.

The Bethlehem ambulance, en route back to the Base Station for a second group of victims, had motor trouble near the Zealand Campground and had to be abandoned.

A word of appreciation should be given the girls at the Highway Office in Lancaster for their untiring work during the emergency. Mrs. Kathleen Doolan and her assistant went out of their way to help wherever they could.

The N.H. Public Utilities commission this week was continuing its investigation into the crash. It was made clear that the mountain railroad had not been closed down by the PUC and that trains would probably be operated on a limited basis within a few days, probably to the Waumbek station which is about ⅓ of the 3½ mile trip to the summit. The railroad which is probably the best-known mountain railroad in the world normally closes for the year on October 15.

Only two of the five employees of the railroad required continued hospitalization: Gordon Chase of Lincoln, a patient at St. Louis hospital, Berlin, with severe burns and Charles Kenison of Jefferson, Lancaster hospital, with burns. Guillean "Rusty" Aertsen, who had abrasions and contusions and Nate Carter who had shoulder and nose injuries, have been discharged.

Little Monica Gross was the daughter of Prof. and Mrs. Charles Gross of Brookline, Mass. Miss Shirley Zorzy was employed as a secretary at Northeast Airlines at Logan International Airport, Boston.

Funeral services were held yesterday morning in Hampton for Eric Davies, and funeral services for Mr. and Mrs. Charles Usher were held this morning in Dover. In New London yesterday afternoon the funeral service for Kent Woodward was held.

Forest Ranger Richard MacNeil of the Ammonoosuc District office in Littleton was among those on the scene to render any assistance possible. He commented:

"I arrived at the Base Station at 7:30 p.m., contacted the State Police officer in charge and offered the assistance of the Forest Service. Lt. Genest felt that there was enough help on the scene and said he would contact me if we were needed.

"My first thought upon reaching the Base Station was—where did they manage to get so many ambulances?

"I remained at the Base until the first load of injured people came down, then rode the next train up to the scene of the accident.

"At the scene of the wreck I saw Conservation Officers, State Police troopers, AMC personnel, Forest Service personnel and volunteers. All were working together. About 8–10 injured people were still there and we began to load them into litters.

"As we began I saw two things which made a lasting impression on me.

The first of these was a young man who had been on the wrecked car, but had been uninjured. He was doing an excellent job of comforting and reassuring the injured people and assisted in loading them into litters. The other thing which impressed me was the sight of three teenage girls. They had gotten off another train to help. They were giving reassurance to a couple who were both severely injured, and were doing a good job in calming them.

"I remained at the scene until the bodies were loaded on a car and then rode down.

"The weather was very cooperative—mild temperature and very little breeze—very strange weather for Mt. Washington.

"The lack of adequate communication from the wreck to the base made the rescue operation somewhat difficult. An efficient two-way radio setup would have helped.

"Naturally the most impressive thing was the tragedy itself. Beyond that was the tremendous spirit of cooperation between many agencies, those already mentioned plus Fire Departments, rescue squads, and just plain people who felt that they could help."

1988

Thanksgiving High

Warren and Ginny Martin

From their diary

Warren and Ginny Martin, formerly residents of Whitefield, N.H., and now living in the Conway area, worked in the Mount Washington Observatory's summit museum for five summers during the late 1980s and early 1990s. Previously, the couple were employed together at the Mount Washington Hotel in Bretton Woods. For the Thanksgiving holiday of November 1988, the Martins were invited to spend the weekend atop Mount Washington in the Observatory's headquarters in the Sherman Adams Summit Building. The following is their account of that memorable holiday occasion.

Wednesday, November 23

Temp. 18, winds 42 mph, gusting to 105 out of the NW, visibility 90 miles. These were the statistics we were given before our trip. The winds at the base were almost nil as we gathered at the Glen House. The entire trip would be taken on the auto road and we would not be going the alternate route across the mountain. We loaded suitcases, people, pies, cookies, and various homemade goodies into the Observatory truck and drove two miles up the auto road where everything was transferred to the waiting Thiokol.

A total of nine people, eight riding inside the machine, one riding on top with the luggage, were on their way. It became very apparent the trip was going to be icy, but the views were so overwhelming, that we ignored the icing. Ginny sat in the front with the driver. She was entrusted with holding the Thanksgiving pies on her lap, making sure they were all delivered intact. Only once, when the door next to her sprang open, did we think this trip might be more than any of us had bargained for. But the trip was without further incident until we arrived at the service road.

The driver told us that the road was iced over pretty bad, adding that we might have to walk the rest of the way to the Summit House [a/k/a the Sherman Adams summit building]. However, he was going to try the ascent, but requested that should the machine start to slide backwards, he would appreciate no screaming from the group, as this would be quite unnerving. He reassured all that if we did slide, we would only bounce off rocks and land back in the parking lot. Everyone took a deep breath and up we crept, inching our way until we reached the top. Shouts and cheers of great relief echoed across the top of Mount Washington. We made it! God bless Ken Rancourt, Thiokol driver extraordinaire . . .

How strange the summit looked. The doors to the building were all boarded up for the onslaught of winter. Everywhere you looked there was rime ice. The winds had picked up and were gusting to 105 mph, yet, we could see 90 miles in any direction. We unloaded the Thiokol and weighed everything we brought up, including people, to see what our total weight was. Everything, including the pies, weighed in at 2,716 lbs. and the driver concluded this weight was responsible for us making it up the service road . . . ballast. We all agreed, but also added that prayers helped too!

As soon as our unpacking was over and everything in place in the building, we went to the observation room to see the sights. The ravens were flying overhead, as they did in the summer, hoping someone would throw out some bits of food. The sun made the ice and snow glisten. The Atlantic Ocean gleamed on the horizon; everything took on a new look and feeling for us. We were happy to be here together and stood in awe at the beauty of Mount Washington on this Thanksgiving eve.

The sunset was spectacular, the star-studded sky was breathtaking. Day One of our adventure was great.

Thursday, November 24 (Thanksgiving Day)

Temp. below zero, winds 70–75 mph, gusting to 104, visibility was measured in feet. Most of the day was spent preparing the vegetables and fixings for the "great dinner" which was going to take place that evening. When we started to pack the Thiokol to bring people and food to the TV building, the winds were gusting to well over 104 mph. They were so strong that we couldn't get out of the machine and had to wait between gusts to be able to open the doors. Someone had to grab us as we exited, so we would not be blown away. Once inside the TV building, the festivities began. Everything tasted so good. In fact the turkey was the best one we have ever eaten, maybe because of the great effort it took to get there, or maybe just that Art and Donny are such great cooks!

By 9 p.m., the weather had cleared, so we became adventurous and walked back to the Summit House, Ken driving the Thiokol back alone. We did pretty well for the first hundred yards, then the wind gusts picked up and there were bodies flying in every direction. We were hurled against the cement pillars that line the walkway to the Summit House. We huddled— actually we were pinned against those uprights—along with the others who were deposited there in the same fashion as we, until the wind subsided. When it did, we all made a beeline for the building. We enjoyed the safety and warmth of the building and the comradeship of our friends as we stood looking out over a moonlit mountaintop, silently giving thanks for our blessings.

Friday, November 25

Temp. 13, winds 84 mph, gusting to 132, visibility 60 miles. We are still full and are eating less, but we don't miss a mealtime. The day presented us with clear skies and panoramic views. We had a fantastic sunset, a magnificent moonrise, and an earthquake.

We were sitting down to our evening meal. The 6 p.m. obs were completed, when the telephone began to ring off the wall. People were calling from New York, Vermont, Maine, New Hampshire and Massachusetts, asking us about an earthquake which was occurring. This came as a great surprise to us, since the only thing we felt was the pressure and vibration of winds gusting to 132 mph, and we had no idea the earth below was trembling. Since the Mount Washington Observatory has no equipment for measuring earthquakes, the Weston Observatory in Massachusetts was called and we learned that the quake had registered a six on the Richter Scale. They told us it was located 90 miles north of Quebec City and it was felt as far away as Washington, D.C. The night took on a new momentum as the phone continued to ring and the information concerning the quake was related to uneasy callers.

Saturday, November 26

Temp. 25, winds 53 mph, gusting to 110, visibility 80 miles. Today was an eventful day as far as weather was concerned. We were treated to the phenomena of seeing umbrella clouds, a broken inspectre, and a sunset that defies description. Umbrella clouds look like giant, white fluffy blankets which sit right on top of the mountains, giving the impression that the mountains are covered with snow, and also making it appear as though there are mountain ranges in the distance too. This was our first experience with umbrella clouds. A broken inspectre is eerie. When the sun is in the right location and shines through a haze, your body casts a shadow on the clouds of enormous proportions, and there you are walking in the clouds! Mother Nature certainly put on a display for us. Coupled with the invitation from TV to come enjoy homemade pizza for dinner, this was another day to remember. Tomorrow we go home. The Thiokol must be taken down to the Glen House to have its tracks sharpened.

Sunday, November 27

Temp. 42, winds 50 mph, gusting to 81, mostly cloudy with low haze, visibility 40 miles. Today, we go home. Only four of us, including the driver, are going. The other family of four left Saturday afternoon and walked down the auto road. At 11:11 a.m. we left the summit and we arrived at the Glen House two hours and four minutes later. We thought the trip up the auto road was an experience, but little did we know what the descent would hold for us.

The snow had filled in the road in some places and slush filled in the road at others. Ken had to plow our way down, going back and forth several times over and over the same spot, pushing the snow over the side of the road. We were in the back part of the Thiokol, and as Ken backed the machine up, we were at times suspended over the road, looking down into air and fog. We did not expect this, nor were we ready for this experience. The looks that passed between us thankfully were not recorded, since it was the look of sheer terror. At this point, we wished that we had been riding in the front seat with the driver and not in the rear. Live and learn. We crept, we crawled, we plowed and plowed and plowed, we slid . . . we made it!

When we had reached the base, we all sat in the machine for a few minutes to catch our breath. Ken told us that after a trip like that he feels as if he has put in a full day's work. What an extraordinary man he is, and he wears so many different hats; the main one being the meteorologist for the Observatory, but the one we will always remember is the Thiokol driver par excellence.

We said our good-byes to Ken, to Mount Washington, and looked forward to seeing them both in May, when we would return to the Museum to once again work as attendants.

The burning question everyone has asked is, "Will you ever do this again?" Warren says "probably," while Ginny answers, "Call me from the top, Warren, when you get there!"

The Thanksgiving of '88 will always be special to us and it will be numbered among our finest memories.

Summer 1992

The Unknown Soldier of Mount Washington

Peter Crane

From *Mount Washington Observatory News Bulletin*

*For the last 11 years, Peter Crane (1954–) has been employed by the Mount Wash-
ington Observatory, and is currently serving as MWO's Director of Programs.
Crane first visited the White Mountains during his high school age years, and
quickly fell in love with the region. His was formerly employed by the Appalachian
Mountain Club at its Pinkham Notch Camp and spent one year working for the
U.S. Forest Service, primarily doing trail maintenance work. Crane received his
undergraduate degree from Harvard University and his graduate degree from the
University of Pennsylvania. Besides his interest in White Mountain history and
lore, Crane is also active as a trail adopter on the White Mountain National Forest, and is a member of the all-volunteer Androscoggin Valley Search and Rescue
organization and president of the N.H. Outdoor Council.*

READERS of the *News Bulletin* are accustomed to our notices of accidents,
particularly fatal accidents, that occur on Mount Washington. The purpose
of these articles is not a morbid fascination with these tragic incidents, but
rather to help make people more aware of the potential dangers which are
associated with the mountain, and especially with skiing, hiking, and climbing here. Most of the news which we present with regard to such occur-
rences is recent, but occasionally we are presented with some new information on older events which we feel should be brought to our readers' attention, especially when it has to do with "one of our own."

A reading of William Putnam's recent volume, *The Worst Weather on Earth*, gave us a shock. On page 74 we found the following passage:

> ... *Private William Seely ... was a 29 year old farmer from Seneca Falls, New York, who had been signed up for less than a year and barely arrived at Station 46 (the Mount Washington summit station) when his slide-board got away from him on a trestle and he received fatal injuries ...*

A quick review of the Mount Washington "fatality list" (with variant versions maintained by the Observatory, A.M.C., the U.S. Forest Service, and Mount Washington State Park) indicated that Private Seely's untimely death had gone unnoted! While the only other Mount Washington weather observer to die in the line of duty—Private William Stevens, who died of "paralysis of the left side" on the summit on February 26, 1872—had been given the simple honor of recognition, Seely had disappeared from the active historical record.

While the Signal Service log in the Boston Public Library deals mostly with meteorological matters and does not mention the incident that led to Seely's death, information on the hapless man and his passing is available from United States Army records in the National Archives and from contemporary news accounts. We felt the compulsion to consult these sources, having unduly neglected the memory of our forebear for so long.

According to Seely's enlistment papers, he joined the Army in Saint Louis, Missouri, on August 16, 1872, at the age of 29. The papers indicate that he was "born in Seneca Falls, New York, and (was) by occupation a farmer," (unfortunately, the early records of Seneca Falls were destroyed in a fire in 1881). He was single and had no children. He enlisted for the standard term of five years. The recruiting officer certified that Seely had "brown eyes, brown hair, fair complexion, is 5 feet and 5¾ inches high." The officer also endorsed that standard statement that the recruit "was entirely sober when enlisted"—sufficient evidence to suggest that, in that day and age, they had a goodly number of potential recruits that were not sober at the time. Added to Seely's enlistment papers were the remarks "Residence when enlisted Saint Louis, Mo." and "Enlisted in the General Service for assignment to the Signal Service U.S. Army."

At this point we do not know what brought Seely from Seneca Falls to Saint Louis; nor do we know what path he took from the Gateway City to Mount Washington. Sadly, we do know which route he was taking down the summit on Saturday, June 28, 1873, as an account in Littleton's *White Mountain Republic* for Thursday, July 3, gives us the following information:

On Saturday last, as Wm. Seeley (sic), employed in the Signal Service on Mt. Washington, was sliding down the railroad track on one of the apparatus used for that purpose, (he) was run into by a comrade, whose sled became unmanageable, and was seriously injured. He was brought to this village by Mr. E. Cox of the Marshfield House, and taken to Jennison's Hotel, where he lies in critical condition.

Editions of *The New Hampshire Register and Farmer's Almanac* for the era note a Union House operated by a William Jenerson (*sic*); Eastman's *The White Mountain Guide Book* for 1873 refers to a boarding house of William Jennison, which had room for 20 people at 7 to 14 dollars per week. Apparently only primitive medical care was available in Littleton at that time; though there were four physicians and one homeopathic practitioner listed in the *Register*, the Littleton Hospital was not dedicated until 1907. We can only speculate, but perhaps Seely was attended by Dr. Frank Tifft Moffett, M.D. According to Dr. Charles M. Tuttle, writing on "The Profession of Medicine" in *Exercises at the Centennial Celebration of the Incorporation of the Town of Littleton, July 4th, 1884,* Moffett "will be long remembered by the members of the signal service as the physician who ascended Mt. Washington in mid-winter, 1872, and took charge of the remains of the first member of the corps who died at the summit station" (page 165).

The next issue of the *White Mountain Republic*, that of Thursday, July 10, 1873, completed Seely's sad tale:

William Seeley (sic), who was injured in the descent of Mount Washington, as announced last week, died on Wednesday, the 2d, at Jennison's Hotel. He remained unconscious from the time of the accident till his death.

The "Final Statement" of the Army for Seely asserted that at the time of his death, the soldier was 30 years old and died "by reason of wounds received from falling through the trestle work of the Railroad on Mt. Washington, New Hampshire, in the line of his duty." Seely's remains were buried at Littleton's White Mountain Cemetery, the name of which was changed to the Glenwood Cemetery in 1877. According to James R. Jackson's *History of Littleton New Hampshire*, "The northeast corner (of Glenwood Cemetery) is set apart for the burial of persons without family or strangers in the town," and there were laid to rest both Seely and his predecessor Stevens (Volume III, page 511). Two simple headstones mark these soldiers' graves. While both observers died as privates, the headstones refer to each of them as sergeants—evidently an error, but we won't begrudge the men their posthumous promotions.

Seely's tragic rendezvous with the devil's shingle underscores the hazards associated with that form of transportation on Mount Washington. Putnam (pages 70–71) relates another serious, but not fatal accident which befell Sergeant O.S.M Cone as he attempted to slide down the railway tracks on January 27, 1878. The same author (pages 73–74) also notes that about ten years after Seely's death another observer, Private P. J. Cahill, came to grief between Long Trestle and Jacob's Ladder. On October 27, 1883, the soldier broke his leg in two places and received severe scalp wounds, such that he had to spend two months off the mountain recovering. A colleague attributed the injuries to "too much slideboard."

F. Allen Burt, in *The Story of Mount Washington*, noted that slideboards were used for "early-morning delivery of special editions of *Among the Clouds*," (page 115) but it does not appear that the devices were regularly used by the paperboys. We know they were used, at their peril, by weather observers, but it seems they were most frequently utilized by railway workers. Burt, who considers them "the most picturesque, and hazardous, method of transportation on Mount Washington" (page 100) claims that "no one but workmen were ever permitted to use them, as it required both experience and strength to manage a slideboard safely." While he acknowledges that two accounts exist of women traveling on the devices, there is no evidence that a woman ever rode a slideboard alone. He also notes that the three-mile trip was customarily achieved in ten minutes, with the record an astonishing two and three-quarters minutes (pages 100–101).

We do not know exactly when the slideboard was invented. We can only assume that it wasn't very long after work began on the railroad in 1866; we know that they were used by members of the Huntington-Hitchcock expeditions in the fall of 1870. It is not clear when use of the devices ended. Frederick Kilbourne, in *Chronicles of the White Mountains*, published in 1916, claims that a fatal accident by an employee using a slideboard "cost the Railway Company several thousand dollars in damages and made evident the liability to mishaps of this kind," and thus caused the discontinuance of the use of the slideboard (page 245). This would date the end of slideboard use in 1916 at the very latest, but Burt states that "about 1930, because of several deaths over the years, slideboards were permanently banned" (page 110). Donald Bray, in *They Said It Couldn't Be Done*, would seem to side with Kilbourne in suggesting that the banning may have occurred shortly after the August 23, 1906 death of Alexander Cusick, evidently the employee to whom Kilbourne refers (page 70). Cusick, of Websterville, Vermont, had nearly 30 years of experience working for the Railway, but evidently lost control of his slideboard below the base of Coldspring Hill, near the foot of the mountain; another railway worker who was descending ahead of Cusick

Three men ride down the mountain on slideboards similar to the one
used by Pvt. William Seely in 1873.

barely escaped being hit by him. Offering evidence against a 1906 ban of the devices is the article "Kindellan v. Mt. Washington Railway," by Guy Gosselin (*MWONB*, Vol. 17, No. 2, June 1976) which refers to a non-fatal slideboard accident which occurred to a Cog Railway worker on July 17, 1908. Testimony offered in 1910 stated that "during a period of 20 years or more, three or four accidents had occurred through slideboards in collision, and for a time their use was forbidden," which indicates that their use was not forbidden in 1908, and suggests that their use was still authorized in 1910. (One of the accidents, a September 28, 1900 crash of two railroad workers which resulted in serious injuries to one, is noted in an article by Douglas Philbrook, *MWONB*, Vol. 29, No. 1, 1988, page 10.)

Two additional fatalities can be blamed on ill-thought-out attempts to slide down the Cog Railway tracks. On August 5, 1919, Harry Clauson, 19, of South Boston, Massachusetts, and his companion Jack Lonigan, 20, of Boston, tried to travel down the Railway on "an improvised sliding board made of two planks." They quickly lost any semblance of control and plunged to their deaths "about 100 yards above the half-way station." A companion, John Jansky, 18, "fell off the board right at the start and thereby saved his life, getting out of the affair with only a scraped knee," according to the *Littleton Courier*, of August 7, 1919.

There have been occasional reports of bold (or perhaps fool hardy) adventurers trying out home-made slideboards on the cog railway tracks in the 1940s and 1950s, but such reports are difficult to confirm. Changes in the design of the center cog rail have eliminated the slide flanges against which early slideboard brakes once acted, making this dangerous and sometimes deadly activity even more hazardous than when Seely and Cusick took their last, lethal rides.

We hope that this long overdue notice will correct the record with regard to our fellow observer Seely's death by giving the soldier the dubious distinction of a place on Mount Washington's list of tragic victims. He has been the "unknown soldier" of Mount Washington; let him be unknown no longer. In chronological order, he would be considered the sixth person to perish on or as a result of activities on the mountain, following his colleague Private Stevens, William Seely, *"Ave atque Vale!"*

June 19, 1992

Darby Field,
His Time, and Our Times

Laura and Guy Waterman

Presented at the Darby Field Symposium, Mount Washington
Observatory, North Conway, New Hampshire

*Outdoor writers and mountain enthusiasts Laura and Guy Waterman, from East
Corinth, Vermont, are co-authors of four books, including* Forest and Crag, *a
monumental work on the history of hiking in the northeastern United States.
Laura (1939-) was formerly an editor for several New York publishing companies, and at one time was associate editor of* Backpacker *magazine. Guy (1932-)
is an accomplished jazz pianist, former speechwriter (for three U.S. Presidents),
and, like his wife, an accomplished hiker and technical climber. Among the published books to their credit are* Backwoods Ethics, Wilderness Ethics, Forest
and Crag, *and* Yankee Rock and Ice.

A CONTEMPORARY of Darby Field's, the Seventeenth Century essayist,
Joseph Addison, once complained: "We are always doing something for
Posterity, but I would fain see Posterity do something for us." Well, Mr.
Addison and Mr. Field, as humble representatives of Posterity 350 years
later, we today are doing something for you with this Symposium.

In gathering to honor Darby Field, his Indian guides, and their ascent of
June 1642, we who assemble here are conscious of more than just one hike
and just a few individuals. Our backward view encompasses an era, an historical context, a young community of immigrants, an old community of
original settlers, and a very old mountain.

* * *

It is a very different world in 1642. We should keep in mind that this 1642 ascent was closer in time to Columbus' voyage—not only closer to Columbus than to our own time, of course, but also closer in time to Columbus' voyage than to Lewis and Clark's expedition to the Missouri River in 1805. That is to observe that Field was closer to the principal European discovery of the eastern seaboard of this continent than he was to the opening of the American West. In other words, he belongs to the age when civilization (as the European colonists saw it) fought a precarious struggle for the toe-hold on the shore of wilderness, the outcome by no means certain, rather than to the boisterous, optimistic era of expansion and westward ho.

Darby Field lived closer in time to Joan of Arc than to us; closer to Dante and Chaucer; closer to the Black Death and the Battle of Agincourt—people and events which we think of as far, far away in time.

When Field climbed this hill, John Milton had not yet written *Paradise Lost*. Rembrandt had not yet painted *Aristotle Contemplating the Bust of Homer*. Bach had not yet composed *The Well Tempered Clavier*.

This was a New England that did not yet know Jonathan Edwards or Samuel Adams; neither Ralph Waldo Emerson nor Emily Dickinson; neither Sherman Adams nor Ted Williams. Yet the seeds of future greatness were already sown: Harvard College had been running for six years; in 1640 (two years *before* Field's trip) Roger Williams and his co-founders of the Plantation at Providence had drawn up a covenant pledging "to hould forth liberty of conscience"; and in May 1642, less than one month before Field set out, delegates from Plymouth, Connecticut and New Haven met with those of the Massachusetts Bay Colony in Boston and agreed upon articles of Confederation, presaging a political union which bore earth-shaking fruit in 1776. But the results of these small beginnings lay far in the future, and are not our concern today.

Today we should try to revisit the world of 1642. First, we shall recognize that this Symposium brings together close students of Darby Field scholarship and of the colonial and Native American culture of that era—and those who simply love Mount Washington or the Observatory and who know nothing more about Darby Field than that he founded an inn or restaurant in the area or something. So let us start with a brief review of what little is known about Darby Field.

There are, of course, no primary sources. For those who have pulled together the fragments, our best informant is Warren W. Hart, a prominent climber and leader in the Appalachian Mountain Club, who researched and wrote two articles on Darby Field for *Appalachia*, one published in 1908, the other in the Tricentennial year of 1942.

According to Hart, Field was born in 1610 in Boston, England, a coastal town approximately 100 miles due north of London. The Field family was locally prominent—Boston Brahmins before there was a Boston on this side of the Atlantic, we might almost say.

As early as 1636, when in his mid-twenties, Darby Field had moved to Boston, in the New World, having left England probably because of religious controversies then rampant. By 1638 he was again moving for religious reasons, and in that year helped the Rev. John Wheelwright form the town of Exeter, New Hampshire. If he lived in Exeter at that time (which is uncertain), that fact would require us to identify Bob Bates, the great Harvard mountaineer of the 1930s, veteran of adventurous climbs in Alaska and on K2, as the second most important mountaineer from Exeter, New Hampshire.

By 1642, according to Warren Hart, Field was living at Oyster River or Durham Point, in what is known as Durham, New Hampshire.

It is known that he was illiterate, that at some point he married; had five children, several of whom became reasonably prominent in colonial history; and eventually died about 1649, not quite 40 years of age. Among his descendants are some who have worthily upheld his mountaineering spirit; Parker Field, a President of the Appalachian Mountain Club during its early years; and David Field, a President of the Maine Appalachian Trail Club in recent times.

Warren Hart's researches discarded as undocumented and almost certainly false the fairly common reference to Field as an "Irishman." Hart also failed to document evidence for another allusion, in a speech of about 100 years ago, to Field as "wide-mouthed." No doubt when he first saw the beauty of Mount Washington he was open-mouthed, but whether the resulting orifice was wide or narrow, Hart was unable to establish.

Whether from Exeter or Durham, Field is thought to have journeyed up the coast to the Maine settlement of Saco, thence up the Saco River toward a known Indian town in the vicinity of what we now call Fryeburg.

Actually, as recently as the last 10 years, we have personally found that even this simple description can place one in unexpected difficulties. When we first drafted our chapter on Darby Field for *Forest and Crag*, we wrote about what we just stated; that Darby Field set out up the coast to Saco and on up the Saco River, and so forth. Now, we wanted to be sure our description passed muster with the best White Mountains authorities, so we asked a number of scholars to review our draft. (We wanted to catch errors before they appeared in print, not after.) The first expert who reviewed this chapter draft happened to be an ocean sailor, and he informed us that you do not go up the coast from New Hampshire to Maine; you go *down* the coast—

something to do with prevailing winds or currents; why you hear Maine
called "Down East." So we corrected our manuscript to read Darby Field set
out down the coast," and so on. Well, our next scholar was *not* a sailor, and
he said I'm looking at your sketch map and it's perfectly clear Field went *up*
the coast, not down. So now we had a problem. And if you look in *Forest
and Crag* now you will see that the text reads: (Darby Field) "set out *along*
the coast . . ."

Once Field reached the White Hill, or Agiochook, or whatever he and
his companions called it, what happened?

For 342 of the 350 years since the event, White Mountain historians had
only a single source to consult, the journal kept by Governor John Winthrop
of Massachusetts. Here is what Winthrop told us:

> His [Field's] relation at his return was, that it was about one hundred miles
> from Saco, that after 40 miles travel he did, for the most part, ascend, and
> within 12 miles of the top was neither tree nor grass, but low savins, which
> they went upon the top of sometimes, but a continual ascent upon rocks, on
> a ridge between two valleys filled with snow, out of which came two branches
> of Saco river, which met at the foot of the hill where was an Indian town of
> some 200 people. Some of them accompanied him within 8 miles of the top,
> but durst go no further, telling him no Indian ever dared go higher, and that
> he would die if he went. So they stayed there till his return, and his two In-
> dians took courage by his example and went with him. They went divers times
> through the thick clouds for a good space, and within 4 miles of the top they
> had no clouds, but very cold. By the way, among the rocks, there were two
> ponds, one a blackish water and the other reddish. The top of all was plain
> about 60 feet square. On the north side there was such a Precipice, as they
> could scarse discern to the bottom.

What was the route of ascent? Until 1984, based on the Winthrop account, most of the experts placed the route as going up from Pinkham
Notch.

In Lucy Crawford's *History of the White Mountains*, originally published
in 1846, the author gives Field's route as "near Tuckerman's Ravine.

The first careful examination of the question by someone with a scholar's
credentials was by Edward Tuckerman, in his chapter "Exploration of the
White Hills" in Starr King's *The White Hills*, published in 1959; Tuckerman
was certain Field went up Boott Spur and thought it "unlikely" he went up
the Ellis River.

The next writer to publish an independent analysis seems to have been
Frederick Tuckerman, in a 1921 article in *Appalachia*; this second Tucker-

man was less confident of which approach to Boott Spur was used, saying that the route went "up the valley either of Rocky Branch or of Ellis River."

In 1930 John Anderson and Stearns More published *The Book of the White Mountains*, in which they opted for the Montalban Ridge.

In 1942 Warren Hart came out for the Ellis River and the east ridge theory.

Frederick W. Kilbourne, a most respected source on the White Mountains, hedged on this question: he placed the route on "the ridge (Boott Spur) between Tuckerman's and the valley of the Dry, or Mount Washington River"; there are three or four ridges between these two ravines, and Kilbourne didn't say which was Field's route.

But then came the now-famous "second source."

The coming to light of dramatic new evidence about a seventeenth century event is a rare and wondrous happening. Those attending this meeting are probably familiar with the facts, but for the record, and because it was such a tenuous journey for that frail second source to make its way down to us, let's briefly remind ourselves what happened.

Through the centuries during which Winthrop was considered the solitary source, a letter written by a Maine magistrate named Thomas Gorges sat silently in the wings unnoticed. Gorges served as deputy governor of the province of Maine, on behalf of his cousin in England who had received a charter for Maine in 1639. Gorges was thus on the scene near the mouth of the Saco River when Darby Field came up, down, or along the coast, and walked into town wide-mouthed. On June 29, 1642, Gorges wrote a letter to his cousin relating what he knew of Field's ascent.

The original of that letter was apparently lost. But Thomas Gorges made a practice of rough drafting his letters in copybooks that contained miscellaneous notes and entries. Ten such copybooks were not destroyed. One included the draft of that June 29, 1642 letter describing Field's climb.

For three centuries, totally unknown to the White Mountain scholars or aficionados, these copybooks from the years 1640–43 were held by the Mallock family (into which Gorges had married) in their manor in an obscure English village 3,000 miles from the windswept summit of Mount Washington. In 1948 the Mallock family papers were turned over to the City Library of Exeter, Devon. By this time the Gorges letters were "in a sorry state, having lain neglected, exposed to water and rats . . . water-stained, blotted, frayed at the edges, matted together, disarranged." Yet there, in that ancient, musty, and nearly unreadable copybook, was that slender thread leading back into the oblivion of early colonial times, providing long-forgotten information about the first ascent of Mount Washington.

Still another generation was to pass before the White Mountain community became aware of the find. Finally the Exeter Library called the material to the attention of American colonial history scholars, and in 1978 the Maine Historical Society published an unobtrusive volume under the title *The Letters of Thomas Gorges*. For another six years this volume sat on library shelves before a Vermont history professor (and White Mountain hiker), Gary Thomas Lord of Norwich University, pointed out to White Mountain historians the significant paragraph about Darby Field's climb.

Significant indeed! Gorge's account preceded Winthrop's in time, having been written within a month of the ascent, based apparently on direct evidence provided by Field himself. Since Gorges and Winthrop are known to have been in communication, it is possible that Winthrop had his information secondhand from Gorges or others. In short, 342 years after the event, a second source—and probably an even more direct one—on Darby Field's pioneering climb had come to light.

This conference might be interested in the specific chronology of this discovery.

We were in correspondence with Professor Lord primarily because he was the chief expert on Alden Partridge, a phenomenal walker and mountain climber of the early nineteenth century. On June 15, 1984 Professor Lord sent us some information about Partridge, and enclosed a photocopy of a page from Gorges' letters, with the casual comment: "Do you know about the enclosed letter which sheds 'new' light on Darby Field's ascent of Mt. Washington? I meant to send it months ago."

When we received this Gorges letter, our first reaction was one of discouragement. We had thought there was only one source on Darby Field (Winthrop's). We were dismayed that, in all our consultations with the leading White Mountains historians, none of them had pointed out this second source. We interpreted this as evidence that the White Mountains historians were not taking our research seriously; they had not even bothered to tell us to read this second source.

So we wrote back to the most prominent White Mountains scholars—Douglas Philbrook, Walter Wright, Guy Gosselin—and said something like: "We are embarrassed to have been working on this subject so long and not realized that there was this much pertinent information in a second source published six years ago. Can you tell us: Are there other letters by Gorges or other primary sources of information on Field's ascent?" Well, of course, we got back some interesting replies, the gist of which was: "What second source?" And soon the White Mountains history community was buzzing over Professor Lord's "discovery."

And its implication! Gorges letter included at least one striking new hint of Field's route. Here is what Gorges wrote:

> . . . he travailled some 80 miles as he sayeth & came to a mountain, went over it, & a 2d & a 3d, at length came to a ledge of rocks which he conceaved to be 12 miles high, very steep, uppon which he travailed going to a rocke which he judged 2 miles high, very steep, yet he adventured up, but one Indian accom-paynge him, the most being fearfull. At the top it was not above 20 foot square, wher he sat with much fear some 5 hours time, the clouds passing un-der him makinge a terrible noyse against the mountains. On this mountain, he mett with terrible freesing weather and, on the top of the ledge or rocke & at the foot of them were 2 little ponds, 1 of a curious red colour, the other black. The [latter] dyed his handkerchief very blacke, the former did not al-ter the collours. Ther wer many rattle snakes but he receaved noe harm.

Notice he speaks of going over three preliminary summits before as-cending the final summit cone. This "new" evidence, not mentioned in Winthrop's account, gives strong reason to suspect the Field did not first ascend Boott Spur but rather came up over the ridge where the Crawford Path now ascends, and over Mounts Eisenhower, Franklin, and Monroe. The Gorges letter also emphasizes Field's passing by two ponds—presum-ably the Lake of the Clouds. This has prompted historians to recall that Winthrop said they passed these ponds—quote—"by the way"—unquote. Furthermore, if Field came over Boott Spur and went around the rim of Tuckerman's Ravine, why did not such close and prolonged views of that spectacular cirque receive more attention than the Great Gulf (which he does mention)? The evidence is so vague that the earlier Boott Spur theory cannot be dismissed, but the Crawford Path ridge is certainly now the more likely possibility.

If so, of course, most of the pre-1984 Field scholarship was off the mark; the State of New Hampshire's roadside pullout sign is all wrong; and, im-probably enough, the Darby restaurant in Bretton Woods is closer to his original ascent route than either the Appalachian Mountain Club's Pink-ham Notch Camp or the Darby Field Inn.

However, let us not be smug about the present state of Field scholarship. The sum total of all we know about Field is still very meager, our conjec-tures about this route most doubtful. None of us has cause for complacency about anything we can say about that wide-mouthed mystery man of 1642.

We do not, for example, know why Field and his companions climbed the White Hill. Was it really because it was the highest peak in the north-east? How could they know that? Was he on an early "northwest passage" quest? Was it just for the love of adventure? Or was he lured by rumors of fabulous treasures in the form of precious stones?

We, of course, do not even know that this was the first ascent of the mountain. It is the first *recorded* ascent. In fact, since cliché has become so widely used in mountaineering history, we may also say that it is the first recorded first recorded ascent. We know so few details, and those we think we know are largely guesses based on attaching a lot of conclusions to some vague phrases in the two sources.

So if all that interested us were the minutiae of this 350-year-old adventure, this would be either a very brief or a very dull Symposium.

What gives power and meaning to whatever took place on this rockpile 350 years ago is our own linking this solitary event to its time; and relating them both to our own time and our own association with this great mountain. That now-sometimes-controversial historian of American adventure, Francis Parkman, admonishes us:

> Faithfulness to the truth of history involves far more than a research, however patient and scrupulous, into special facts. Such facts may be detailed with the most minute exactness, and yet the narrative, taken as a whole, may be unmeaning or untrue. The narrator must seek to imbue himself with the life and spirit of the time. He must study events in their bearings near and remote; in the character, habits, and manners of those who took part in them.

So let us muse some more on the world of 1642, hoping to understand better the "life and spirit of the time."

Though Roger Williams and the founders of Harvard College might have a vision of the future, they swam against strong currents in their time. The Stuarts and the Divine Right of Kings still ruled England, though, during that very summer when Darby Field climbed onto strange new ground on Mount Washington, the English Parliament was taking its first steps toward asserting popular rights, faltering steps toward that strange new ground of representative government which led inexorably to the execution of Charles I just seven years later. Thus the seeds of new ideas, of liberty and defiance of privileged authority, were being sown, not only in Rhode Island and Connecticut but in the mother country, seeds of new ideas which were to bear unexpected harvest in Field's adopted continent more than 125 years later.

Yet in 1642 most of Europe still had faith in Absolute Monarchy. Louis XIV, Sun King and perhaps the greatest exemplar of that doomed philosophy, ascended his lofty throne just eleven months before Field ascended his lofty perch. So almost the whole of Louis XIV's long reign lay still to come.

A different world indeed. Galileo died in 1642, the year also in which Isaac Newton was born. There's a symbolic transition in the world of ideas.

Field's ascent is weighty with Symbolic portent for many threads of historic fabric which were as yet unwoven in 1642. His is early for land exploration. The great age of sea discoveries was largely over, but Europeans had traveled little to overland remotenesses. In Africa Grant had not yet visited Ethiopia, nor Burton central Africa. The polar explorations had not begun. Few high mountains had been visited. The Himalayas were rumors. No one in Europe had even heard of the three high peaks of central Africa.

We mentioned that Galileo died in 1642. Recall the reception which his ideas suffered. Darby Field lived in an age and place not yet prepared to decide whether the sun or the earth was the center of the universe, which was yet to burn witches at Salem, and which knew not pianos, nor plumbing, nor peanut butter.

On the plus side, this was a world which had not yet fought two World Wars, nor tore holes in the ozone, nor fouled the oceans. Darby Field could drink from any stream on his mountain without fear of pollution—don't try that today. That exceptionally rare alpine plant *Potentilla Robbinsiana* had not been stepped on, unless Field and his companion or companions did indeed come over or by Monroe, in which case they may have given that little flower (then flowering—it was June) its first taste of hiker impact. When Field sat on the summit, his experience was undisturbed by Air Force training jets or helicopters supplying huts, by bus loads of school kids or transistor radios blaring rock music or large parties of sociable range walkers.

In other words, the exploitation of mountainsides had not yet been decided upon. Field's generation and later ones, including our own, might have made decisions which could have bequeathed to us and to future generations a different, a quieter, a healthier mountain environment.

One large and complex implication of what Field did in 1642, of course, relates to the fact that he was not alone. Indeed, our discussion so far has assumed that it is Darby Field we salute today. It would be equally appropriate to salute his Native American companion—possibly two of them, but more likely just one. (The sources disagree on how many.) Perhaps this unnamed hero, Banquo's Ghost at our celebratory feast, is *more* deserving; Field apparently found the mountain only with the help of local Native Americans. Indeed some might argue that we should really focus our appreciation on those residents of "an Indian town of some 200 people" who declined to enter the sanctuary of the mountain gods, who had the restraint to leave the high, fragile land alone, to respect the realm of alpine terrain, as we of subsequent generations have often conspicuously failed to do.

To muse on the relationship between Field and the Native Americans who were there in 1642—both the one (or ones) who accompanied him to the top and those who lived at the village near the base—is to open up many avenues of inquiry, some of which we hope other speakers may explore today. To consider these topics even momentarily is to be reminded of how little we really know about Field and his era. The seventeenth century French pundit, La Rochefoucauld, a contemporary of Field, warns us that "History never embraces more than a small part of reality."

What was the relationship between Field and the "3 or 4 Indians" who undertook the journey from Pascataqua? Were they friends? Or was it a master-servant relationship? Or an uneasy agreement between suspicious colonist and the wary natives? We do not even know why they undertook the journey, do not even know that the mountain was the original objective. Much has, however, been studied about the relationship between the colonists of New England and elsewhere and the indigenous peoples whom they were beginning to displace. This anniversary observance is an appropriate time to consider that relationship and its impact on the later history of the region.

Nor do we know a thing about the reception which Field and his companions enjoyed at the "Indian towns of some 200 people" which they found "at the foot of the hill," where "two branches of Saco River" came together. (We don't even know precisely where this was. Somewhere around Glen?) Did Field's companions already know the people of this village? Did they head there purposefully, or happen to stumble into town? How were they received? In friendship or with suspicion? Whose idea was it to go up the hill—and why? Did they stay in town long? When they left, what impression remained with the villagers? Did they see portents of the future impact of European colonization? Here again is proper food for thought at this Symposium.

The parallels with Columbus are too obvious to require belaboring. Should we here today honor Field as the hero who opened the way for liberty, prosperity, and the American Dream, and the Mount Washington Observatory? Or should we excoriate him as the first to desecrate the sanctuary, the angel of doom for that delicate ecological balance which the Native Americans had preserved in their northern forest lands, the first mountain exploiter?

Our position on this point will be seen differently by different eyes of different beholders. Just as with Columbus. For example, were we to describe Field as the progenitor of the Cog Railway, the Mount Washington Auto Road and the AMC Hut System, we have many friends who would nod ap-

provingly and prepare to join us in applauding this great benefactor to the
northern New England economy and the pleasures of countless visitors; and
we have other friends who would wince painfully and prepare to join us in
condemning this first step toward the destruction of mountain wilderness.
Perhaps this Symposium will provide a forum for both viewpoints, and more.

Field has given us much. Perhaps the very scarcity of definite facts about his
climb is an advantage. Another contemporary of Field, the English poet
William Davenant, once mused: "How much pleasure they lose . . . who take
away the liberty of a poet, and fetter his feet in the shackles of an historian."
Among the poetic, if not purely historical, legacies which the brief accounts
of that 1642 outing invite us to speculate about, are several which could
equally serve (perhaps will serve) as focal points for discussion today. For
examples:

Field gives us the first report of weather atop Mount Washington. He
was the Joel White or Ken Rancourt of 1642, broadcasting (through his reporters, Thomas Gorges and John Winthrop) news of "terrible freezing
weather," "thick clouds for a good space," then "no clouds, but very cold,"
all of which sounds like we might have heard them on the radio just this
morning. The sponsor of this Symposium must surely rank Darby Field as
its spiritual great-great-grandfather, the first in that long honorable line of
the world's worst weather observers.

Just within the past few years, the entire northeastern mountain region,
from the Adirondacks to Katahdin, has seen a strong surge of interest in the
well-being of those small alpine ecological communities of which the largest
is to be found in the Presidentials. Consider that Darby Field was the very
first person of European ancestry to gaze upon that unique and wonderful
world above the dwarfed trees. If those are right who report that Native
Americans declined to enter that sacred realm, Field and his small party
were indeed privileged pioneers. They were the first to walk by the Monroe
Flats and Bigelow Lawn, the first to look down upon the Alpine Gardens.
As they were there in June, they saw the alpine flowers in their phase of
glory. Did they appreciate what they saw?

Consider another historic role of Darby Field. His account, as handed to
us by his reporters, includes some outrageous exaggerations, which perhaps
also makes him the spiritual ancestor of many a Mount Washington adven-
turer since. He describes the summit cone as "very steep" (this to a European audience which had seen the Matterhorn, and to us who have hiked
up the Six Husbands Trail or Madison Gulf). He portrays a "precipice" "on
the north side," of which he says "they could scarce discern to the bottom"

(which is a bit extravagant for even such a fine cirque as the Great Gulf); and of course he gives us those mysterious rattle snakes. Those of us assembled here have certainly heard many a similar and many much more implausible anecdotes of adventure on this mountain, especially if you have read some of our past writings.

Consider another of Field's legacies. He tells of dipping his handkerchief in the two ponds, finding that one came out "a curious red colour, the other black." Surely this was the start of alpine areas research which has had such illustrious progeny as the Observatory's long-standing support of and participation in scientific research to this day, not to mention the work of the Center for Northern Studies, the Army's Cold Regions Research and Engineering Laboratory, the White Mountain National Forest's research program, that of the Appalachian Mountain Club, and many renowned individuals, from William Oakes and Edward Tuckerman through Joshua Huntington and Vincent Schaefer and on down to researchers of the present day.

Yet another legacy, and this one is especially pleasing. While we do not know anything about the relations between Field and his guide or guides, we cannot help but observe that they accomplished this (for them) perilous journey *together*. Despite a colonial history of growing hostility between European settlers and displaced natives, here on this mountain, at least on this climb, representatives of the two beleaguered constituencies worked *together* to achieve their goal. Despite vastly different cultural backgrounds and despite the shadow of the future, here at least these twain came *together* to overcome formidable barriers, physical and cultural. Would that our world, our distracted globe, could profit from their humble example.

Finally, and this is a point on which we'd like to close, and to ask you to consider especially carefully: Whatever Field's long-lost views were, whether he was crusading explorer or marauding exploiter, the second-hand accounts of this trip drop just a hint or two of his passion for the mountains. He and his companions "took courage" to make the final ascent; on top they saw "a mighty river" and "a very glorious white mountain" and "such a precipice, as they could scarce discern to the bottom."

Do we read too much from too little to take these shreds as evidence that Field was impressed? Though the transition from mountain gloom to mountain glory awaited a later century, did not Field and his companions see majesty and beauty on the mountain height—"a mighty river," "a very glorious white mountain," "such a precipice, as they could scarce discern to the bottom."

We would like to honor Darby Field and his anonymous companion as the first who felt the power and magnificence of the Presidential Range, the first who stood on that awe-inspiring height, amid terrible freezing weather, who listened to the sounds of the infamous wind, who saw the incomparable views of range on range, who felt the glory of a mountain world which dwarfed the stature and feeble powers of two small men, yet which permitted them to stand there as two living atoms in a vast and marvelous landscape.

Eighty-four years ago, in his pioneering research on Field, Warren Hart admonished: "The mountains are themselves the noblest monuments to his memory." We who follow in their footsteps should never fail to perceive the power and the glory of these mountains. Never take them for granted. Never fail to stop a moment and take the measure of that view from on high, to watch the wind whip swirls of snow across the mountainside, to see a sunset with gratitude.

In all that we remember today about Darby Field, his companion, and the mountain they climbed, let us all remember it is the mountain which brought Darby Field here and it is the mountain which brings us back. It is the mountain which held in its grip Ethan and Lucy Crawford, Jacob Bigelow and Francis Boott, J. Rayner Edmands and Madame Pychowska, Joe Dodge and Sherman Adams, and so many more. This is the mountain where Lizzie Bourne lay down to die and Benjamin Ball squatted under his incredible umbrella for night after night. This is the mountain where Toni Matt dove down the headwall to immortality, where Julian Whittlesey cut icy steps up Pinnacle Gully, where the merrymakers from Lancaster whooped it up to christen the northern peaks, where Albert Dow was buried in an avalanche on a mission of rescue, where Tony McMillan's fertile brain conceived a hundred pranks, where Brad Washburn and Casey Hodgdon traced the rugged contours, where Thomas Starr King, as well as many an anonymous hiker since, has stood in silent rapture taking in the wide wonder of this landscape.

It is the splendor of Mount Washington which we must honor today and for all time, the vision of precipice and wind and glorious white mountains and wild untamed weather which we preserve and value. The mountain, not our petty intrusions which we call improvements (our roads, our huts, our helicopters, our hardened trails); the yet wild mountain brought Darby Field here and it is the mountain which brings us back.

In this push button computerized age, humanity needs access to wilderness and wonder. We need recourse to difficulty. We need to encounter nature and nature's gods in ways that fully impress us—as they impressed two tiny travelers in 1642 — with the enormous power of one mountain, its beauty, its wild untamed energy.

Can we hold on to this spirit of wilderness? Can we preserve those opportunities for stillness and solitude, for wonder, for the freedom of the hills, for difficulty and adventure and genuine risk? Can we pass on to future generations a little of the spirit which Darby Field and his companions felt in 1642? We must keep our values in focus, and ourselves. May this be the legacy of Darby Field.

Selected Bibliography

Among the Clouds. Mount Washington, N.H.

Appalachia. Journal of the Appalachian Mountain Club, Boston.

Belknap, Jeremy. *The History of New Hampshire, Vol. III.* Boston, 1792.

Bliss, L. C. *Alpine Zone of the Presidential Range.* Edmonton, Canada. 1963.

Burt, F. Allen. *The Story of Mount Washington.* Hanover, N.H.: Dartmouth Publications, 1960.

Burt, Frank H. *Mount Washington: A Handbook for Travellers.* Boston, 1904.

Crawford, Lucy. *The History of the White Mountains, From the First Settlement of Upper Coos and Pequaket.* Portland, Maine, B. Thurston & Company, 1886.

Cross, George N. *Dolly Copp and the Pioneers of the Glen.* 1927.

Daniell, Eugene S., III, ed. *AMC White Mountain Guide.* 26th edition. Boston: Appalachian Mountain Club, 1998.

Drake, Samuel A. *The Heart of the White Mountains, Their Legend and Scenery.* New York: Harper and Brothers, 1881.

Eastman, Samuel C. *The White Mountain Guidebook.* 7th edition. Boston: Lee and Shepard, 1867.

Goldthwait, Richard P. *Geology of the Presidential Range.* New Hampshire Academy of Science, 1940.

Gosselin, Guy A., and Hawkins, Susan B. *Among the White Hills: The Life and Times of Guy L. Shorey.* Portsmouth, N.H.: Peter E. Randall Publisher, 1998.

Hitchcock, C. H. et alia. *Mount Washington in Winter or The Experiences of a Scientific Expedition Upon the Highest Mountain in New England—1870–1871.* Boston: Chick and Andrews, 1871.

Kidder, Glenn M. *Railway to the Moon.* Littleton, N.H., 1969.

Kilbourne, Frederick W. *Chronicles of the White Mountains.* Boston: Houghton Mifflin Company, 1916.

King, Thomas Starr. *The White Hills: Their Legends, Landscape and Poetry.* Boston: Crosby and Ainsworth, 1859.

Littleton Courier (The), Littleton, N.H.

McAvoy, George E. *And Then There Was One.* Littleton, N.H.: The Crawford Press, 1988.

McKenzie, Alexander A., II. *The Way It Was: Mount Washington Observatory, 1934–1935.* 1994.

Monahan, Robert S. *Mount Washington Reoccupied.* Brattleboro, Vt.: Steven Daye Press, 1933.

Mount Washington Observatory News Bulletin. North Conway, N.H.

New Hampshire Profiles, Portsmouth. N.H.

Pote, Winston. *Mount Washington in Winter: Photographs and Recollections, 1923–1940.* Camden, Maine: Down East Books, 1985.

Putnam, William Lowell. *The Worst Weather on Earth.* Gorham, Mount Washington Observatory, 1991.

Putnam, William Lowell. *Joe Dodge: One New Hampshire Institution.* Canaan, N.H.: Phoenix Publishing, 1986.

Ramsey, Floyd W. *Shrouded Memories: True Stories from the White Mountains of New Hampshire.* Littleton, N.H., 1994.

Randall, Peter E. *Mount Washington: A Guide and Short History.* Third Edition. Woodstock, Vt.: Countryman Press, 1992.

Spaulding, John H. *Historical Relics of the White Mountains, Also a Concise White Mountain Guide.* Boston, 1855.

Sweetser, Moses F. *The White Mountains: A Handbook for Travellers.* 4th edition. Boston: James R. Osgood and Company, 1881.

Sweetser, Moses F. *Chisholm's White Mountain Guide.* Portland, Maine: Chisholm Brothers, 1902 edition.

Teague, Ellen Crawford. *I Conquered My Mountain.* Canaan, N.H.: Phoenix Publishing, 1982.

Torrey, Bradford. *Nature's Invitation: Notes of a Bird-Gazer, North and South.* Boston: Houghton, Mifflin and Company, 1904.

Ward, Julius H. *The White Mountains: A Guide to Their Interpretation.* New York: D. Appleton and Co., 1890.

Washburn, Bradford. *Bradford on Mount Washington.* New York: G.P. Putnam's Sons, 1928.

Waterman, Laura and Guy. *Forest and Crag: A History of Hiking, Trail Blazing and Adventure in the Northeast Mountains.* Boston: Appalachian Mountain Club, 1989.

White Mountain Echo and Tourist's Register. Bethlehem, N.H.